Socialist Women

Socialist Women

european socialist feminism

in the nineteenth and

early twentieth centuries

edited by

MARILYN J. BOXER

&

JEAN H. QUATAERT

 Elsevier · New York

NEW YORK · OXFORD · SHANNON

ELSEVIER NORTH-HOLLAND, INC.
52 Vanderbilt Avenue, New York, New York 10017

Distributors outside the United States and Canada:
THOMOND BOOKS
(A Division of Elsevier/North-Holland
Scientific Publishers, Ltd)
P.O. Box 85
Limerick, Ireland

Library of Congress Cataloging in Publication Data
Main entry under title:
Socialist women: european socialist feminism in the nineteenth
             and early twentieth centuries
  Bibliography: p.
  Includes index.
    1. Women and socialism—Case studies. 2. Feminism—
Europe—History—Case studies. 3. Socialism in Europe—
History—Case studies. I. Boxer, Marilyn J.
II. Quataert, Jean H.
HX546.S635   335′.0094   77-16618
ISBN 0-444-99042-9
ISBN 0-444-99050-X pbk.

Manufactured in the United States

Designed by Loretta Li

*We dedicate this volume
to the memory of the women
whose stories are told
in the following pages.*

Contents

vii

Preface

This book is a history of the search by women and men for human liberation. It deals with the efforts of women and working-class men, two powerless groups with common aspirations, to join in their struggle for a more equitable social order. Presenting case studies in the relationship of socialism and feminism in nineteenth- and early twentieth-century European history, it recovers a lost heritage of brave women whose work remains largely unknown, and uncovers a historical process about which much has been surmised but little research actually performed. By grouping seven essays on a single theme, this collection provides material for comparative studies through which strengths and weaknesses, similarities and differences in styles of leadership, policies of parties and histories of nations are illuminated. It is intended for the classroom, the general reader, and all interested in social and political movements of the dispossessed.

Like the subjects of this volume, the authors work in a context of feminist awakening. Each of us has been profoundly influenced by the social and intellectual unrest of the 1960s in North America. Since history, to paraphrase Croce, is a dialogue between the present and the past, contemporary concerns influenced our choice of historical issues for investigation. By 1973, our research had advanced to the point that four of us presented papers in two sessions at the annual meeting of the American Historical Association. Rose Glickman, a commentator at one of the sessions, sparked interest in cooperation on a book, and recruited a fifth collaborator. When Glickman's research took her to the USSR, the present editors inherited her job; we wish to thank her for all her efforts. In 1975 the A.H.A. again provided a meeting ground where additional contributors were solicited and the book took its final shape.

To thank individually all of those whose counsel and cooperation facilitated this work would be an impossible task. We hope simply that our book in some measure merits the support and encouragement we have received from friends, family, teachers, colleagues, librarians, and archivists. The editors have been rewarded already by the exhilarating experience of collaborating on a mutually engaging task.

Socialist
Women

1 • The Class and Sex Connection: An Introduction

• Marilyn J. Boxer
Jean H. Quataert

I

In the course of the nineteenth century, two groups on the periphery of power met in a struggle for a more just and equal society. Spurred by notions of progress and by principles of equality and liberty, women and the working class rejected inherited concepts of a naturally hierarchical order. Underpinning the process of social reconstruction were the demographic and industrial revolutions which began in the late eighteenth century. In that world of transition, however, old social values lived on to retard the realization of new ideals.

Nineteenth-century Europe called the problem of a newly emerging political and social structure "the social question." "The woman question," as it was known, addressed the related issue of the role of women in the society undergoing radical change, where the domestic economy was giving way to the factory system and the amateur healer and teacher had been replaced by the trained and certified professional. If the traditional woman disappeared, what type of "new woman" might take her place?

Responses to the question varied greatly. They ranged from the "cult of true womanhood" in Victorian England and America, which emphasized the weakness of women and called for the perpetuation of domesticity, to schemes raised by continental feminists for their full and equal participation in public and private life. While social thinkers of many political persuasions

1

dealt with the challenge, the strongest support for sexual egalitarianism came from parties of the left, which proposed the most radical solutions to the "social question" as well. In particular, socialist leaders assumed that women and the working class should, on the basis of the common experience of social powerlessness, unite in the struggle to extend the promises of the French Revolution of 1789 to all men and all women. Despite the outstanding efforts of such liberal thinkers and feminists as John Stuart Mill and Mary Wollstonecraft, it was the socialist movement that offered the strongest and longest-sustained assistance to women seeking redress of past injuries and freedom for future development. Socialists formulated the first political theory to encompass the rights of women and the political parties that they later founded were the first to inscribe women's rights in their programs and to open the doors of their meetings to females. In 1891, the Second International, an association that guided the international socialist movement, mandated that member parties advocate the equality of women.

In many European countries, women responded by joining the cause. By the outbreak of World War I, for example, females comprised 16.1 percent of the membership in the German Social Democratic party (some 175,000 women), 2–3 percent in France (probably no more than 1,000), while in the underground in Czarist Russia they made up about 15 percent, and in the terrorist movement of the 1870s and 1880s their representation reached one-third. In addition, female socialists founded their own branch of the Second International, headquartered in Germany, held international conferences to coordinate their activities in 1907 and 1910, and symbolically set aside one day—International Women's Day—to demonstrate for their feminist political reforms. A new alliance of women and workers had entered the political arena.

The paths of feminism and socialism sometimes intersected, sometimes ran parallel. From Flora Tristan to Juliet Mitchell and from Marx to Marcuse, socialists and feminists have assumed that the two social movements are necessarily complementary. Socialism is an optimistic faith, as is feminism. The two philosophies share the eighteenth-century Enlightenment's assumption that man and woman, adequately fed and properly educated, can reconstruct the world and make it, if not perfect, at least a much better place for the masses of mankind and womankind. If the rather immodest goal of socialism is the achievement of a world of abundance in which "the free development of each is the condition for the free development of all," the aims of feminism are equally expansive, encompassing no less than the vision of ending all interpersonal as well as international strife. In terms of the ideal there is, in fact, little difference. Strong similarity exists also in the affective expressions of many socialists and feminists, all of whom tend, seeing evil about them, to lay moral blame on the men who hold power. Both groups are quintessentially antiestablishmentarian. But those who have sought to commit themselves in practice to the dual goal of working-class and women's liberation have found unresolved issues and experienced personal conflicts. For socialism and feminism can also conflict. The ambiguities in the relationship of the two "isms" form a central theme of this collection.

The present volume, then, explores the strengths and the weaknesses in the alliance of socialism and feminism as it was forged in the nineteenth and early twentieth centuries. The seven women historians whose essays are included here stand at the crossroads between two relatively new and fast-growing areas of scholarship, women's history and working-class history. To date, historians in both fields have largely ignored the conjuncture of the two historical movements. Mirroring the assumptions of their historical subjects, working-class historians have seen socialist women as carbon copies of male workers and have failed to grasp the pervasive feminist component in their battles. Historians of women have skewed their work twice over: the focus has been mainly on the experiences of *middle-class* feminists active in the Anglo-American world. This collection fills a triple gap: it deals with *working-class* women and their feminist struggles in the countries of continental Europe.

The authors of this volume commence with a common purpose. Having read the basic texts of socialist literature on

women, each sets out to examine the origin and nature of socialist feminism in a specific country and to assess socialist feminist
theory critically by investigating specific women involved in
the socialist movement. All authors focus, in varying degrees,
on the life experiences of prominent socialist women who, as
feminists, confronted the dual and difficult commitment to both
sexual and social liberation. The subjects' careers, choices, successes, and failures vividly capture, in personal terms, the dilemmas involved in the need to reconcile loyalties to class and
to sex. Beyond reading records of party congresses, published
speeches, essays, and biographies, most of the authors have
conducted extensive archival research to find the personal papers that reveal the private experiences and beliefs so crucial in
penetrating the facades of public figures.

To be sure, in each society women active in left-wing politics
were atypical, standing out from the masses of womankind by
virtue of their commitments to socialism and feminism as well
as their political, organizational, and oratorical activities. Because of this uniqueness, however, they are fascinating figures
whose biographies allow us to raise new questions and reach
new insights. Such materials can be used to identify and isolate
the very factors that set these women apart from the norms.
From biographical data we can also learn a great deal about the
social and psychological forces that facilitated or hindered
women's political mobilization as well as the meaning of political activism in individual cases. We can observe the process of
politicization generally neglected in historical studies—why did
these female leaders become politically active? Were they
awakened by jarring recognition of their own sexual oppression
or by growing outrage at social conditions of poverty and deprivation? Was it a complex combination of the two experiences?
Why did they become socialists? Especially in their career activities we see highlighted the often overlooked interface between private and public spheres of life. As several essays suggest, some politically active women were atypical only in so far
as they were politically awakened. As young girls and women
at home or in factories and workshops, their life course could be
quite typical. Much information on the social condition of

women inside and outside the home can be obtained from a study of the subjects' lives prior to their embracing a political cause.

Committed to radical change, the subjects shared similar aspirations, and they used a common vocabulary that is reflected in this collection. Therefore, it seems useful here to offer definitions of key terms. By *socialism* we mean the movement for the economic and political reconstruction of society on an egalitarian cooperative basis, through some form of workers' control ranging from early mutual cooperatives to public ownership of the means of production. The time frame of this book spans two distinct phases in the history of socialism: a "utopian" and romantic era in the decades of the 1820s through the 1840s and a "scientific" Marxist period after 1848. It encompasses as well a plethora of theories subsumed under the label socialist that makes precise definition difficult, i.e., collectivism, evolutionary socialism, Kautskyism, populism.[1] During the early "utopian" period, socialists were committed to vague notions of equality, cooperation, and humanitarianism and to the belief that a new social order based on these principles was obtainable. Marx inherited these goals and transformed socialism into a movement of the proletariat, the industrial wage earners, committed to the acquisition of political power through some form of revolutionary activity. As his heirs interpreted his theories, socialists favored trade union activity to improve wages and working conditions and also worked for practical reforms that would hasten the revolution. Although many and, in some cases, most of the persons attached to socialist organizations in Europe were artisans or employees of small shops rather than large factories and although a substantial number were intellectual rather than manual workers, after the midcentury they increasingly viewed themselves as proletarians and sympathized with the working class. To them, everyone associated with the ruling classes was "bourgeois."

The designation *feminist* we apply to all those in the nineteenth century who supported express efforts to ameliorate the conditions of women through public *organized* activity, be it for educational, legal, political, economic, or social purposes.

5

Beyond that, as the reader will quickly note, concensus breaks down. In the Russian case studies, the authors equate feminism with separatism. Rather than impose our own definitions, we have encouraged such latitude in the hopes of capturing national nuances and differences as well as changes over time in the meaning of terms. Actually, to label many of our subjects "feminist" reflects more the historian's need to categorize, order, and give meaning to the chaos of the past than contemporary usage. Socialist women in Imperial Germany, for example, vehemently rejected the label "feminist" (*Frauenrechtlerinnen*) not only to distinguish themselves from middle-class "women's righters" but to emphasize their adherence to the *workers'* struggle for liberation. To us, however, these German socialists appear decidedly feminist.

With these caveats aside, it does seem necessary to distinguish, more precisely, between socialist feminist and bourgeois feminist. This book is about *socialist feminists*—women who saw the root of sexual oppression in the existence of private property and who envisioned a radically transformed society in which man would exploit neither man nor woman. They opted to join the movement for radical reconstruction, convinced that their feminist goals would be realized fully and finally in the new society. Some, like the Russian radicals in the early 1870s, discarded their feminism for all practical purposes in joining the social struggle; more typically, socialist feminists fought the dual battle for both socialist and feminist goals simultaneously but they saw their feminist program as a means to hasten the advent of socialism. Thus, they all were plagued by the thorny question of priorities, the resolution of which varied from woman to woman and country to country.

Bourgeois feminists, in contrast, owed their ideological heritage to liberalism or some national variant thereof and envisioned significant improvement in women's status without social revolution. They sought to integrate women into a capitalist structure reformed by changes in social customs such as the double standard as well as by elimination of barriers to equal education, employment, and political power. To socialist feminists, achievement of equality with men who labored long hours for subsistence wages under capitalism would only perpetuate social injustice. Formal equality without structural change in the economic and social system would bring little improvement in the daily lives of the mass of womankind.

If theory distinguished socialist from bourgeois feminists, so did more practical issues of recruitment tactics, propaganda targets, and organizational affiliation. Bourgeois feminists tended to remain politically independent, loosely connected to liberal and center parties in parliament, organized in a multitude of associations pursuing a variety of goals from welfare and educational reform to the vote. Socially, the backbone of the movement was middle class, mostly teachers, white-collar workers, and leisured wives searching for a more meaningful existence. In contrast, socialist feminists, as part of the working-class movement, sought close organizational ties to their respective socialist men. In practice, they limited their efforts to the needs of working-class women—in factories, at home in domestic service or industry, or in proletarian households. Socialist feminism owed its social genesis to the growth in industrial female labor, even though throughout the period under investigation the component of the total female work force in factories was less than in agriculture, domestic service, and the home industries.[2]

The degree of contact between socialist and bourgeois feminists apparently reflected the role of class hostility in the politics of each socialist movement. In France prior to 1900, the theoretical concept of class hostility played such a minimal role that women affiliated with the socialist movement such as Aline Valette and Paule Mink could work in concert with bourgeois feminists. Around the turn of the century, many French socialists came to accept Louise Saumoneau's portrayal of bourgeois feminists as class enemies and distanced themselves from a feminism embracing women of all social strata. In the early 1890s, the Italian Socialist party permitted its leading woman, Anna Kuliscioff, to be active both in bourgeois feminist and socialist causes. In contrast, in the same decade a leading German bourgeois feminist, Lily (von Gizycki) Braun, was forced to denounce the bourgeois women's platform in order to adhere to the jealously class-oriented German Social Democratic party. National differences and personal commitments prescribed varying solutions to common problems.

II

Socialist feminists drew sustenance from a common ideological heritage. The idea that only thorough structural change in the economic and political order could achieve the equality of the sexes is traced to the systems for universal reform created by Frenchmen in the early nineteenth century. Saint-Simon, his followers, and Fourier envisioned societies in which male ascendancy, along with traditional political and economic patterns, would be overturned. According to Fourier, social evolution required elevation of the position of women. "Social progress and changes in [historical] periods depend upon the progress of women toward liberty." A drastic reordering of family life would be essential to the advancement of society. Although these "prophets of universal love" had little influence on their own community, they exerted a lasting impact on social analysts concerned with improvement of human life. Their ideal, "From each according to his abilities, to each according to his needs," was relayed by Marx to generations of his socialist descendants through the *Critique of the Gotha Programme* (1891). In a less famous document, a personal letter written in 1868, Marx paraphrased Fourier: "Social progress can be measured exactly by the social position of the fair sex (the ugly ones included)."[3]

While Marx designated his predecessors "Utopian Socialists," and sought to supersede them with his "scientific socialism," he incorporated several aspects of their work, including the connection between socialism and feminism. Although use of the generic terms such as *humanity* allowed the socialists to avoid profound analysis of the role of women in society, and although neither Marx nor his followers applied dialectical reasoning toward study of the contradictions inherent in the female condition, they nevertheless contended that all women were

8

oppressed by private property and would be liberated only under socialism.

Though Karl Marx was not a dedicated feminist and never fully explored the implications of his theories for women, he did recognize that both as productive workers increasingly employed outside their homes and as partners in marriages that were influenced by monetary relations, they, too, suffered the effects of industrial capitalism. Women, like working-class men, had become "instruments of labor." In one of the most popular socialist tracts, the *Communist Manifesto* (1848), Marx and Engels established the relationship of capitalism and the "woman question" through their assessment of the impact of capitalism on family life. Marx, the practical politician, also created a precedent for the participation of women in socialist politics by naming a woman, Harriet Law, to the General Council of the International Workingmen's Association (First International, 1864–1872) and by promoting the organization and admission of groups of women workers. The first call for the collaboration of working men with women, however, had antedated Marx by some twenty years and, like the early ventures in socialist feminist theory, had come from France. It was Flora Tristan, an illegitimate and impoverished woman of French and Peruvian ancestry, who had first attempted to achieve feminist goals through organized efforts to emancipate the working class. But her story remained little known; and for the most part at midcentury, working-class men responded negatively to changes in the traditional domestic roles of women.

While working-class women had always worked and, along with half-grown children, had been expected to earn their share of family subsistence, they had remained close to home or at least under proper patriarchal surveillance. Neither the economically—and sexually—autonomous "new woman" who entered radical circles in the character of Vera in Chernyshevsky's popular novel *What Is to Be Done?* (1863), nor the nimble-fingered spinsters who appeared in previously male-only workshops were welcomed by working-class men. The Proudhonist mentality, which saw the patriarchal family workshop as the basis of the ideal cooperative workers' society, remained strong among workers in the First International (and lingered long after). While in Russia the middle- and upper-class new woman gained acceptance in radical circles and sometimes moved from a search for personal autonomy to conspiracy for social revolution, a more positive commitment by socialist organizations to solving "the woman question" waited, for the most part, until the late decades of the century.

Although the structural changes that underlay the development of the woman question—removal of "women's work" from the home, mechanization that increased the productive capacity of women workers, and economic growth—continued unabated, the impetus for closer association between socialists and feminists reached its peak in the decade of the 1890s when both groups decided to organize for political power. The social groundwork had been laid with the permanency of industrial female labor, low wages, and competition between male and female workers; the ideological justification had been prepared by both Marx's closest collaborator and by one of his leading disciples. The publication of Engels's *The Origin of the Family, Private Property and the State* (1884) and August Bebel's *Woman Under Socialism* (1883; first published in 1879 as *Woman in the Past, Present and Future*, but later revised to incorporate much of Engels's work) strengthened the theoretical links between socialism and feminism. The two works quickly became favorite reading among European socialists. Translated into many languages, serialized and paraphrased in socialist periodicals, quoted endlessly, reprinted numerous times (Bebel's book appeared in its fiftieth edition in 1913), they achieved "canonical status" within the movement.[4]

Engels declared in the preface to *The Origin of the Family* that his publication, following close on Marx's death, was intended to place before the public the unpublished work of the master theorist. Using extensive notes that Marx left on his readings of the anthropological works of J. J. Bachofen, J. F. McLennan, and Lewis H. Morgan, Engels had assembled the material and fulfilled Marx's intention. Thus establishing credibility, he developed a thesis purporting to show that an evolution in the form of relations between the sexes had accompanied a progression of stages in the development of society. In the earliest of times, known as savagery, human beings, living in tribes, held property in common, engaged promiscuously in sexual relations and cooperatively supported all offspring, who necessarily carried their mothers' names. Despite a very primitive level of economic development—or, rather, because of it— it was a golden age of communal living, especially for women who enjoyed the power termed, by Bachofen, "Mother-Right" (*das Mutterrecht*, sometimes taken to mean mother-rule or matriarchy). In response to technological development, social relations changed, going through a stage of "barbarism" whose corresponding form of sexual relations was "the pairing family," an unstable union that served, Engels thought, to protect women from the demands of promiscuous sex. Finally, with the development of increasing wealth and "civilization," men decided—for unspecified reasons—to accumulate private property and, in order to perpetuate their hold on it, to appropriate and subordinate individual women in the form of marriage we term monogamous. By forcing women to limit their sexual relations only to their husbands, thus assuring "legitimate" succession, they developed to satisfy their own desires a system of exchanging sex for money. Thus monogamy, Engels asserted, functioned only for women while men enjoyed the benefits of its companion institution, prostitution. The development of private property had caused the "world historical defeat" of the female sex, and restoration of woman's rightful place in the social scheme would follow only from its transcendence.

Despite the teleological cast to his solution, which envisioned the end of women's oppression only after socialist revolution and the restoration of communism, Engels did offer some immediate advice. The means to female emancipation lay in the entrance of women into "socialized production." Far from lamenting the "industrialization of women," Engels, like Marx, saw it as a progressive force.

It fell to the leader of German Social Democracy, August Bebel, however, to trace in detail the history of women in Western civilization from the depths of degradation imposed by Christian and capitalist society to the heights of equality in the com-

11

munist future. Bebel's *Woman under Socialism* is a long narrative history replete with citations, from Tertullian's assertion, "Woman, thou art the gateway to hell," to data on the socioeconomic origins of German prostitutes. After several hundred pages packed with fascinating and instructive tales—one learns that a medieval church council decided by a majority of one that women do indeed have souls and that some advanced societies such as New Zealand and certain American states (despite their capitalist economies, a fact ignored by the author) have already accorded political equality to the subjugated sex— the author described a society so advanced technologically that machines and electrical appliances do all the hard work, assuring to workers the pleasures of both abundance and leisure and, finally, to women as well as men sexual freedom and personal autonomy. Woman in the future, Bebel declared in the essay to which he allotted only six of three hundred fifty pages, is "socially and economically independent; she is no longer subject to even a vestige of dominion and exploitation; she is free, the peer of man, mistress of her lot. Her education is the same as that of man, *with such exceptions* [italics added] as the difference of sex and sexual functions demand."[5] Without pausing to consider either the nature or the implications of such exceptions, which might lead into questions of family structure, child support, and the sexual division of labor in the socialist state, he asserted that the new woman of the new world would enjoy sexual as well as social and economic equality with man. "Class rule will have reached its end for all time, and along with it the rule of man over woman," he concluded, thus "proving" his assertion that the "solution of the Woman Question coincided completely with the solution of the Social Question."

If Engels's book rested on the faulty assumption that communally held property could not coexist with the subjection of women and posited an unproven correspondence between stages of evolution and forms of marriage, Bebel's glossed over many problems, including that of assuring personal freedom to individuals in a technologically advanced society planned for maximum efficiency. Except to support the increasing participation of women in production, neither dealt with the process of

12

transition to the new world of equality for women. It was simply announced by both authors that *after the revolution* women would be equal partners in the socialist society. And, given the obvious suffering of women in capitalist society and the self-righteous assumption of moral superiority over the bourgeoisie prevalent among nineteenth-century socialists, assertion made manifest the truth. There were few philosophers among the socialist leaders, and those who might have tried to develop a more thorough theoretical basis for relating the woman question to the social question—perhaps Jean Jaurès from humanitarian motives or Rosa Luxemburg, as an exercise in dialectics —lacked the interest.[6] This failure prepared the way for conflict and confusion when socialists sought to put into practice what they considered their theory on women. But the details are to anticipate much of the human drama in the following essays.

III

In this volume, the authors trace the impact of an idea. By examining the history of socialist and feminist relations in five nations, all heirs to a common tradition regarding the roles of women, they show that despite national differences similar themes emerge. Heard from the beginning in the lonely voice of Flora Tristan, to the end in the struggle of Aleksandra Kollontai was the insistence that class could not be separated from sex nor personal relations divorced from politics and that the only successful revolution would be a total one. The French utopian socialists, as Joan Moon points out, had compared the "prostitution of labor" to that of "love," and had called for sexual equality along with class equality, for moral along with economic reform (Chapter II). If in an industrializing society workers became "wage-slaves," all women, whatever their class, marrying for economic survival and gaining thereby legal masters, became prostitutes. Still it was not against marriage or men that Tristan railed but against the dehumanization inherent in the denial of women's "natural rights." Reminding French workingmen that until 1789 they, too, suffered disinheritance

13

and that they still lacked control of their lives, she developed her thesis that workers were women's natural allies. But, Moon notes, if Tristan glimpsed the possibilities of a union of the "pariahs" of both sexes, she was also the first in a long series of socialists and feminists who "saw only their potential for mutual development and ignored the reality of their incompatibility." Themes of conflict, competition in the workplace, and male insistence on patriarchal privileges in the family also emerged at the beginning of our story.

Barbara Engel, demonstrating further the value of biographical studies for the analysis of political socialization, also traces the development of a potential socialist feminist synthesis in the lives of women who belonged to the Chaikovskii circle in Russia during the 1870s (Chapter III). Seeking selfhood, these women struggled first against patriarchal family patterns. "For them," Engel notes, "feminism was a personal not a social solution." Radicalized by their own life situations, they sought and found allies among men on the political left, developing with them a new consciousness of the scope of social problems. The women on whom Engel focuses all ultimately subordinated their feminism to political radicalism. Feminism served them as a stage on the route to revolutionary politics. Particularly in the life of Sofia Perovskaia, Engel demonstrates the tensions between the feminist goal of self-development and a commitment to socialist action. In Perovskaia's martyrdom the tensions were not resolved but only obscured. Indeed, because of the tendency of the Russian women to compartmentalize their feminism and their radical politics, the problems of women as women were lost and the women question ceased to be considered a political problem and feminism a political movement.

The conflict between theory and practice emerges more clearly in the studies of France, Germany, and Italy in the heyday of the Second International, 1889–1914. In countries with the institutions of parliamentary democracy, where socialist parties opted to contest for political power, the potential existed for a mutually advantageous alliance of the liberators of workers and women. The essays by Marilyn J. Boxer, Jean H. Quataert, and Claire LaVigna demonstrate the shortcomings of the synthesis (Chapters IV, V, and VI). Each author deals with the search for a political strategy by women rooted in or identified with the organized working class, and all credit the socialists with good intentions. In fact, it was the resources offered by the working-class parties that in part attracted women to socialism. According to LaVigna, for example, Kuliscioff enjoyed a larger arena and stronger support for her talents in the Italian Socialist Party than the incipient feminist movement in Italy had to offer. Likewise as part of the so-called state within a state, which German Social Democracy became, Clara Zetkin had access to means of communication, an audience, and an ideology well beyond the wherewithal of any middle-class feminist. For feminists in Imperial Germany, Quataert declares, "the socialist subculture provided the most supportive milieu" and "spearheaded efforts" to improve the situation and status of women. In the French case, an exception that proves the rule, Boxer shows that party organizations withheld material support not only from socialist feminists but also from indisputably proletarian women seeking only to bring other women to socialism. For Louise Saumoneau and her colleagues, rejection of bourgeois feminism brought moral and ideological satisfaction rather than any concrete political advantages.

Once in the socialist camp, socialist feminist leaders faced the vexing question of developing a truly viable connection between class and sex. The three case studies here show that ambivalences and even conflict surfaced when women pressed their male comrades to put their feminist promises into practice. Quataert speaks of the "uneasy" alliance between the two social movements in Germany, LaVigna writes of the "Marxist ambivalence" toward women in the Italian context, whereas, in the case of France, Boxer suggests the development at times of an adversary relationship. Equivocation was not all on the part of men. These cases demonstrate that socialist women also at times failed to advance their feminist goals for fear of disrupting proletarian unity. For example, on the main feminist demand of the epoch, the women's vote, the movement hesitated. The French party and at critical times the Belgian and Austrian socialists as well, fearing the issue might embarrass them at the polls, refused to support women's suffrage actively. Problems of priority inherent in the dual commitment were shared by other activists such as, for example, members of national parties in the international labor movement and ethnic groups within national organizations. This issue in socialist women's history offers another perspective on radical political experience.

Although socialists equivocated on political issues, they never squarely faced the more sensitive question of women's role in the family. For to deal with women as mothers and wives (or "reproducers" as socialist feminists put it today) was to raise a specter that haunted continental socialists: fear that socialism required dissolution of the family. It did. Transcendence of private property would necessarily mean the equality of women only if the basic unit of society for purposes of production and consumption became the individual and if the traditional family, resting on the unpaid labor of women, were destroyed. But could a social movement that threatened to upset the precarious stability of the social order hope to win power and influence? The exigencies of party politics required soft-pedaling criticism of family relationships. Some socialists, like Aline Valette in France, followed continental bourgeois feminists who, while critical of male supremacy, sought to strengthen and conserve the family as the center of women's lives. In this, the bourgeois and socialist feminists of continental Europe distinguished themselves from most Anglo-American feminists of their time who sidestepped the issue altogether. Others tended to focus their attack on an abstract "bourgeois" family while ignoring the sufferings of women at the hands of working-class men.

The one who most clearly understood the fundamental importance of family reconstruction was Aleksandra Kollontai (Chapter VII). During her brief tenure as commissar for social welfare, the Bolshevik party passed family legislation specifically designed to destroy the old social order by liberating women. The new laws, which established equality of the sexes, provided for easy divorce and abortion, and abolished the distinction between legal and so-called illegitimate children, led to the proliferation of irregular marital unions. In 1926, the Bolsheviks introduced a revised family code that regularized these free unions and required larger contributions by men to family maintenance. Intended to protect women and children as well as reduce the level of governmental obligations, the measure in effect reduced the autonomy of women. Only Kollontai, who had advocated replacement of the nuclear family by social institutions, protested. The Soviet Union's leading woman took a feminist stance, as Beatrice Farnsworth clearly shows. Yet in the end, even Kollontai gave up her struggle and "join[ed] the leadership in mythmaking"; one of the most persistent of socialist myths being that the Bolshevik Revolution did indeed liberate women.

In the very years that saw the Russian advances undone, yet another European socialist party pledged itself to an integrated program envisioning wide-ranging transformation of patterns of work, sex roles, and values. Socialist women in Catholic Austria during the 1920s won promises from their party to support legal free abortion and birth control as well as revision of marriage and divorce laws. Ingrun Lafleur's essay demonstrates the staying power of the socialist tradition during a period of European reaction on the woman question. "The Austrian women socialists," she notes, "took a more advanced position of social issues than any other group in Europe, with the exception of those few involved in the temporary experiments on family life occurring in Soviet Russia." Their program addressed not only economic and political issues but also the personal development of women. But it represented a vision of a few, increasingly at variance with the temper of the time.

In reviewing the history of European socialism in relation to women and the "woman question," we must distinguish between ideology and reality. That socialist activists themselves blurred this distinction was one of their failures. The major concrete achievement for women was passage of restrictive but protective legislation for female factory workers. Realization of the broader goals of social and familial equality would have required not only attainment of political power but, perhaps more important as shown by the Soviet case study, transcendence of social institutions and categories of thought that dominated the nineteenth and much of the twentieth centuries. Such transcendence is asking the impossible. To their credit, socialists found new ways of analyzing women's situation and included them in the task of social reconstruction. But their analysis remained limited and their institutions and behavior reflected the biases of their times. Although the dynamic connection between the crucial social categories of class and sex has yet to be forged satisfactorily, nonetheless the life experiences of early socialist feminists provide an instructive and inspirational legacy.

N O T E S

1. A useful introduction to socialist theory is Albert Fried and Ronald Sanders, eds., *Socialist Thought: A Documentary History* (New York, 1964).
2. This has been pointed out in several recent articles. See especially Patricia Branca, "A New Perspective on Women's Work: A Comparative Typology," *Journal of Social History* 9, no. 2 (Winter 1975): 129–53. We are clearly dealing with the work experience described in Branca's Model II.
3. *Théorie des quatre mouvements et des destinées générales* (Paris, 1967), p. 147; Frank E. Manuel, *The Prophets of Paris* (New York, 1962), pp. 9, 313–14; Marx, *Letters to Dr. Kugelmann* (New York, 1934), p. 83.
4. George Lichtheim, *Marxism: An Historical and Critical Study* (New York 1961), p. 241.
5. *Woman under Socialism* (New York 1971), p. 343.
6. Jaurès, the charismatic leader of moderate French socialism, known for his devotion to humanitarian idealism, totally ignored the problems of women. Luxemburg, the Polish-born leader of the radical wing of German socialism, one of the few socialists of the Second International to struggle seriously to extend Marxist analysis, considered the woman question a trivial and tangential issue (see Chapter V).

2 • Feminism and Socialism: The Utopian Synthesis of Flora Tristan

• S. Joan Moon

It is hardly surprising that the first tentative alliance of socialism and feminism took place in the France of the July Monarchy, 1830–1848. France was, after all, the home of the Revolution, and memories of gallant struggles and battles died slowly. More specifically, the Revolution of 1830 brought the upper bourgeoisie of bankers and industrialists to power, dashing the hopes for a political voice of republican intellectuals and the laboring classes who had helped overthrow the Restoration. Disillusionment quickly set in, manifest by workers' strikes such as the Lyon silkworkers' insurrection in 1834. The autonomous workers' protests heralded a new age as did the French socialists—from the Utopians to Louis Blanc and his National Workshops—who also were grappling with the world emerging out of the French Revolution and the industrial transformations. Flora Tristan was a bridge between the working-class movement of unions and crafts and the socialist efforts to formulate a vision of the new society. As Moon writes, she was the first reformer to attempt to establish sexual equality through the emancipation of the working class. Where did Flora's feminism originate? What was her understanding of women? How did she join feminism and socialism? What tasks did Flora assign to women in bringing about the new society?

The basis of this chapter was a paper read at the 88th Convention of the American Historical Association, December 28, 1973, San Francisco, California.

FLORA TRISTAN. From Jules-L. Puesch, *La Vie et l'Oeuvre de Flora Tristan, 1803–44* (Paris, 1925).

Disorder and disbelief appeared to rule the July Monarchy as the values of industrial capitalism usurped the traditions of preindustrial France. Utopian socialists interpreted this displacement in terms of moral and social decadence. They pointed to the prostitution of labor and love as the most visible sign of the materialism, egotism, and exploitation of their age; they promised workers and women a better future. Their socialism surpassed the programs of workers who sought to improve their condition through the establishment of trade unions, mutual aid societies, and producers' associations. It proposed complete social transformations that organized work in accordance with human passions and capacities. Their feminism transcended the demands of reformers who wished to educate women in order to prepare them for their civilizing role within the patriarchal family. It envisioned new social relationships based on freedom and equality between the sexes.[1]

But how were these gentle worlds of class and sexual harmony to be achieved? Disdaining mass action and violence, utopian socialists optimistically relied upon exposition, example, and philanthropy to provide the pacific impetus for social change. The first reformer to attempt to synthesize feminism and utopian socialism by securing sexual equality through the self-emancipation of the working class was Flora Tristan.[2]

Flore-Célestine-Thérèse-Henriette Tristan Moscoso's brief life (1803–1844) was an impassioned search for identity and purpose. Until her early teens, Tristan gloried in being the "excessively sensitive and proud" daughter of Mariano de Tristan, an aristocratic Peruvian colonial in the Spanish army, and Thérèse Lainé, a middle-class French émigré from the Revolution. Tristan's parents lived comfortably in Paris on a small annuity, and occasionally, when the ships managed to run the English blockade, money arrived from her father's extensive estates in Peru. When Tristan was four years old, her father suddenly died. To conserve her meager funds, Thérèse Tristan moved to the country with her young daughter and infant son. For the next ten years, Flora Tristan, who considered early childhood a critically formative period, lived on the memories of those first few years and dreamed of assistance from her wealthy uncle, Pio de Tristan. After the death of her brother, Tristan and her mother returned to Paris to live in poverty among "murderous thieves and prostitutes" near the Place Maubert.[3] Around 1818, Tristan learned the full details behind her family's drastic change of fortune when she needed a birth certificate to obtain a marriage license. The French state had seized her father's house as alien property because it did not recognize the validity of her parents' religious ceremony. Thus Thérèse Tristan was legally neither widow nor heir, and Flora Tristan, child of an irregular union, was illegitimate.

Although Tristan considered her illegitimacy an "absurd social distinction," her fiancé's father prevented the marriage.[4] Forced by poverty to seek work as a colorist in a lithographic shop, within the year Tristan married her employer, André Chazal. The next four years were marked by constant illness, her indifference to her two sons, and increasing dissension with a husband who attempted to push her into prostitution, she later claimed, to pay off his gambling debts.[5] Early in 1825, perhaps aware that she was again pregnant, Tristan left Chazal, thus acquiring another mark of illegitimacy, for the Napoleonic Code forbade such wifely independence.[6] For the next fifteen years, Tristan led a life of protest against the misfortunes of her birth and the inequities of her marriage. Robbed of her inheritance and her freedom, she detested the fabrications necessary to support her children and to protect her precarious independence. To secure a job as a lady's maid to an English family, she left her two sons and infant daughter with her mother and posed as a *demoiselle,* a "young lady." Although she found the work humiliating (she later destroyed all records of the experience), it evidently provided the necessary funds to obtain a preliminary legal separation from Chazal. By 1829 she was again living in France as the "Widow Tristan."

From 1830 to 1833, Tristan, absorbed in her own marital and economic problems, moved only on the periphery of feminist and socialist activities.[7] Chazal, learning that his wife had finally succeeded in obtaining a small annuity from her Peruvian uncle, renewed his persecutions in humiliating scenes that constantly impressed upon Tristan the servile nature of marriage. Resuming her posture as a demoiselle, Tristan sailed for Peru in 1833 to press her claims to her birthright. But that birth, her uncle maintained, was illegitimate. He did, however, agree to continue her small yearly income. Frustrated by the concealment of her marriage and motherhood, angered by her uncle's selfishness, Tristan's awareness of being a prisoner of social conventions and a stranger to her family intensifed; she saw herself as a pariah.[8]

When Tristan returned to Paris in 1834, the Peruvian money allowed her time to write and to establish contacts with the utopian socialists. As a result of her travels, Tristan recognized the universality of her own experiences as a woman; in the writings of the utopian socialists she found the formulas to express her feminism. Her first works reveal the intimate union she forged between personal experience and utopian socialist theories. *On the Necessity of Welcoming Foreign Women* (1835) combined a call for the establishment of associations to shelter women travelers with appeals for universal love and internationalism. *Peregrinations of a Pariah* (1838) described her trip to Peru, and although she later considered it dominated by her own self-suffering, it contained intense passages on the anguish of other women. *Méphis* (1838), a semiautobiographical romantic novel, recounted the tragic love of Maréquita for Méphis, and while Tristan constructed the characters as her own alter egos, their message was the utopian socialist dream of woman as the moralizer of humanity.[9] Her growing fame as a professional pariah, however, was marred by persistent problems with Chazal, who became increasingly jealous of her influence on their daughter, of her small annuity, and of her literary successes. In 1838 he made a nearly fatal attempt on her life, and the sensational trial resulted in national publicity for Tristan. Chazal was sentenced to twenty years hard labor; Tristan had her portrait painted for *Charivari*.[10] After successfully applying for the restoration of her maiden name, she became legally Madame Flora Tristan.

Freed from her marital problems (but not her conjugal ties, of course), Tristan faced the loss of her economic independence when Uncle Pio de Tristan, angered by her frankness in *Peregrinations*, canceled her annuity. Now completely dependent upon her writings, Tristan turned her pen to a country she had frequently visited—England.[11] Exhibiting more than a touch of Anglophobia, she described the "serious, unsociable, suspicious, cowardly" Londoners, with their irritating climate, their decadent, materialistic society, and their exploitative social and economic institutions that reduced women and workers to a nullity. She compared the enslavement of workers by their masters to the subjugation of women to their husbands. She described the dehumanization of person and purpose shared by workers and women; she called both pariahs. During her trip, she "rediscovered" Mary Wollstonecraft's *A Vindication of the Rights of Woman* (1792) with its appeal to natural rights and education. From her encounters with the Chartists she witnessed the power of popular association led by an educated and devoted working-class elite. While visiting a public asylum, she met a mad Frenchman who, believing himself to be the Messiah, gave her a small cross and commissioned her to go through the world preaching the new law of woman's emancipation and the reign of God. Profoundly moved by the experience, Tristan saw in him not insanity, but the same "holy indignation" against the servility, corruption, and hypocrisy of society expressed by Jesus, Saint-Simon, and Fourier.

The publication of *Promenades through London* (1840) brought Tristan new success as a social critic. Now she turned her attention to the French working class; she read socialist and working-class pamphlets on association and the organization of work; she debated with workers, socialists, and literati in her small Parisian salon. Her heightened consciousness of working-class misery was responsible for the forward to the 1842 "popular edition" of *Promenades*, which dedicated the book to workingmen and workingwomen, and exhorted them to claim their rights. By 1843 Tristan had prepared a new manuscript that prescribed the means of obtaining sexual equality and working-class association. However, her efforts to interest the working-class elite in its publication failed, she explained, because the "stupid, bestial, crude, vain" workers preferred flattery to frankness. Finally she resorted to a door-to-door self-raised subscription to launch her "good and useful" book, the *Workers' Union* (1843).[12] In 1844, not content with the printed word, Tristan decided to take her message directly to the workers. From spring to late fall, from Auxerre to Bordeaux, in taverns, workshops, rooms, and rented halls, she preached her gospel of love, union, and work. Fatigued by chronic illness, spied upon by the police, rebuffed by the clergy and the bourgeoisie, often ignored or misunderstood by the workers, her few successes at establishing workers' circles nevertheless sustained her faith in her mission. In her diary, detailed observations on working-class conditions are increasingly confounded with flights of religious fervor.[13] Pariah no longer, she was the Messiah, spreading the gospel to save women, workers, and the world. She begged God for ten disciples, for three; in truth she believed, and only intermittently, in just one convert, her "spiritual" daughter, Eléonore Blanc. By the time Tristan reached Bordeaux in November 1844, she was fatally ill with typhoid. Four years later, "thankful workers" erected a monument at Bordeaux "To the memory of Madame Flora Tristan, author of the *Workers' Union*."

As a writer, Tristan's lack of formal education fades before her passionate convictions and an innate sense of description. Her best portraits are of women, from the elaborate toilette of Maréquita to the body-deforming labor of Montpellier washerwomen. Often she wrote with a frankness that bordered on tactlessness, and excused it in the name of "truth." Some works are lengthy and repetitious, filled with insignificant details, bursting with individual indignities and social injustices. In her pursuit of facts, she embodied the concern with social data that established the first half of the nineteenth century as the "prime age of statistics."[14]

But she wrote not just to describe, but to transform reality, contrasting what men and women were with what they should be. At her best, contemporaries complimented her on her "masculine" style, and hastened to remind their readers that the author was a woman. Few who met her could forget it. Tristan was an extremely magnetic woman, with her dark brown eyes filled with the "fire of the Orient," her Grecian nose, and her magnificent black hair which even at her death was only slightly "spangled with a few silver threads."[15] Her vibrant and harmonious voice was by turns animated and pensive, and she spoke with facility and persuasion. But because of her nature, dialogues soon turned to dicta. Uncompromising with her "principle," impatient with criticism, intolerant of deviation, critics considered her too vain and too utopian.[16] She insisted that she was not anxious to please, to be found beautiful, or to be loved. She stated that she had loved only twice, and her later liaisons evidently were not physical.[17] Her professed love was humanity; her dream, to establish a world of equality and love through the peaceful transformation of a decadent society.

Tristan's feminist and socialist vision was strongly influenced by the Saint-Simonian and Fourierist schools of the 1830s. Young Parisians of both sexes became devoted, although often temporary, disciples.[18] Flora Tristan never denied a master, never deserted a system, because she never identified with one.[19] Both philosophies promoted theories of human nature and historical progress that condemned the present exploitation of women and workers and projected sexual equality and social harmony as the highest stage of human development.

To the Saint-Simonians, human nature was at once rational, emotional, and active; but this tripartite equality dissolved before their preference for feeling over reason and action, and their elevation of artists and moral teachers above scientists and administrators. While some men might excel in the emotive faculty, the Saint-Simonians assumed the romantic position that all women did. The qualities of passion, sweetness, love, and peace that characterized woman's nature determined her role as the moralizer of man, assuaging his bestial instincts and tempering his intellectual sterility.[20] Woman and man, cooperating as a couple composed of distinct but complementary natures both in the private and public spheres, would insure woman's equality with man without risking her competition. The Saint-Simonian theory of progress viewed history as the alternation of egotistical critical periods with altruistic organic ones, accompanied by the gradual peaceful elimination of antagonism for association. Their own transitional age was characterized by the inferiority of women and the exploitation of the "largest and poorest class," because indissoluble marriage and inherited wealth had created domestic and social inequalities and inutilities. They saw themselves as prophets of a new age of universal association, regulated by the formula of social utility, in which women would be fully emancipated and work would be organized on the principles of the compatibility of industrial interests and the development of dominant natural capacities.

Through journals, missionaries, experimental communities, and "workers' degrees," the Saint-Simonians attempted to convert the people by their examples of brotherly love. But in 1831, the new morality proposed by the charismatic Prosper Enfantin scandalized Paris. Insisting that morality should accord with human passions, he defined love as either constant or mobile and approved legal or nonlegal relations reflecting the two natures.[21] When some *femmes libres*, "free women," adopted the new ethic, women's emancipation became identified with free love. In the midst of internal tensions created by the new doctrine, the government charged the school with immorality and imprisoned its leaders. From his prison cell, Père Enfantin approved the search for the Mère who would complete the Supreme Couple. After his release from prison in 1833, he led the faithful remnants of his flock to Egypt, seeking the *Femme Messie*, "Woman Messiah" who would promulgate the definitive moral law that would establish peace and universal association.

The dissolution of the Saint-Simonian hierarchy during Enfantin's imprisonment provided the opportunity for two disciples, Désirée Véret and Marie-Reine Guindorf, to found a woman's journal, the *Femme libre* (*Free Woman*) hastily changed by their successors to the *Femme nouvelle* (*New Woman*) to avoid charges of moral license.[22] In open opposition to the masculine domination of the school and in place of the imposed dictates of a single female messiah, they advocated the self-elevation and association of women of all classes. Equating the struggle of women with that of the people, they called for "Truth. Union. Freedom for women, freedom for the people through a new organization of home and industry."[23] Strongly influenced by Fourier and their own proletarian backgrounds, the writers of the *Femme libre* argued that woman's role as moralizer and educator required not only her domestic equality, but her economic independence as an individual rather than as part of a couple. The journal, however, suffered from its own lack of material security and disappeared after two years of sporadic publication.

When Tristan returned from Peru in 1834, the Saint-Simonians were widely dispersed, their journals defunct, their doctrines ridiculed. Her attention was drawn to the rival philosophy of Charles Fourier. Fourier, purporting to describe human nature as it really was, identified twelve passions exhibiting over 800 shades of expression, haphazardly distributed among children of both sexes.[24] While he considered women to have the same passions as men, he could not entirely free himself from the romantic tradition of stressing woman's emotional nature and women predominated in the affective passion of love. In Fourier's stadial and cyclical theory of history, the passion of love, which varied in form depending upon opportunity of expression, constituted the pivotal mechanism for periodic change, and the extension of privileges to women became the index of all social progress.[25] His own period, civilization in decline, was characterized by the repression of passions; women had no freedom to love and workers lacked the right to work. The repression of love was especially evident in marriage, family life, adultery, and prostitution. Fourier's discovery of the "butterfly" passion rendered the notion of undying love contrary to human nature; therefore, the accepted love relationship of civilization—monogamous, indissoluble marriage—was a repressive institution, characterized by pure brutality and deadly boredom, only temporarily relieved by the sudden "pin prick" of the senses. Family life was the most defective social unit conceivable, sad and monotonous, false and immoral, the principal source of egotism and antisocial behavior. Fourier estimated that most women, finding no fulfillment in skimming the souppot, justly despised an occupation that stifled their character. Woman's passions, thwarted by unsatisfying labor, emerged as vices, and adultery and immorality became the inevitable result of civilization. For Fourier, there could be no such thing as a "free woman" in any period that lacked the guarantees to assure women their complete emancipation and equality. One right step, however, would be to establish women's economic freedom, so that they would never again have to prostitute themselves in loveless marriage or in the streets.[26]

The position of the workers in civilization paralleled that of women. There could be no such thing as the much-vaunted Saint-Simonian dignity of labor given the current working conditions that forced men into deadening, degrading, even feminine occupations. Who could blame the workers for despising work when they lacked the most basic of human rights, the right to work; that is, the right to labor in accordance with natural inclinations at a satisfactory level of subsistence. It was understandable, therefore, that the workers' passions would be expressed in personally and socially destructive vices such as gambling and drinking.

But for Fourier, civilization would gradually yield to harmony, the total economic and moral transformation of society which reflected rather than changed human nature, where individual passions were completely in accord with social interests. To workers, this meant the true dignity of work, the final reconciliation of man's God-given duty with his pleasures. For women, harmony signified the true *femme libre*, the complete educational, professional, and amorous equality of the sexes. The transformation to harmony could be hastened by the establishment of experimental phalansteries, which Fourier hoped would be achieved by philanthropic action. He also appealed for women to play an important part in accelerating the change. He suggested that women writers set aside their egotism, open their eyes to the fate of their sisters, and find a means to shatter the chains of civilization. They must become "Women Liberators."[27]

In general, Tristan accepted the utopian socialist theories of human nature and historical progress. Like the Saint-Simonians, Tristan defined human nature as a "great trinity" of capacities. She spoke of the need to develop the total intellectual, material, and moral capacities of the workers; she especially insisted upon the full use of woman's capacities in order to provide for

29

individual and social progress. "According to a simple calculation," she announced, "it is evident that wealth will indefinitely increase the day when women (half of the human race) are called upon to bring the sum of their intelligence, their strength, and their ability to social activity."[28] Tristan also elevated feeling over reason and action and contrasted the natural self, filled with a boundless capacity for universal love, with the artificial self, characterized by atrophied feeling. The unflattering portraits that Tristan painted of working-class women and men reflected the social distortion of their true natures.

In the romantic tradition, Tristan also defined woman's nature primarily in terms of feeling; love was the "pivotal passion" of all her thoughts and the motivator of all her actions. Tristan, however, de-emphasized sexual and familial love in favor of universal love. There existed a constant tension between her idealization of love and the reality of her personal relationships. The teenage girl who deified love as the living thought of God became the spurned fiancée. The unhappy, ill, pregnant wife of a mediocre artist longed for a passionate and exclusive love for a man ennobled by the grandeur of his sufferings. And the woman who keenly felt her own passionate nature defined herself as a pariah, continually forced to control her passions. Of the three men Tristan loved, her adored father died suddenly, her young love supposedly committed suicide rather than defy his father, and the third coldly rejected her "grand passion."[29] Whether from frigidity, a fear of social censure, a desire to remain independent, a hatred of men, or a latent homosexuality (it certainly was not from lack of opportunity), Tristan avoided sexual relationships. For Charles Fourier, only partially anticipating psychological alternatives, repressed passions invariably resulted in vices. But from a Freudian viewpoint, Tristan succeeded in sublimating her passions at a higher level, and at that level, no restraint was necessary. Only humanity could be her lover; it alone was worthy of her; it alone was faithful. "To serve humanity," she cried, "is a devouring passion with me. I would give my life, I would sell my soul to be able to serve it."[30] "This love," Méphis warned Maréquita, "will not betray you, and at twenty as at sixty, you can love it passionately."[31]

30

It was humanity that Tristan professed to love In Eléonore Blanc, her "spiritual" daughter: "Oh, what a sublime love that has nothing to do with sex. Nothing unforeseen will sully it."[32] She interpreted this preference for Eléonore over her daughter, Aline, as proof that spiritual creations were superior to those of the flesh. While the utopian socialists strove to rehabilitate the flesh through the emancipation of sexual desires, Tristan tried to transcend it through the overcoming of sexual attraction. While Enfantin's theory of sexual mobility shocked the bourgeoisie, Tristan's concepts of sexless love confounded the workers.

With the Saint-Simonians and the Fourierists, Flora Tristan cried out in the wilderness that theirs was a critical transitional age, the expiring gasp of a decadent civilization awaiting a rebirth.[33] To her, history was the Saint-Simonian struggle and intermingling of individual and social interests, where materialism promoted morality and egotism became an instrument for universal good. In this moral world, as Saint-Simon stated, a philosopher was not only an observer, but an actor whose opinions regulated society.[34] Tristan came to believe that she was an agent of divine providence, a *Femme Guide* whose purpose was to march ahead of the masses, to proclaim the truth, to enlighten the people in spite of themselves and regardless of personal suffering. As a pariah, Tristan's physical sufferings and mental anguish over her marital and economic situation had consumed her thoughts. But from suffering for herself, she learned to suffer for others. During her tour, her torments rivaled the pains of the saints: "No, but never have Jesus, the apostles, or the Christian martyrs felt one hundreth the anguish that I endure."[35] Her apostolic faith in a martyr's mission of love increased daily during those final months, until she saw herself, as did Saint-Simon, as the new Messiah.

This society is evil; I wish to change it, to regenerate it. I wish to save the world which is perishing. . . . The Jewish people were dead in abasement, and Jesus raised them up. The Christian people are dead today in abasement, and Flora Tristan, the first strong woman, will raise them. Oh, yes, I feel in myself a new world—and I shall give this new world to the old one which crumbles and perishes.[36]

31

Both the utopian socialists and Tristan believed that the natural superiority of the moral elite would be readily recognized and accepted by the people. With this attitude, Tristan was understandably picqued when the people showed a reluctance to be saved, and wondered what she would do if "these miserable, blind people by their stupidity prevent me from helping them."[37] Tristan's *Femme Guide* is ideologically closer to Enfantin's illusive *Femme Messie* than to Fourier's pen-wielding *libératrices*, but the *Femme Messie* constituted a complement to the Père, and Tristan, like Fourier, rejected the concept of the couple. Tristan as *Femme Guide* marched alone, with two changes of shoes to keep her feet dry.[38]

"Poor women, poor mothers," cried Tristan that last summer in southern France, "my sisters, I swear I will deliver you."[39] Her feminist vision derived its substance from her experiences as a woman, although she couched it in utopian socialist expressions. Tristan discovered that all women, without vocation or profession and dependent upon marriage, were pariahs. Her feminism transcended all class and national boundaries, for no woman could escape the "helotism" of modern marriage, with its indissoluble nature, patriarchal structure, and double standard. Like Fourier, Tristan denied that even a woman of wealth could be completely free. Her fictional *femme libre*, Maréquita, whose money allowed her to leave her husband, was still limited by education and bound by social conventions. She lived a life of uselessness. Tristan's Peruvian experience revealed the repressive nature of family life for rich women. The middle-class English girl, detailed by Tristan in *Promenades*, was educated for a married life that robbed her of all domestic utility and reduced her to a thing, a doll, a baby-making machine; she vegetated rather than lived.

For a woman of the people, uneducated and unskilled, marriage was much worse, according to Tristan.[40] In a semiautobiographical sketch, she traced the life of a young girl, subjected to an uneducated, brutal mother until twelve, apprenticed to an exploitative patron, hardened and cruel by twenty. The early nineteenth century considered the single workingwoman to be a transitory economic element; contemporary statistics indicate that she could not afford to live alone, that marriage was a means of survival. For Tristan, however, marriage was less an economic necessity than an escape from parental tyranny. But it was an illusory haven, for the working-class marriages described by Tristan were without love and happiness because they lacked equality. Woman, by law subject to her husband, was also inferior due to her smaller earning power. This master-slave relationship was the constant source of dissension between the spouses. The husband sought respite in taverns, gambling and drinking. For the wife, there was no refuge; she endured pregnancies, illness, unemployment, and misery, constantly surrounded by demanding children, cooped up in a wretched hovel. Thus Tristan explained the contrast between the nature of the working-class woman and the sweet, good, sensible, generous nature of woman in terms of domestic and economic inferiority.

Tristan's descriptions of working-class life are commonplace in the picturesque and social literature of the period that vividly depicted the lack of familial relations that turned the working-class children to a life of crime and fused the laboring classes with the dangerous classes.[41] Children, Tristan warned, brutalized by harassed and fatigued parents, locked up in unhealthy rooms, left to themselves, to neighbors, to the streets, soon turned to a life of vagrancy, thievery, and prostitution.

The "proliferation of common prostitutes" was a phenomenon of urban life in early nineteenth-century Paris.[42] Tristan, acquainted with Parent-Duchatelet's study of Parisian prostitutes, concluded from her own observations that most working-class women lived on "a little work, a little thievery, a little begging, and a lot of prostitution."[43] Denying the premise that prostitution was an inherent and inevitable aspect of society, Tristan attributed it to economic inequities. Prostitution was caused not by a lapse in morals, but by a lack of bread, by the exploitation of women and their exclusion from secure jobs and equal wages. "A poor workingwoman," Tristan observed, "earning fifty centimes a day cannot live, and in order to have bread, and often to work, she prostitutes herself to a manufacturer or a shopman who gives her work only on that condition."[44] It was not, then, for the niceties of life that women of the people turned to prostitution, but for the necessities.

Tristan's early remedies for the subjugation of women were marriage reform, educational equality, and vocational training. With Enfantin and Fourier, Tristan opposed the indissolubility of marriage, arguing that since God has given continuity to only a small number of our affections, to impose immutability was unnatural and would be joining what God has sundered.[45] But petitions for divorce were presented almost yearly during the 1830s without result.[46] And divorce, even if reinstated, would only increase the misery of uneducated and unskilled women. Influenced by the educational theories of the Welshman Robert Owen, Tristan proposed the establishment of state-supported infant schools for girls and boys of all classes.[47] Placed in school at age two, children would remain there, living communally free of all class and sex privileges, until primary school. By age sixteen, their education and vocational training would assure their love of humanity and insure them a job. But the French infant schools, although subject to royal ordinance, were privately funded, few in number, and inadequate in hours, nutrition, help and hygiene.[48] The Guizot Law of 1833, "the first constitutive charter of primary education in France," did not provide for the establishment of girls' schools, and the first female vocational schools lay in the future.[49] By what means, then, could Tristan liberate her sisters?

Tristan discovered her answer in a socialist vision that united her own personal experiences and utopian socialist theories with the emerging French labor movement. As a worker, Tristan suffered the deprivations of ill-paying labor. Her journeys to England sharpened her awareness of the wretched existence of the working class as well as its potential for social upheaval. From the utopian socialists, she learned of the liberating effects of industrialism and the inevitability of universal association. In the labor movement, with its message of working-class utility, action, and unionization, she found the means to realize the abstract sexual and social harmony of the utopian socialists.

From 1830 to 1833, while Tristan pursued her inheritance and the utopian socialists spread their gospels, Parisian work-

34

ers, disappointed with the results of the July Revolution, subjected to continued economic crises, and demoralized by the increasing mechanization of their crafts, erupted in strikes, riots, and demonstrations. Through journals and pamphlets, a skilled working-class elite attempted to channel these spontaneous and sporadic actions into a conscious movement of working-class unity. These artisans, who retained their traditional skills but who feared losing control of the means of production, tried to create a "producers' ideology," which promoted their own utility over that of the idle capitalists.[50] With utility, came an emphasis on solidarity, for they recognized that exploitation, competition, isolation, and misery were the common lot of all workers. Appeals for political reforms, dimmed by the government's refusal to realign its liberal economic policy, yielded to nonviolent worker-initiated action through association. "Let us unite" and "Union and strength" became the mottoes of the working-class elite. In place of trade unionism and mutualism, the leaders called for the establishment of producers' associations, supported by weekly contributions that would allow workers to purchase the means of production. Proposals were drafted not only to associate within a craft, but for particular crafts to federate through a general association governed by a central committee.

These early attempts were checked by the Law of Associations, which stringently regulated the size and purpose of working-class associations.[51] Workers turned to mutual aid societies or to secret societies of resistance that supported Blanqui's abortive coup in 1839. That same year, the economic crisis that hit France precipitated the mass strikes of 1840 and stimulated new demands for reform.[52] Between 1839 and 1844 a new working-class elite joined socialists in proposing plans for the organization of work. Adolphe Boyer, a compositor, urged the government to provide working-class representation on councils of arbitration that would gradually transfer the means of production to working-class control.[53] A new working-class newspaper, *Atelier*, encouraged workers to establish partial producers' associations, which would gradually become general through the absorption of all workers in that trade, and eventually expand into a universal association preserving both elements of cooperation and competition.[54] The worker-reformers of the Compagnonnage—an ancient secret society of skilled workers organized into two rival vertical orders—hoped to unite hundreds of thousands of skilled workingmen. Agricol Perdiguier, who first revealed the secrets and structures of the Compagnonnage, criticized its rivalry and violence, and called for the unification of the two orders. Pierre Moreau argued against any reform of the Compagnonnage short of its total absorption into his own rival "Union," which would then serve as the nucleus for a universal society of equality and assistance. Moreau's plans were approved by Gosset, the "father of the blacksmiths," who proposed the creation of a general association guided by a central committee elected by local groups and funded by a two-franc initiation fee.[55]

Influenced by these labor theories, Tristan called for the immediate self-emancipation of all workers utilizing existing associations to form a general union whose purpose was to create a self-conscious, powerful working class in order to bring about the full material, moral, and intellectual transformation of society. From the utopian socialists, Tristan adopted a theory of progress that saw the working class as the historical successor to the middle class. According to providential plan, the bourgeoisie, larger and more useful than the nobility, had formed a class in 1789; it was now time for the workers to create the "largest and most useful class." Since the Saint-Simonian concept of association moved from the particular to the general, Tristan's series went from isolated workers, to partial societies (such as extant mutual aid societies or the Compagnonnage), to a federated workers' union. A yet higher form of association would be worldwide, and in a celebrated footnote, Tristan called for the internationalization of the working class.[56]

Through the Union, the workers could claim their natural rights, especially the all-important right to work. Tristan derived the *right to work,* a Fourierist term, from the bourgeois guarantee of property rights. She argued that the laboring skill of the working class represented a form of property, "propriété de bras"; therefore, this property must be guaranteed through the right to work and the organization of labor.[57] To complete this right, she added the right to political representation, the right to educational and vocational instruction, and the right to "daily bread," which she rather ambiguously defined as the possibility of living completely independently.[58]

Tristan also argued that since the working class included women, these natural rights must be extended to them. But in case workingmen did not recognize the inherent justice of freeing "the last slaves still remaining in French society," she appealed to their self-interest by contrasting their present domestic and social misery with their future happiness once women were granted equality.[59] For Tristan, the working-class woman's domestic and economic utility, although limited by a lack of education and inferior salary, provided her with a potential far exceeding that of her sex in other classes. Just as the workers were the largest and most useful class, Tristan apparently considered working-class women to be more numerous and useful than their aristocratic or bourgeois sisters. Their functions as workers, teachers, and moralizers required education and vocational instruction.

> Let the women of the people receive from infancy a rational, solid education fit to develop all their good tendencies, so that they may become able workers in their crafts, good mothers capable of raising and guiding their children . . . and so that they may serve as moralizing agents for men on whom they exercise influence from birth to death.[60]

Tristan asked the workingmen to recognize the principle of woman's equality; to acknowledge the urgent need to give women of the people an equal moral, vocational, and intellectual education; and to implement this equality by equal treatment in the home and in the Union.[61] In this way, women would not only share in the "moral" rights of 1789 and 1830, but in the material benefits derived from the right to work, to organize, to political representation, to instruction, and to daily bread. Tristan thus hoped to secure the guarantees of woman's domestic equality, education, and economic independence that utopian socialists considered necessary for moral regeneration.

The equality accorded to working-class women would gradually spread to all women. Tristan's feminism proceeded upward from the working masses rather than percolating downward from the privileged classes.

> Workers, be sure of it. If you have enough equity and justice to inscribe into your Charter the few points I have just outlined, this declaration of the rights of women will soon pass into custom, from custom into law, and before twenty-five years pass you will then see inscribed in front of the book of laws which will govern French society: THE ABSOLUTE EQUALITY of man and woman. Then, my brothers, and only then, will human unity be constituted.[62]

For Tristan, the federal and international formation of the working class was therefore a means to an end, the constitution of humanity, a constitution that depended upon the equality of the sexes. The equality of women, far from being a proposal "woven into the general scheme" of the Union, formed the necessary prerequisite for the social and moral transformation of civilization.[63]

The actual construction of Tristan's Union was simple. Existing societies would elect seven-member correspondence committees of men and women to register all interested workers, taking special care to enroll women. These committees would then elect a central committee. A hierarchy of committees would gradually be established between small villages, the major cities, and the central committee in Paris or Lyon. Tristan estimated that there were five million workingmen and two million workingwomen, but that the potential size of the working class was around twenty-five million, for she counted on the interest and support of all who suffered from the inequalities of property.[64] At a yearly contribution of two francs per worker, this would mean a treasury of fourteen to fifty million francs per year. Some of the money would go to support missionaries sent out to convert more workers. Another part of the capital would be used to employ a defender to represent working-class interests in the national assembly and to solicit funds and enlist the sympathy of other classes. Tristan did not detail the defender's program, other than to say that he would be concerned with legally obtaining the right to work and with the organization of work. The defender was Tristan's alternative to universal male suffrage as demanded by the workers of *Atelier* and to select female suffrage as advocated by the bourgeois feminists of the *Gazette des femmes*.[65]

The largest amount of the funds would be spent on the construction of workers' "palaces." Tristan, borrowing freely from Owen and Fourier, envisioned the palaces as combination workshops, farms, and residences for two to three thousand people. Half of the inhabitants would be the elderly and the infirm, who would retain their dignity and utility through limited labor. The other half would be children, equally divided between the sexes, from age six to eighteen. Working-class boys and girls, and a few middle-class students, would receive the same general and specific education in subjects that would promote a love of humanity, develop their intelligence, train their bodies, and prepare them in two crafts suitable for earning a living. Work in the palace approached Fourier's harmonic description; all inhabitants worked at a variety of tasks that reflected their personal inclinations and everyone received a share of the profits. As subscribers to the Union increased, additional palaces would be built in each department. The image emerges of a vast grid of palaces covering France in which working- and middle-class children learned the value of work, the necessary trades for economic security, and the essential equality of humanity. Tristan admitted that many of the details for the Union would have to be worked out, that she sketched only the outline for immediate action: "This Union is a bridge thrown between the dying civilization and the harmonious social order envisioned by superior spirits."[66]

Tristan's "naive" socialism is considered to contain two seeds of mature socialism: the self-emancipation of the working class and the workers' international.[67] While self-emancipation was a common theme of the working-class elite by 1843, two concepts distinguished Tristan definition. First, she viewed the working class as a self-conscious entity of all workers, skilled and unskilled, male and female. But despite its potential numerical superiority (twenty-five million out of a population of thirty-six million) and productive capacity, she saw it only in legal, peaceful opposition to its historical predecessor and contemporary exploiter, the bourgeoisie. Although she did not hesitate to raise the threatening specter of twelve million uneducated and unemployed workers before the eyes of a recalcitrant middle class who failed to see the social benefits to be derived from improving the lot of the workers, she advised the workers against the use of force. A few contemporary critics perhaps recognized the potentials for social divisiveness present in the formation of a self-conscious working class opposed to a self-interested middle class, and warned against it as an "unhappy thought."[68] A second aspect of self-emancipation as developed by Tristan centered around her particular idea of association. The Workers' Union contained few of the aspects of the producers' associations that distinguished the federalism of the 1830s. The majority of the funds went not to purchase the means of production, but to build palaces. These combination workshops-farms-residences functioned as moral, educative, and economic units. The Union, with its self-governing hierarchies of committees, with its grid of worker-financed and controlled departmental palaces, has been likened to later syndicalism. Contemporary opponents labeled it a "state within a state" capable of dividing the nation into two camps.[69]

The international aspect of the Union has been vastly overrated. Appeals for universal fraternity already existed in the secret societies of resistance, in the Compagnonnage, and in the articles of *Atelier*. While later socialists considered her notion of a workers' international to anticipate Marx, internationalism for Tristan was primarily a logical progression drawn from Saint-Simonian concepts of expanding associations and was independent of economic development. The suggestion that internationalism was the book's raison d'être is not only erroneous, but deceptive, since it diverts attention from the really important "seed," the equality of women as the preparatory step to social transformation.[70]

Tristan's feminism embraces the major demands of early nineteenth-century feminists for domestic, educational, and economic equality. Tristan implicitly accepted the idea that marriage was the goal of women, and argued for alternatives within, rather than to, its structure. Monogamous marriage would be natural and moral only by allowing divorce and by establishing equality between the spouses. Tristan offered both social and individual justification for women's education. First, she argued that a mother was all important in the training of children and therefore needed to be educated to fulfill this role, a position previously advanced by Fénelon and Rousseau. But in her proposals, Tristan turned the education of children over to infant schools at age two or to the palaces at age six. Since there is a strong suggestion that the children would live in the palaces, woman's educative function would at best be part time. Secondly, she demanded education as a means of developing woman's natural capacities and talents, an essentially utopian socialist argument that benefited both the individual and society. She based her arguments for economic equality on the Fourierist position that woman's moralizing role required her material independence. Only with economic freedom could women be free from prostitution, the most obvious stigma of social immorality. The superior morality that traditionally had confined women to the private sphere here provided the means to the public realm. For Tristan, woman's economic independence included vocational training and the opportunity to learn any craft, not just "feminine" trades. It also meant that wages should be commensurate with utility, rather than fabricated upon woman's supposedly lesser needs, frugal nature, or inclusion as part of a domestic unit. Woman as wife, mother, and worker fulfilled her nature. But such fulfillment, as Tristan realized, depended upon a total transformation of the social order. In this transformation, Tristan accorded women little action. Unlike her emphasis on working-class self-emancipation, Tristan assumed that women could not free themselves.[71] Women's emancipation required the action of workingmen.

Integral to Tristan's synthesis of feminism and socialism is the preliminary decision of the workingmen to grant the principle of sexual equality. By recognizing the equality of workingwomen, the workingmen would open the door not only to feminism, but to socialism. Without this decision, the working *class* would not be created, since the formation of the Union, the tangible sign of worker solidarity, required the admission of workingwomen. Without the Union, with its political defender to promote the right to work and with its palaces to develop values and vocational skills, there would be no moral and material transformation of humanity. For Tristan, feminism and socialism were not parallel movements that could proceed at independent and unequal speeds; they were mutually dependent. Only through the mediating action of the workingmen could the principle of sexual equality be realized; only through the moralizing influence of women could human potentials for social harmony be actualized. Lacking the deterministic dialectic of the Marxists, Tristan relied upon reason and self-interest to convince the workingmen. She thus imparted to her synthesis a quality of immediacy. There was no awaiting a socialist revolution; only a moral decision was required. But would the workingmen make it?

Parisian pamphlets and journals written by skilled workers during the July Monarchy expressed an increasing concern with the misery of the workingwoman.[72] They encouraged inquiries into salaries, working conditions, and the moral effects of working outside the home. They attributed low salaries primarily to competition with other women, with men in feminine trades, and with prison, convent, and even military labor. They were also aware of the injustice of considering the workingwoman as an auxiliary wage earner, when, in many cases, she was the sole support of the family. Workingmen were especially concerned about conditions that threatened woman's morality, such as being employed beside men, being forced to carry a *livret* (a record of debts and employment), and being encouraged to cultivate tastes that led to prostitution. The resultant picture of the workingwoman was not promising: the single woman was constantly fatigued, encouraged to live beyond her means; a wife was forced to leave the cares of the household and work long hours for low pay; a mother, working without rest, was prevented from fulfilling her "holy duties."[73]

Four themes emerge from these articles: women, single or married, were seen as a source of competition; women and men seemed to be reversing roles; women belonged in the home performing household tasks and raising children; and the way to improve the lot of women was by increasing men's salaries. Workingwomen were clearly identified as a source of substitute, cheap labor, lowering men's salaries and hindering strikes for higher wages. *Atelier* warned the typographers that the real danger to their trade was not mechanization, but feminization.[74] In certain cloth-printing trades, workers protested female competition by going out on strike and by avidly opposing the establishment of special associations to train women in skilled trades.[75] Competition sometimes forced men to extremes: working in "female" trades (which shocked the bourgeoisie and angered workingwomen), and performing woman's domestic duties. *Atelier*, in discussing the workers' situation in England, complained that a reversal of roles had occurred. Formerly the man had provided for his dependents; now his wife and children supported the family, while the husband, "crying with rage, attends to the cares of the household and the preparation of food."[76] The journal warned of a similar trend in France. Workingmen reacted by disparaging the lesser productive value of woman's work in the workshops and factories and by magnifying her educative, moral, and housekeeping roles in the home. To these workers, woman's nature was emotional; her character was defined in terms of self-sacrifice, devotion, and love; her life was familial rather than individual; her weaknesses demanded man's assistance; her "kind attentions and chaste caresses" alleviated the daily misfortunes and fatigues.[77] The goal of association envisioned by these workers was to increase the salary of the workingman in order to allow his wife to quit the workshop and return home. There, doing a little piecework, she could perform her duties as wife and mother.[78]

The skilled workers who commented on Tristan's Union were divided as to its socialist practicability (for example, most pointed out that such association was illegal), but united against its feminist pretensions. From her first attempts to obtain working-class support for the publication of the *Workers' Union*, Tristan encountered opposition to the chapter on women. At a reading of the manuscript before a committee of the *Ruche po-*

pulaire, a Saint-Simonian working-class journal, workers criticized her for mistreating women of the people. One woman charged her with humiliating all women by asking for such rights, as women enjoyed divine ones. Tristan preferred to attribute the negative reaction to her frank discussion of working-class family life rather than to the question of women's rights.[79] She should have heeded the advice she later received from *"la femme Soudet:"* "You do not know the workers. They have not yet reached the point of being just to women and of having faith in them. If my husband presented your idea to his colleagues, they would laugh in his face."[80] Reviews of the book in working-class newspapers concentrated on its socialist aspects, ignored or ridiculed its feminist issues, and commented approvingly on its masculine style or critically on the masculine pretensions of this "O'Connell in skirts."[81] When Tristan visited Lyon, the idea that such a book could have been written by a woman was so foreign to the workingmen that they accused Tristan of fronting for a fearful male author.[82] Two Lyonese skilled workers wrote that they agreed that women were poorly educated for their natural tasks, but they chidingly lectured Tristan on the nature of those tasks. "Woman's life is the life of the home, the domestic life, the inner life." "To man discussion in assemblies, troubles and labors, wars and dangers. To woman the tranquil and uniform life needed to raise and provide children with early instruction. From the savage state to the present society, woman has always been consecrated to the inner life." But her domestic position, they admitted, should not be that of a slave. Through education, woman would become the equal of man, exercising on him a legitimate and salutary influence, but without expressing any independent ideas. To these workers, equality meant that woman exchanged a master for a tutor. The working-class literature and the workers' responses to Tristan's feminism confirm the fact that during the July Monarchy, the skilled workers were elevating the workingwoman to the same lofty and economically unproductive pedestal occupied by her bourgeois sister.

The utopian socialists masked the threat present in woman's equality by creating "couple-workers" and by constructing future societies where competition was part of a cooperative whole. The *Workers' Union* contained no such illusions. Tristan's socialism embodies a radical feminism that freed woman from the home and placed her on a competitive footing in the market place. Working-class socialism reveals a domestic feminism that granted women equality within the home at the cost of economic independence. To workers, association without workingwomen was not only possible, since most societies excluded women and there were few female societies, but economically and morally preferable.

Feminism and socialism, parallel in desires and nourished by the social conditions of the July Monarchy, contained both conflicts and accords. Tristan saw only their potential for mutual development and ignored the reality of their incompatibility. With her death in 1844, her Union was essentially forgotten. Four years later, Marx and Engels laid the groundwork for a new unity of feminism and socialism that, by assuming a dependency between economic relations and male domination, predicted the emancipation of women as the consequence of a social revolution that would abolish private property. In Marxist terminology, Tristan had achieved only a utopian synthesis, for she placed before the workers a concept of equality whose realization depended upon moral acceptance rather than upon the inexorable laws of economic development. Time alone would determine whether or not the Marxist "scientific synthesis" of feminism and socialism would fare much better.

N O T E S

1. Charles Fourier is credited with the invention of the word *féminisme*. However, E. Silberling, in his *Dictionnaire de sociologie phalansterienne* (Paris, 1911), makes no mention of the word. Pierre Leroux takes credit for the word *socialisme*, in an 1834 article on the Lyon strike, reproduced in David Owen Evans, *Le Socialisme romantique: Pierre Leroux et ses contemporains* (Paris, 1948), pp. 223–38; see also R. Picard, "Sur l'origine des mots *socialisme* et *socialiste*," *Revue socialiste* LI (1910): 379–90.
2. The classic work on Flora Tristan remains Jules-L. Puech, *La Vie et l'oeuvre de Flora Tristan, 1803–44* (Paris, 1925); see also his articles,

"Flora Tristan et le saint-simonisme," *Revue d'histoire économique et sociale*, 13th yr., no. 2 (1925): 207–15 and "Un romancière socialiste: Flora Tristan," *La Revue socialiste* LIX (jan–juin 1914): 132–46. An excellent analysis is contained in Marguerite Thibert, "Féminisme et socialisme d'après Flora Tristan," *Revue d'histoire économique et sociale*, 9th yr. (1921): 115–36, which is enlarged in her book, *Le Féminisme dans le socialisme français de 1830 à 1850* (Paris, 1926). In the past few years, a new interest in Tristan has produced Jean Baelen, *La Vie de Flora Tristan* (Paris, 1972); Dominique Desanti, *Flora Tristan: la Femme revoltée* (Paris, 1972); Charles Gattey, *A Biography of Flora Tristan: Gauguin's Astonishing Grandmother* (London, 1970); Marie M. Collins and Sylvie Weil-Sayre, "Flora Tristan: Forgotten Feminist and Socialist," *Nineteenth-Century French Studies*, 229–34; Leslie R. Rabine, "The Other Side of the Ideal: Women Writers in Mid-Nineteenth-Century France (George Sand, Daniel Stern, Hortense Allart, Flora Tristan)" (Ph.D. dissertation, Stanford University, 1973), chap. 5; Laura S. Strumingher, "Les Canutes: Women Workers in the Lyonese Silk Industry, 1835–48" (Ph.D. dissertation, University of Rochester, 1973), chap. 5. For bibliography prior to 1925 see Puech, *La Vie*. Works since then also include Edwin Hedman, "Early French Feminism" (Ph.D. dissertation, New York University, 1954); Edouard Perrin, *Un Précurseur féminin des temps nouveaux: Flora Tristan* (Saint-Etienne, 1938); Catalina Recavarren de Zizold, *La Mujer mesianica: Flora Tristan* (Lima, Peru, 1946); Maximilien Rubel, "Flora Tristan et Karl Marx," *La Nef* (jan. 1946): 68–76; Lucien Scheler, *Flora Tristan: Morceaux choisis* (Paris, 1947); Luis A. Sanchez, *Una Mujer sola contra el mundo: Flora Tristan la pariah* (Lima, Peru, 1961); Margaret Goldsmith, *Seven Women against the World* (London, 1935), chap. 3.

3. Puech, *La Vie*, p. 9.

4. Flora Tristan, *Pérégrinations d'une paria, 1833–34*, 2 vols. (Paris, 1838), I, 47.

5. For Chazal's version of the marriage see André Chazal, *Mémoire à consulter pour M. Chazal contre madame Chazal*, Tribunal Civil de 1re instance de la Seine, 3e Chambre (7 fev. 1838).

6. For an analysis of the laws pertaining to women, see Jane Cerez, *La Condition sociale de la femme de 1804 à l'heure présent: la problème féministe et la guerre* (Paris, 1940).

7. In *Pérégrinations*, II, 228–29 Tristan notes that she had participated in the July Revolution of 1830, but does not go into any details.

8. Tristan, *Pérégrinations*.

9. *La Necessité de faire un bon accueil aux femmes étrangères* (Paris, 1835); *Pérégrinations; Méphis*, 2 vols. (Paris, 1838).

10. During the proceedings, she filed a *Pétition pour l'abolition de la peine de mort;* see *Journal de peuple* (16 dec. 1838).

11. Flora Tristan, *Promenades sur Londres* (Paris, 1840). In the preface she notes she visited England four times—in 1826, 1831, 1835, and 1839. Nothing is known of the 1831 and 1835 journeys.

12. Flora Tristan, *L'Union ouvrière* (Paris, 1843). Two subsequent editions were published in 1844.

13. Flora Tristan, *La Tour de France, journal inédit, 1843–44*, Preface by Michel Collinet, notes by Jules L. Puech (Paris, 1973).

14. Louis Chevalier, *Laboring Classes and Dangerous Classes in Paris during the First Half of the Nineteenth Century*, trans. by Frank Jellinek (New York, 1973), p. 49.

15. Jules Janin, "Madame Flora Tristan," *La Sylphide*, II ^{e} ser., Tome I (1845), 3–8, 17–20; Sebastien Commissaire, *Mémoires et souvenirs*, 2 vols. (1888), I, 108–109 quoted in Tristan, *La Tour*, p. 47; Puech, *La Vie*, pp. 119–21.

16. George Sand, quoted in Puech, *La Vie*, p. 285, fn. 1 and Victor Considérant, "Lettre à Flora Tristan," included in the second edition of *Union* and reproduced in the third edition (Paris and Lyon), p. xiv.

17. Tristan, *Pérégrinations*, I, 47.

18. Frank E. Manuel, *The Prophets of Paris* (Cambridge, Mass., 1962), pp. 2–3.

19. Tristan, *Promenades*, p. 355; Tristan, unedited letter to M. le directeur de la *Phalange*, quoted in Herbert Bourgin, *Fourier, Son contribution à l'étude du socialisme français* (Paris, 1905), p. 544, fn. 5.

20. For the Saint-Simonian concepts of women, see: *La Femme libre* (1832–34); *le Globe* (1830–32); *l'Organisateur* (1829–31); *Oeuvres de Saint-Simon et d'Enfantin*, 47 vols. (Aalen, 1964), XLII, 9; XLIV, 23; XLV, 47–51. For secondary works on the utopian socialists that have reference to feminism, see: H.-R. d'Allemagne, *Les Saint-Simoniens* (Paris, 1930); C. Bouglé, *Chez les prophètes socialistes* (Paris, 1918); Camille G. Charlety, *Histoire du saint-simonisme* (Paris, 1931); A. Cuviller, "Un Schisme saint-simonien: les origines de l'école buchézienne," *Revue du mois*, XXI, nos. 125–26 (mai-juin 1920), 494–532; David Evans, *Social Romanticism in France* (New York, 1969); H. J. Hunt, *Le Socialisme et le romanticisme en France* (Oxford, 1935); Jehan d'Ivray, *L'Aventure saint-simonienne et les femmes* (Paris, 1928); Manuel, *The Prophets*; Thibert, *Le Féminisme*; Edith Thomas, *Les Femmes de 1848* (Paris, 1948) and *Pauline Roland: socialisme et féminisme au xix ^{e} siècle* (Paris, 1956).

21. Prosper Enfantin, *Religion Saint-Simonienne. Réunion générale, séance du samedi 19 novembre* (1831).

22. Suzanne V. [oilquin], *Souvenirs d'une fille du peuple ou la saint-simonienne en Egypte, 1834–36* (Paris, 1866), p. 96.

23. Logo from *La Femme nouvelle* (subtitled *Apostolot des femmes*), p. 73. For a hostile contemporary account, see Anonymous, "Chronique de la quinzaine, 14 nov. 1832," *Revue des deux mondes*, ser. 1, VIII (Paris, 1832): 492–95; and for recent interpretations, Thibert, *Le Féminisme*; and Evelyne Sullerot, *La Presse féminine* (Paris, 1963).

24. Charles Fourier, *Théorie des quatre mouvements et des destinées générales* (Paris, 1967, c. 1808). See also Bourgin, *Fourier;* Jonathan Beecher and Richard Bienvenu, *The Utopian Vision of Charles Fourier, Selected Texts on Work, Love, and Passionate Attraction* (Boston, 1971); E. Dessignolle, *Le Féminisme d'après la doctrine socialiste de Charles Fourier* (Lyon, 1903); Manuel, *Prophets;* Riasanovsky, *The Teaching of Charles Fourier* (Berkeley and Los Angeles, 1969).

25. Fourier's statement has often been quoted by feminists: "Les progrès sociaux et changements de période s'opèrent en raison du progrès des femmes vers la liberté; et les décadences d'ordre social s'opèrent en raison du décroissement de la liberté de femmes. ... En résumé, l'extension des privilèges des femmes est le principe général de tous progrès sociaux." *Théorie*, p. 147.

26. See Zoe Gatti de Gamond, *Fourier et son système,* 2d ed. (Paris, 1839); J. Czynski, *L'Avenir des femmes* (Paris, 1841); and Clarisse Vigoreux, *Paroles de Providence* (Paris, 1834).
27. Fourier, *Théorie,* p. 156.
28. Flora Tristan, *L'Union ouvriére,* 3ᵉ ed. (Paris and Lyon, 1844), p. 49.
29. Tristan, *Pérégrinations,* I, 47.
30. Tristan, *La Tour,* p. 43.
31. Tristan, *Méphis,* I, 61–62.
32. Tristan, *La Tour,* p. 120.
33. Manuel, *The Prophets,* pp. 1–10.
34. Manuel, *The Prophets,* p. 300.
35. Tristan, *La Tour,* p. 247.
36. Tristan, *La Tour,* pp. 109, 139.
37. Tristan, *La Tour,* p. 141.
38. Tristan, *La Tour,* p. 34.
39. Tristan, *La Tour,* p. 216.
40. Tristan, *Union,* p. 53.
41. Chevalier, *Laboring Classes,* pp. 119–20.
42. Report of June 4, 1828, A. N. F⁷ 6772 quoted in Chevalier, *Laboring Classes,* p. 267.
43. A.-J.-B. Parent-Duchatelet. *De la Prostitution dans la ville de Paris, considerée sous le rapport de l'hygiène publique, de la morale et de l'administration* (Brussels and London, 1838, c. 1836); Tristan, *La Tour,* p. 164; Tristan, *Promenades,* chap. 8.
44. Tristan, *La Tour,* p. 89.
45. Flora Tristan, *Pétition pour le rétablissement de divorce,* A. N., Chambre des députés, no. 133, Pet. 71, 20 dec. 1837.
46. Léon Abensour, *Le Féminisme sous le règne de Louis Philippe et en 1848,* 2ᵉ ed. (Paris, 1913), p. 43.
47. Tristan, *Promenades,* pp. 324–54.
48. E. Levasseur, *Histoire des classes ouvrières et de l'industrie en France de 1789 à 1870,* 2 vols., 2d ed. (New York, 1969, c. 1904), II, 150–51; for a contemporary comment see *Ruche populaire* (nov. 1844), 212–13.
49. Levasseur, *Histoire,* II, 144; Puech, *La Vie,* p. 274, fn. 3.
50. For the workers' movement of the early 1830s see *l'Artisan* (26 Sept.–17 Oct. 1830); Efrahem, *De l'Association des ouvriers de tous les corps d'état* (Paris, 1833); Grignon *Les Réflexions d'un ouvrier tailleur sur la misère des ouvriers* (Paris, 1833); *Journal des ouvriers* (19 sept.–12 dec. 1830); Jules Leroux, *De la Nécessité de fonder un association* (Paris, 1833); and for analysis see Octave Festy, *Le Mouvement ouvrier au début de la monarchie de juillet* (Paris, 1908) and David H. Pinkney, *The French Revolution of 1830* (Princeton, N. J., 1972).
51. For working-class legislation, see Edouard Dolléans, *Histoire du mouvement ouvrier,* 2 vols. (Paris, 1936), I.
52. For strikes, see Jean P. Aguet, *Les Grèves sous la monarchie de juillet* (Geneva, 1954) and Peter Stearns, "Patterns of Industrial Strike Activity in France during the July Monarchy," *American Historical Review,* LXX, (Jan. 1965): 371–94.
53. Adolphe Boyer, *De l'Etat des ouvriers et de son amélioration par l'organisation du travail* (Paris, 1841).

54. *L'Atelier* (sept. 1840 à juillet 1850), 3 vols. (Paris). For a contemporary evaluation of workers' journals see J. Lerminier, "De la littérature des ouvriers," *Revue des deux mondes*, XXVIII, 4ᵉser. (15 dec. 1841); for historical analysis see Armand Cuvillier, *Un Journal d'ouviers, l'Atelier (1840–1850)* (Paris, 1954 c. 1914) and Georges Weill, "Les journaux ouvriers à Paris, 1830–70," *Revue d'histoire moderne et contemporaine*, IX (1907–08): 89 –103.

55. Agricol Perdiguier, *Le Livre du compagnonage*, 2 vols. (Paris, 1841 c. 1839) and *Mémoires d'un compagnon* (Moulins, 1914 c. 1852); Pierre Moreau, *De la Réforme des abus du compagnonage* (Auxerre, 1843) and *Un Mot aux ouvriers de toutes les professions* (Auxerre, 1841); J. Gosset, *Détails sur quelques Compagnons-Forgerons* (Paris, 1843). For historical analysis see Emile Coornaert, *Les Compagnonnages en France du Moyen Age à nos jours* (Paris, 1966) and E. Martin Saint-Léon, *Le Compagnonnage* (Paris, 1901).

56. Tristan, *Union*, p. 74, fn. 1.

57. Tristan, *Union*, chap. 2.

58. Tristan, *La Tour*, p. 191.

59. Tristan, *Union*, p. 70.

60. Tristan, *Union*, p. 62.

61. Tristan, *Union*, pp. 70–72, 108.

62. Tristan, *Union*, p. 71.

63. George Lichtheim, *The Origins of Socialism* (New York, 1969), pp. 68–70. Lichtheim misunderstands the importance of Tristan's feminism.

64. Tristan, *Union*, p. 6. Tristan, like most reformers of the July Monarchy, spoke of and to only the skilled workers. Her figures, however, seem to include the industrial proletariat. Cf. those given in Levasseur, II, 288.

65. Tristan, *Union*, pp. 23–43, 79. Her model for this was probably Daniel O'Connell of the Catholic Association. She seems to have had Victor Considérant, a Fourierist, in mind for the job. *Union*, p. 38.

66. Tristan, *Union*, p. 71.

67. Lichtheim, *The Origins*, pp. 68–70.

68. *Nouveau Monde* (July 1843). The author of the article also believed it was unrealizable.

69. *Echo de la fabrique de 1841* (15 fev. 1844), review of *Union ouvière*; Cf. Ferdnand Pelloutier's later statement that the *Bourses* were to become a "State within a State," in his *Histoire des Bourses du Travail* (Paris, 1902), p. 146, quoted in Irving Louis Horowitz, *Radicalism and the Revolt against Reason: The Social Theories of Georges Sorel* (London, 1961), p. 31.

70. G. D. H. Cole, *A History of Socialist Thought*, 3 vols. (London, 1953), I, pp. 185–88, stated that Tristan wrote the book to publicize the idea of a Workers' International.

71. For the political efforts and suffrage reform, see Abensour, *Le Féminisme*. Attempts to create women's associations were characteristic of the *Saint-Simoniennes;* see Adèle de Saint-Armand, *Proclamation aux femmes, sur la nécessité de fonder une société des droits de la femme* (Paris, 1834) and Femme Voinier and Femme Lefevre, *Association de femmes: Société du progrès* (Paris, 1839); for a hostile reaction to the idea that they were an economic pressure group, see the correspondence between the Société de

Marie (women hatmakers) and the *Union* (jan. 1844), 4 and (mars 1844), 2–3.

72. See for example, articles in *Atelier*, *l'Union*, and *Ruche populaire*; pamphlets by Boyer, *De l'Etat*; Efrahem, *De l'Association*; A. Egron, *Le Livre de l'ouvrier* (Paris, 1844); Moreau, *De la Réforme*. For the conditions of working-class women, see Caroline de Barrau, *Etude sur le salaire du travail féminin à Paris* (Paris, n.d.); Michel Chevalier, *Questions des travailleurs* (Paris, 1848); Emile Chevallier, *Les Salaires au XIX siècle* (Paris, 1887); Julie-Victoire Daubié, *La Femme pauvre au XIX siècle*, 3 vols. (Paris 1869); Théodore Fix, *Observations sur l'état des classes ouvrières* (Paris, 1849); H.-A. Frégier, *Des Classes dangereuses de la population*, 2 vols. (Paris, 1840); Ernest Legouvé, *La Femme en France au dix-neuvième siècle* (Paris, 1864); Paul Leroy-Beaulieu, *Le Travail des femmes aux XIX siècle* (Paris, 1873); Jules Simon, *L'Ouvrière*, 2d ed. (Paris, 1861); J. C. Paul Rougier, *Les Associations ouvrières* (Paris, 1864); Vée, *Du Pauperisme et des secours publics dans la ville de Paris* (Paris, 1845); Louis Villermé, *Tableau de l'état physique et moral* (Paris, 1840).

73. *Atelier* (mars 1845), 86; (30 dec. 1842), 31; (juin 1841), 77; *Union* (fev. 1846), 9–12; *Ruche populaire* (juillet 1841), 21–27; (mars 1844), 72–76; (avril 1844), 135–40; (août 1844), 231–36).

74. *Atelier* (mai 1841), 70; (juin 1844), 158.

75. Chevallier, *Les Salaires*; *Atelier* (dec. 1841), 28; (mai 1844), 124; (sept. 1844, 186; (jan. 1846), 251–52.

76. *Atelier* (juin 1844), 137–39; (mars 1844), 87.

77. Boyer, *De l'Etat*; *Atelier* (jan. 1844), 63; (fev. 1844), 66ff.

78. *Atelier* (jan 1841)36; (dec 1847), 367; (dec 1845), 230; (jan. 1846), 251-52; Efrahem, *De l'Association*; Moreau, *De la Réforme*, 65; *Ruche populaire* (mai 1844), 135–40.

79. Tristan, *La Tour*, p. 13.

80. Quoted in Puech, *La Vie*, pp. 166ff.

81. *Union* (dec. 1843), 4; *Union* (dec. 1844), 4; *Echo de la Fabrique de 1841* (Lyon), no. 59 (15 fev. 1844), 1–2; *Atelier* (31 mai 1843), 71–72.

82. Tristan, *La Tour*, p. 66.

83. Letters from Louis Vasbentir, 11 juin 1843, and S. Hugont, 17 juin 1843 reproduced in Puech, *La Vie*, pp. 470–81.

3 • From Separatism to Socialism: Women in the Russian Revolutionary Movement of the 1870s

• Barbara Alpern Engel

Russia of the 1860s and 1870s was in ferment. The eman-cipation of the serfs in 1861 had generated tremendous excite-ment throughout Russian society. Among the by-products was a women's movement dedicated to the spread of education as a necessary precondition to women's economic independence. As important, burning new questions were raised by bureau-crats and idealistic scions of nobles regarding the intellectuals' role in society. Once conscious of the ways in which the ruling classes had minimized the impact of peasant emancipation, they formed literally hundreds of groups over the next decades, dedicated to "serving the people" and spreading socialist ideas. One such group, the Chaikovskii circle was, as Engel writes, "the first in Russia in which women played an active and independent role." Just as Russia had its own unique tradi-tions—indigenous Russian socialism, or populism, saw the peas-ant village as the foundation stone of a new socialist Russia— so the association of feminism with radical politics differed from the utopian and later Marxist syntheses. It served as a stepping-stone to a commitment to social revolution. Yet Rus-sian women faced a common issue that affected socialist femi-nists throughout Europe. What should be their organizational ties to men? While coming to grips with their own identity, Russian women opted for "separatism," but later joined with men (and discarded their feminism) for the revolutionary struggle. What led the women in the Chaikovskii circle to abandon feminism for socialism? What did the loss of feminism

Group portrait: Sofia Leshern von Gershfeld *(top)*; **Aleksandra Kornilova** *(left center)*; **Sofia Perovskaia** *(right center)*; **Anna Vilberg** *(bottom)*. From the Russian journal *BYLOE* (August 1906).

mean to Russian socialism? Did Russian women share assumptions about women's nature with Flora Tristan?

During the 1870s, the Russian radical movement reached massive proportions. Thousands of young people, primarily students, took part in an attempt to initiate social revolution in Russia. In self-development circles they prepared themselves for action, then moved out among "the people"—peasants and sometimes factory workers—to share their socialist ideals. About 15 percent of these young people were women.

One of the first, and one of the most important, groups to emerge in the early 1870s was the Chaikovskii circle. Lacking any explicit ideology, the members of this group based their association on communal ideals and shared ethical principles. Their motivation was a sense of duty to "the people" (the peasantry); their aim, to spread socialist propaganda by both legal and illegal means; their ultimate goal, a peasant-based social revolution. The Chaikovskii circle had neither rules nor formal membership and judged its members according to their morality and their commitment to the cause of the Russian people. Between 1871 and 1873 the circle moved from self-development and the distribution of legally printed books to conducting socialist propaganda among factory workers and peasants.

The Chaikovskii circle was the first in Russia in which women played an active and independent role. Because of its informal organization, estimates of the group's membership vary, but thirty members, plus fifteen associates, is the one most commonly agreed upon.[1] Ten of the members were women: Sofia Perovskaia, Aleksandra and Liubov Kornilova, Elizaveta Koval'skaia, Sofia Leshern, Olga Schleissner, Aleksandra Obodovskaia, Anna Kuvshinskaia, and Larissa Chemodanova. They took part in every facet of the circle's activities. In fact, the group itself originated from the merger of two independent circles: a group of medical students led by Mark Natanson, and a women's circle, centered around Sofia Perovskaia and made up of students attending the newly opened Alarchin courses for women.[2]

53

The opening of the Alarchin courses in the spring of 1869 marked a new stage in the Russian women's movement. The movement had emerged soon after the emancipation of the serfs in 1861 and its founders, three middle-aged, relatively well-to-do noblewomen, aimed initially at helping women to become economically independent by creating inexpensive housing, and employment for them. They soon realized that without proper training economic independence was impossible, so they launched a struggle for higher education that led to the establishment of the Alarchin courses in 1869, a course for "Learned Obstetricians" in 1872, and a women's college in 1878. During the early stages of the movement, radical men helped women in a variety of ways. Because they saw the liberation of women as one aspect of their overall attack on authoritarian social relations, men lent money and expertise to assist in organizing communes and collectives, and sometimes entered chaste, or fictitious marriages solely to free women from "family despotism."[3] Liberated women, they hoped, would swell the still meager ranks of opposition by assuming a position alongside men.

By the early 1870s, these hopes began to be realized. The generation of women who enrolled in the Alarchin and other courses usually began as feminists, seeking education as a necessary step toward personal autonomy. But education, even autonomy, rarely remained an end in itself. At school they came into contact with a whole range of new ideas that urged them to action, not for themselves but for the good of society as a whole. Under the influence of these ideas, many abandoned feminism altogether to merge with the struggle for social revolution. For such women, feminism had become a way station on the road to revolution. The women of the Chaikovskii circle were among the first to travel this road.

The Alarchin courses, by bringing together a new generation of women, initially provided an enormous boost to the women's movement. The courses, nonetheless, fell short of the original goal of a university for women. They offered no degree, and the lectures were scarcely more sophisticated than those offered in the Alarchin boys' high school where the women's classes convened from six to nine each evening. But so great was the enthusiasm that they generated—and so low the overall quality of women's education—that graduates of teachers courses (the most advanced then available to women) joined graduates of high schools and boarding schools as students. The first group of students included Sofia Perovskaia, Aleksandra Kornilova and Ekaterina Koval'skaia. Of different backgrounds, but sharing an intense desire for knowledge, these three young women typified the new generation.

Sofia Perovskaia was born in 1854, the fourth child and second daughter in an old aristocratic family. During Sofia's childhood, her father, Lev Perovskii, occupied a series of powerful positions, serving as vice governor of Pskov and Tavrich, then as governor of St. Petersburg. He was relieved of this last post in 1866, when a revolutionary attempted to assassinate Tsar Alexander II. Sofia's childhood was not particularly happy. Her parents got along badly, and the children often had to witness their quarrels. A despotic and ambitious man, Lev Perovskii enjoyed the power of a governor's post and the entry into aristocratic circles it provided. This made him extremely critical of his wife, whom Sofia practically worshipped. Raised in the provinces, of relatively modest background and poorly educated, Varvara Stepanovna infuriated her husband by her shyness and provincialism, and by preferring domestic duties to social life. As his career advanced, their relationship became increasingly strained. When Perovskii would criticize his wife, the young Sofia would invariably take her mother's part. His rude, occasionally brutal, behavior left her with a lasting antagonism toward her father and a tendency to distrust all men.

Sofia's education reflected the vicissitudes of the family fortunes. Until she was twelve, tutors and a German governess instructed her, then Lev Perovskii lost his post, leaving the family without income and deeply in debt. This destroyed the study plan her mother had devised for her. On their small estate in the south of Russia, where mother and daughters retreated in 1865, Perovskaia was free to read as she chose in her grandfather's excellent library. Vasilii, her older brother, helped to channel her interests. During the summers, he would visit the country, bringing the latest books and articles that they would read and discuss in their mother's presence. On the basis of these readings and her own limited experience, Sofia at fifteen had become a "devotee of feminism" (*zhenskii patriot*) prepared to dedicate her life to the struggle for women's rights. She was overjoyed to hear about the Alarchin courses, for they provided her with a long-awaited opportunity to study systematically.[4]

Soon after she arrived in St. Petersburg she made friends with Aleksandra Kornilova. Only two generations removed from the peasantry, the Kornilov family lived modestly but well on the proceeds of a flourishing trade in porcelain. The mother had died of cholera in 1853, six weeks after the birth of Aleksandra, her seventh child in ten years of marriage. Unwilling to impose a stepmother on his children, Ivan Kornilov, their father, refused to remarry. Kornilov was a remarkably progressive man, an exception to the customary conservatism of the Russian merchantry, and he permitted his children an unusual degree of freedom. His only son Aleksander was a full-fledged "nihilist" who had a powerful influence on the whole family on account of his personal behavior and his merciless criticism of all superstition and prejudice. His younger sisters followed his lead. In 1866, Vera, then seventeen, enrolled in a teacher training course, an act that seems unobjectionable enough now, but which at the time was considered rather indecent. She made friends there, brought them home, and introduced them to her sisters, Nadezhda, Liubov, and Aleksandra. She also took them along with her to the gatherings of progressive society that were a characteristic feature of the mid-1860s. These gatherings lasted far into the night, but their father never tried to stop his daughters from going about unescorted in the evening. "I can't hire four governesses for them," he would laughingly tell their aunt, who was appalled by their "nihilist" appearance. Even in high school, Aleksandra had occasional conflicts with school authorities, which almost prevented her from gaining a first prize at graduation.[5]

Elizaveta Koval'skaia began attending the Alarchin courses soon after they opened. She came from Kharkov, in the south of

Russia, where she had been born a peasant, the illegitimate child of a noble father and a serf mother. Various dates, 1849, 1850, 1852, are given for her birth. She spent her early years as a serf, self-conscious about her illegitimacy and all too aware of her precarious position. "I was tormented by nightmares: I dreamt that they were selling me," she later remembered. That her father could sell her mother, but not the reverse seemed to her particularly unjust, and this combination of sexual and class oppression left a lasting impression. Only when she reached seven did her father agree to register her mother and her as free citizens.[6] (Osip Aptekman, a comrade, writes that it was Elizaveta herself who somehow convinced him.) Her father, Sol'ntsev, subsequently made her his heir and tried to transform her into a lady, but neither freedom nor wealth could erase the lessons of those early years. After a struggle with her father, she enrolled in a high school where a friend introduced her to the literature of the 1860s. In high school she organized a study circle, first of girls and then of both sexes. "We concentrated on social issues, but we also read papers on the natural sciences, astronomy, physics and other branches of knowledge [. . .] Chernyshevsky was one of our favorites—particularly his novel *What Is to Be Done?* with its exploration of the woman question."[7] Her father died shortly after she graduated, and Elizaveta used the property she inherited to get up evening classes for working women. In her classes, she always placed special emphasis on women's issues. When the police started to harass her school, Koval'skaia decided to go to St. Petersburg and attend the Alarchin courses.

The Alarchin courses, by providing the first opportunity for women of such diverse backgrounds to meet and get to know each other, brought new perspectives to Russian feminism. Soon after the courses opened, women began to gather in discussion groups in apartments around the city. "In these circles, the center of debate was always the woman question, although political and social themes were touched on in passing. The meetings of women were numerous, and so frequent that one barely had time to go from one to another,"[8] wrote Koval'skaia. But this was feminism with a difference. No longer was the beneficiary to be the individual herself. Autonomy had become a necessary step to social action. Still, in the struggle to attain that autonomy, they became highly critical of traditional institutions. Her friends, Aleksandra Kornilova remembered, were "trying to liberate themselves from the stagnant past and all tradition, from the family and from the marital authority that had enslaved them, preventing them from entering the broad path of self-development and work for the good of society."[9] In some ways, their ideas about personal life were far more radical than their critique of the social system.

Marriage, with its endless childbearing and household responsibilities, seemed particularly oppressive. The subject of free love never arose, since in the absence of effective contraception it was hardly a viable alternative. Instead, many simply rejected marriage, courtship, and all the trappings of traditional male-female relations. Aleksandra Kornilova recalled: "I had not the slightest inclination to marry anyone at that time. I despised ladies' men [and] I pitied the students who were mothers, absorbed by child care and petty household concerns. Courtship seemed either funny or coarse to me."[10] Perovskaia shared these views. In 1870 when the Franco-Prussian War broke out, Perovskaia sided with the Germans mainly because she found the French frivolous and overly inclined toward love affairs, according to her friend Aleksandra. Her brother Vasilii recalled a talk they had around this time, in which his sister denounced early marriages. Such marriages, she argued, "don't even allow the organism to develop properly. Maturity is reached around thirty or so, and if people feel sexual desire earlier, it's only because of the abnormal conditions of city life."[11] Later in the decade, Perovskaia became "fictitiously" engaged in order to assist a political prisoner. When her mother mistook the engagement for a real one and congratulated her daughter on behalf of the family, Perovskaia flew into a rage. "And even if it were real," she cried, "it's still too intimate to make such a fuss about."[12] The memoirs of other women of the period demonstrate the same tendency to downplay personal life. They tell us almost nothing about relationships with men, even when those relationships were evidently intense and loving. Koval'skaia, born Sol'ntseva, had married before she left Kharkov, but in her memoir she devotes only a sentence or two to her husband, Iakov Koval'skii, and not a word to their relationship.[13] To these women, involvement constituted danger; and not only the very concrete danger of being overwhelmed by petty household tasks, but the more abstract danger of being trapped in conventional femininity. If to feel sexual love was to be feminine, then these women would reveal no such weakness—at least not in their memoirs.

They sought to escape conventional femininity, not to redefine it or to expand its prerogatives. It was the public, not the private, sphere that mattered. They wanted independence, which to them meant the freedom men had to act in the interests of society as a whole. Although unconventional in their aspirations, they did share with their contemporaries certain assumptions about woman's special moral qualities, her greater readiness to sacrifice herself for others. This, too, qualified their desire for autonomy and prepared them to abandon their own struggle to serve "the people." Still, to act effectively they needed independence, for which only knowledge could provide the key. As Kornilova put it: "Knowledge alone could liberate a woman from material and intellectual enslavement."[14] More than just a means to economic independence, knowledge would grant freedom from men's tutelage, would indicate the proper path to action.

The desire to understand things for themselves gave a special intensity to women's groups. Elizaveta Koval'skaia has left us a description of one meeting held at the Kornilov's. As she entered, Aleksandra came to greet her at the door. "She was short and strongly built with close-cropped hair, and she wore an outfit that seemed almost to have become the uniform for the advocates of the 'woman question': a Russian blouse, cinched with a leather belt, and a short, dark skirt. . . . In general, she looked more like a young boy than a girl." Kornilova made the newcomers welcome.

She greeted us warmly and led us into a large room where around twenty women, divided into groups, were conversing animatedly. A few sat quietly, listening. So many women were smoking that it was difficult to breathe in the room. The hostess returned to her evidently unfinished argument, leaving us to make our own way in the new surroundings. Ginsburg (a medical student who had brought them there) left at once, without stepping foot into the room: the meeting consisted exclusively of women.[15]

Koval'skaia quickly became absorbed by an argument between a tall, stately blonde and a short brunette—Sofia Perovskaia. Perovskaia's appearance, that of a young girl, almost a child, made a great impression on her.

Her plain costume set her apart from others: a modest grey dress with a small white collar that somehow looked clumsy on her, like a school girl's uniform—you could see that she was totally oblivious to her appearance. The first thing you noticed was her broad, high forehead. Below the large forehead were eyelids drawn slightly downwards towards her temples; her grey-blue eyes seemed rather evasive, but held a kind of stubborn inflexibility. Her expression was distrustful. When she was silent, her small, childlike mouth was tightly shut, as if she feared saying something superfluous.[16]

The two women were arguing over whether or not men's and women's circles should remain separate. The blonde insisted that there was no reason to divide them; Perovskaia contended that joint meetings would be harmful since "men, as the more educated, would undoubtedly make it difficult for women to think independently."[17]

The issue was a very real one, with a practical as well as a psychological dimension. Radical concerns sometimes conflicted directly with women's needs, especially the needs of women students. The very presence of women in lecture halls constituted a significant victory, and that made it hard for them to support the activities of radical male students, whose protests promised women nothing while providing the government with an excuse to destroy recent gains. When student riots erupted in Moscow in 1869, some women students asked the men to call them off, concerned that the ensuing repressions would close their courses, too. The identical problem arose in St. Petersburg. In March 1869, a woman student wrote to a friend:

Things are terrible here in Petersburg. The students of the medical academy have started rioting and the result, of course, is that the medical academy is closed.... Sixty students have been arrested and many have already been exiled to far-off places. But what is worst for us is that women who were being allowed into the academy will of course be kicked out again.[18]

Sometimes differences even existed between the educational interests of men and women. In Kharkov, for example, disagreements arose when women's study circles first merged with men's in the winter of 1866–67. "The men wanted only to study science, while we were drawn to questions of real life (*zhivoi zhizni*)" remembered Koval'skaia.[19]

In addition, fear of male dominance led some women to see the presence of men as a genuine threat to their autonomy. This was all the more true because women often remained very sensitive to male expectations. In a male-dominated society, it was natural to want acceptance by men you respected, to want to fit into their notion of what a woman should be. The problem was not only that men would try to take over women's groups; but that women felt tempted to acquiesce. To all this, separatism provided the most straightforward solution.

By the late 1860s, women who wanted to could exclude men, because they had become less dependent on them. A growing minority of women had fought free of their families and had begun to live on their own. Women's networks—still few, fragile, and concentrated in urban areas—existed to provide support. And women, mainly teachers, had begun to assume positions from which they could influence others. Anna Kuvshinskaia, for example, later joined the Chaikovskii circle, but in 1870–71 she taught in a parochial school for girls in Viatka. Before they fired her for "sowing the seeds of nihilism," Kuvshinskaia managed to influence a number of her pupils. One of them later wrote: "I'm indebted to our teacher, Anna Kuvshinskaia, for giving me intellectual direction and a political perspective." She taught them to read, obtained books for them, and had them read aloud to each other while they did needlework.[20] Another of Kuvshinskaia's students was Larissa Chemodanova, who also joined the Chaikovskii circle. Before coming to St. Petersburg, Elizaveta Koval'skaia had been active among women for years.

The message they conveyed was primarily but not exclusively feminist. However much they might emphasize the woman question, it remained one facet of a larger critique inseparable from other social issues. Indeed, their concern with women's issues inevitably led them elsewhere in search of answers. When she taught the women workers of Kharkov, Koval'skaia quickly learned that passionate agitation on the woman question was not enough. Her students would become aroused, but she could provide them with no program for action, for, as she put it: "I myself had no idea how injustice could be righted."[21]

The need for a more comprehensive world view led Perovskaia and Kornilova in new directions too. In the spring of 1870, a professor at the Forestry Institute offered to teach qualitative analysis to interested students. Perovskaia (whose parents had gone abroad), Aleksandra Kornilova, and a couple of other students took advantage of his offer and settled in Lesnyi, a suburb of St. Petersburg, for the summer. Kornilova and Perovskaia had become close friends, and they would talk endlessly in the evening as they wandered in the park. To protect themselves from unpleasant encounters with soldiers stationed nearby, they disguised themselves in men's clothing, which they borrowed from Perovskaia's brother Vasilii. Femininity obviously remained a problem, and the woman question continued to dominate their conversations, but other issues claimed their attention, too. That summer they read *The Position of the Working Class in Russia* by F. Bervi Flerovskii and *Proletariat* and *Association* by M. Mikhailov.[22]

They, nevertheless, clung to their separatism after they returned to St. Petersburg. A translation of Karl Marx's *Kapital* had recently been published in a journal, and Vasilii Aleksandrov, a medical student, suggested that he, Perovskaia, Kornilova, and a few of their friends form a group to study it. Both Perovskaia and Kornilova refused, because as Kornilova put it: "Very few people were capable of understanding Marx, and we didn't want to take on faith, from somebody else's words a philosophy we could not study ourselves."[23] Instead, they formed a group exclusively of women in order to study the more accessible *On Political Economy* by John Stuart Mill, with commentaries by Chernyshevsky. They intended this circle to grow into a more active one, so they chose their membership with unusual care. On the basis of her work in Kharkov, Koval'skaia was one of the few people asked to join. "This circle is destined to become another, with different goals," Perovskaia announced rather portentiously at their first meeting, but she nevertheless took her studying very seriously. She would stop thoughtfully at each idea, develop it, and raise objections first to Mill, then to Chernyshevsky. It was obvious that she was carried away by intellectual work, and enjoyed it for its own sake, not only as a means to an end.[24]

Formal studies continued to claim a sizable share of their time. Besides attending the Alarchin courses, Perovskaia, Kornilova, and two of her sisters joined a circle of about a dozen women interested in taking geometry lessons from a math professor. Perovskaia turned out to be highly gifted in math, and she started to think seriously of enrolling in the Engineering Division of the Technological Institute, which her brother told her would admit women.

They all lived the lives of students now, attending classes, meetings, study groups, benefits, and so forth, and many drew ever further from their families. Koval'skaia already lived on her own (what had become of her husband she does not tell us). Ivan Kornilov allowed his daughters to do as they pleased (although Vera had contracted a fictitious marriage to escape their "bourgeois existence"). Perovskaia, however, felt terribly restricted. While she remained close to her mother, her relationship with her father had deteriorated still further. He threatened to lock her in the house, and he forbade her friends to visit. This was a declaration of war. Rather than submit, Perovskaia began to stay with various friends. She was only seventeen, however, and possessed no identity papers of her own, so Lev Perovskii could call in the police whenever he wished and force her to return. Several days after Sofia left home, her mother visited the Kornilov's in search of her. "Children have a duty to obey their parents," Varvara Stepanovna argued, as she asked for information as to her daughter's whereabouts. Kornilova stood up for Sofia. "She had a right to disobey her father," she maintained, "once he resorts to force and takes away her chance to study," the key to her liberation. In the name of the individual's right to freedom, Kornilova refused to betray her friend. A few days later, Lev Perovskii called in the police. They failed to locate his daughter, but she grew tired of evading them so she fled with the help of friends to Kiev, where she remained for several months until the combined pressures of his wife and son forced Lev Perovskii to give in. After he capitulated, Perovskii became so enraged that he refused to allow Sofia into his house, and mother and daughter had to visit each other in secret.[25]

This sort of confrontation was something new. Women had, of course, fled their families before, but Perovskaia had defied her father openly, thereby avoiding both the subterfuge necessary for fictitious marriage and the consequent dependence on a man. Her women friends defended her, concealed her, and arranged for her flight to Kiev. Perovskaia thus proved her independence, not only of her father, but of men in general. In her own eyes, a stage of struggle, the struggle for autonomy, had ended. Now she was free to devote herself to the liberation of others. The question was: How should she go about it?

A group of male students at the School of Medicine were raising the identical question. On Vulfovskii Street, fifteen of them lived communally, two per room, sharing their every kopek and dining mainly on horsemeat: the commune would purchase live horses and a veterinary student would slaughter them in the courtyard. They stored the meat in a shed and shared it with other communes. They took turns cleaning and cooking, and when they ran out of food, someone would go out, catch a dog or cat, and cook it, and everyone would eat it.[26] They were organizing among students, and in the fall of 1870, they decided to extend their contacts to women. Two of the men, Mark Natanson and Vasilii Aleksandrov, took to visiting the Kornilov home, but the women remained shy of them. Natanson was kind but patronizing, and Kornilova, conscious of his "superior knowledge and development," could never quite relax in his presence.[27] Still, timidity prevented neither she nor Perovskaia from paying a visit to his commune. They went on an errand, but they were also curious to see one of the communes that had become such a fixture of student life. The visit proved even more exciting than anticipated. They found a policeman at the gate and two soldiers in the kitchen, letting everyone in and no one out. Evidently, there was going to be a search. The police were on the lookout for Vasilii Aleksandrov, but someone had slipped out a window and warned him to stay away. Everyone was in an excellent mood. They drank tea and dined on horse-meat, and whiled away the time in singing and in the animated discussions so typical of the times. Everything struck the women as new and interesting. Soon after the visit, Vasilii Aleksandrov proposed to Kornilova. Threatened with exile, he was preparing to go abroad to set up a printing press, and he wanted her to assist him in his work. This would be a "rational marriage," he explained, for which both partners would require special intellectual and moral preparation. Kornilova, unimpressed, refused him, although she kept quiet about the fact that he failed to attract her much personally.[28] Her women friends heartily approved the refusal. Neither Perovskaia nor Kornilova repeated their visit to the commune. Until the close of the school year, they associated only with the students at the Alarchin courses.

Some of their friends disapproved of this separatism. Aleksandra Obodovskaia, for one, held herself aloof at the women's meetings. Born in 1848, to a merchant family from Simbirsk, she had attended high school in St. Petersburg. Obodovskaia was somewhat older than the other members of her circle and was already involved in conspiratorial work. Olga Schleissner was another opponent of separatism. Schleissner was born in 1850, the daughter of a nobleman from Orel. She had graduated from an elite boarding school in St. Petersburg and then enrolled in the Alarchin courses. Her contacts with radical circles were extensive. Schleissner lived in the same building as the Vulfovskii commune, and was considered a member: she moved easily in that milieu. Koval'skaia once accompanied her to a crowded meeting where they two were the only women present.[29]

Schleissner acted as a sort of liaison between male and female students. Involved both politically and romantically with Natanson, she willingly assisted in his efforts to establish a circle parallel with his own. The Kornilova sisters and their friends seemed likely candidates, so Schleissner gathered information about them (which she supplied to Natanson), argued with them over separatism, and tried in various ways to strengthen the links between men and women students.[30] (It was she who had sent Perovskaia and Kornilova on their errand to the Vulfovskii commune.)

Perovskaia and Kornilova, gravitating steadily leftward, proved responsive to these efforts. At the end of the spring term, they astounded their friends by reversing their previous stance entirely. Koval'skaia learned about it from a member of a women's circle, who dropped in one day, and obviously upset, told her: "Imagine! Kornilova and Perovskaia, who have always spoken against uniting with men's circles, have themselves entered a men's circle." A meeting was held at Koval'skaia's to confront them. The two women came late. Kornilova's manner was relaxed, even a bit defiant, but Perovskaia seemed embarrassed and depressed, if also ready to defend herself. Everyone leveled accusations at them, but a woman who later became a lawyer led the attack. When she was finished, Kornilova took the defensive with the enthusiasm characteristic of her, but no one found her particularly convincing. Perovskaia, on the other hand, refused to defend herself at all. She simply replied: "We are not going to explain anything to you," then rose and walked out with Kornilova. Neither Koval'skaia nor her friends ever found a satisfactory explanation for the shift.[31]

The answer lies in the fact that for these women, feminism had more of a personal than a social significance. That is, the "woman question" addressed the oppression they faced as individuals, helped to free them from "domestic servitude," but it offered nothing to alleviate other social inequities. Only radicalism dealt with those. Autonomy thus became a means and not an end in itself. While still of immense personal importance, it was also valuable because it prepared the way for women to serve society as a whole. Feminism and radicalism were not in conflict with each other, since without freedom, women could not be useful. Separatism was a stage in the process. It arose out of women's need to develop themselves free from self-consciousness and insecurity, out of timidity before men, but not out of dislike of them. Having achieved independence and overcome their timidity, women with a social conscience felt ready to move beyond "personal" struggle. It is no coincidence that Perovskaia joined a men's circle only after establishing her independence from her father. By struggling successfully against him, confronting him "woman to man" so to speak, she had won her place in the larger world. Kornilova, as in so many other things, followed her friend Sofia. "Sofia possessed much greater abilities, and I became subject to her influence," she remembered.[32] The political development of other women followed the same general pattern: successful struggle for autonomy led them to abandon feminism for radicalism.

A significant factor in that evolution was the character of the men of the Chaikovskii circle, with whom the women affiliated. Rejecting hierarchical organizations dominated by a single leader, Natanson and his friends based their alliance on trust and on shared moral principles, on comradeship and egalitarian relations. Formally, they had ceased to be interested in the woman question. It was impossible to separate it from the emancipation of the proletariat as a whole, Aleksandrov once argued during a student debate. Once the labor question was solved, the woman question would automatically solve itself.[33] These beliefs did not prevent them from raising the woman question when they began to organize factory workers. Discussions of women's role, of the family, even of the position of the children helped to instill a revolutionary perspective.[34] The men also participated willingly in efforts to liberate women from "family despotism." They prized all individuals prepared to serve the cause, women especially, so among the tasks they set themselves was to free them. This was, in their eyes, comparable to freeing a political prisoner,[35] a comparison that failed to rob such attempts of a certain romantic quality. Although it took place a year after Perovskaia and Kornilova affiliated with the men, the marriage of Larissa Chemodanova and Sergei

Sinegub serves as an excellent case in point. Chemodanova, sixteen, was a student at a diocese school in Viatka, where Anna Kuvshinskaia, her teacher, had already sown the seeds of rebellion. The daughter of a village priest, Chemodanova wanted to continue her studies and devote herself to serving the people. This her family strictly forbade. They made her a virtual prisoner in her home, and after she once attempted to flee, they tightened surveillance on her and prepared to marry her off by force. She appealed to Kuvshinskaia, who wrote to a member of the Chaikovskii circle to ask for help. Rescue would have to come quickly, the letter warned, since Chemodanova had sworn she would kill herself rather than continue to live under such circumstances. The group decided to arrange a fictitious marriage. They chose Sergei Sinegub as the husband, since his noble birth would make him an attractive son-in-law. They then rented a carriage and a horse, so that Sinegub could arrive in style at the home of Vasilii Chemodanov. Pretending to be the secret lover of Larissa, Sinegub paid her court until the father agreed to let them wed. They spent another month behaving like an engaged couple. It ended with Sinegub actually falling in love with Chemodanova, a feeling that the ethics of his group forced him to conceal. Following the wedding, he brought his bride to Petersburg, and delivered her to a woman's commune. They began to live together as man and wife only after another year, when Sinegub discovered that she loved him, too.[36]

These young men who placed such emphasis on moral behavior had been sensitized by the sixties to issues of importance to women. During the courtship and marriage, Sinegub displayed the sort of tact and delicacy that made him and his friends fit associates for young women seeking autonomy yet also eager to be useful socially. Unlike the men of the sixties, these men could be trusted not to exploit or betray women.

In the spring of 1871, Natanson's group decided to expand their activities by organizing a self-development circle for the summer and inviting selected male and female students. After school ended, Olga Schleissner, Aleksandra Obodovskaia, Sofia Perovskaia, Liubov and Aleksandra Kornilova, Nadezhda

Skvortsova (another student at the Alarchin courses), Mark Natanson, and a number of other men—seventeen people in all—moved into two neighboring cottages at a summer resort. Koval'skaia, who had to go south on account of her health, did not take part. The group set out to define the tasks at hand.[37] Someone, probably Natanson, had already worked out a systematic study program that included physiology, psychology, and political economy. Natanson led their discussions, thereby vindicating some of the women's earlier fears. "He turned our attention to details and made us draw conclusions from what we had read," Kornilova remembered. "It took us a while to notice that the conclusions did not emerge from our heated debates, that Natanson had prepared them beforehand, and that he was leading us in a direction that he himself had charted." Still insecure intellectually and committed to working with men, the women did not protest. When Kornilova's turn came to summarize a chapter of John Stuart Mill, she felt like a student at an exam, unsure of what she knew—although she underwent the test rather well.[38] The group also engaged in mutual criticism in order to get to know each other better and work out their differences in preparation for practical work.[39]

By the end of August, they had chosen as their political work the "cause of the book" (*knizhnoe delo*). They would acquire and distribute books, at low prices, to libraries and to other circles that the group would help to establish. Soon after that decision, Nadezhda Skvortsova and four of the men left the group.[40] The rest made their headquarters in an apartment on Kabinetskaia street. Vera Griboedova (Kornilova) registered as the mistress of the house; Natanson, Chaikovskii, two other men and Olga Schleissner lived there too. Over the next few years, a number of other men and women joined the group. Among the women were Anna Kuvshinskaia, who had been fired from her teaching job for "nihilist tendencies," and Larissa Chemodanova, the young woman she had helped to free.

The group came to be known as the Chaikovskii circle, after Nikolai Chaikovskii, one of the group's organizers. Until its demise in 1874, it engaged in a variety of activities, all aimed at fulfilling the debt that intellectuals owed the people. During the winter of 1871–2 the "cause of the book" flourished, supplied by a printing press run by Vasilii Aleksandrov in Zurich, and by some publishers and booksellers who provided the circle with books at a 30 to 50 percent discount. The books they distributed to provincial circles, together with reading lists to serve as guidelines for self-education. They had managed to establish links in thirty-seven provinces when the government cracked down on them, warning bookstores not to traffic with them and confiscating their books. In any case, many people had grown dissatisfied with work that was limited by necessity to the educated.

Women were among the first to move in a new direction. In the late spring of 1872, Aleksandra Obodovskaia taught in a village school in Tver and then briefly conducted propaganda among the peasantry. That same spring, Perovskaia assisted a village schoolteacher in Samara and then traveled about the countryside alone, vaccinating peasants against smallpox and living the life of the people. In the fall, men and women of the circle began to settle in various sections of the city to organize schools in apartments and conduct propaganda among workers in the evenings and on holidays. Larissa Chemodanova and Anna Kuvshinskaia took part in this work. Aleksandra Kornilova, recently returned from studying women's diseases in Austria, read aloud to workers and talked to them about the Viennese Social Democratic movement. Sofia Perovskaia settled in a small room on the outskirts of the city with Leonid Shishko, another member of the group, and with him ran a school for workers. She also took charge of correspondence with prisoners in the Peter Paul fortress, which she conducted with the help of a policeman someone had bribed. In addition to political work, Perovskaia assumed the role of housekeeper for her apartment, "dragging buckets of water from the Neva, serving as cook and keeping house."[41]

All these efforts proved short-lived. Arrests soon decimated the group, and by the spring of 1874 everyone had been imprisoned. Some, including Perovskaia, Kornilova, and Schleissner, were to resume activity later in the decade, but the Chaikovskii circle as such had come to an end.

The Chaikovskii circle contributed to the Russian radical movement by its ethical tone as much as by its activities. Peter Kropotkin, its best-known member, later remembered: "Never did I meet elsewhere such a collection of morally superior men and women as the score of persons whose acquaintance I made at the first meeting of the circle of Chaikovskii. I still feel proud of having been received into that family."[42] Convinced that they could influence others by their own principled behavior, the members of the group aspired to purity and total self-sacrifice. These qualities radicals (like other members of their society) presumed that women already possessed. The Chaikovskii women "were the purest embodiment of those ideal, endlessly devoted and self-sacrificing women who have so often inspired our poets and novelists," wrote Peter Lavrov, whose ideas helped to shape the generation of the 1870s.[43] It is likely that the women intensified the group's moral fervor. "The feminine influence on the masculine element gave the membership such a moral character," writes one historian of populism.[44] The women were certainly demanding. True to their denial of traditional female roles, they would tolerate no flirtation or sexual advances from their male comrades. Perovskaia, "a rigorist from head to toe, strict, stubborn and consistent," introduced a particularly strong note of asceticism. She was quick to criticize any breach of ethics: at one meeting she attacked a comrade who claimed to be a rigorist, but who allowed himself extra expenditures for clothing. As a result, he was kicked out of the group.[45] Another time, she accused someone of being a ladies' man. By embracing this perception of themselves in a group that valued such qualities highly, the women gained a special influence, above and beyond the activities they shared with men.

But they paid a price. To join the Chaikovskii circle they abandoned their earlier feminism. This meant in practice that professional aspirations sooner or later gave way to political work. Some of the women tried hard to combine the two: Kornilova, for example, studied midwifery in Vienna and women's diseases in St. Petersburg before devoting her time completely to organizing. For a while, Kuvshinskaia attended the courses for "Learned Obstetricians" newly opened in St. Petersburg. In 1873, Olga Schleissner earned a degree in midwifery, but she never practiced it. Perovskaia, released on bail soon after her arrest, trained as a medical aide and worked in a hospital until 1877, when she, too, resumed full-time political work. Abandonment of feminism also meant that women's needs first became subordinated to the struggle of the whole working class and then were forgotten altogether. Even when they organized, radical women rarely focused on their peasant and worker sisters. And of woman-oriented issues—of marriage and the family, equality of education, the right of women to be treated with dignity—they rarely spoke at all.

The pattern would repeat itself in years to follow. Many concerned and intelligent women felt that they had no choice but to move from feminism to radicalism, and it is difficult not to agree with them. The woman question offered no solution to the inequities that pervaded Russian society, and whatever their disabilities, educated women were, after all, highly privileged in comparison to peasants and workers. Moreover, their experience with feminism was not without positive results. It left them free of the traditional constraints on women: it gave them some confidence in their own ideas, and a sense of sisterhood that remained even after feminism was abandoned. Their male comrades, affected by the same ideas, treated them respectfully and as equals. Acknowledging the difficulties that women experienced conducting propaganda, men and women alike agreed that female radicals should be granted no special dispensations. "Let the women who could go to the people like the men, in peasant clothes and as best they could avoid the unpleasantness connected with belonging to the fair sex," they concluded.[46] Nevertheless, feminist battles were far from won —battles not only for the earlier territory of education and personal autonomy, but battles also in the more personal realm of love, sex, and marriage. The time may not have been ripe for struggle in those areas, but when it subsumed the woman question to the question of the working class as a whole, the left ceased to deal creatively with those personal issues. Never, as a movement, would it return to them again.

NOTES

1. Franco Venturi, *Roots of Revolution* (New York, 1966), p. 481.
2. There is considerable disagreement on this point. Most Western historians, Franco Venturi, *Roots of Revolution*, included, date the Chaikovskii circle from 1869, that is, well before the women joined it. But very few of the members of Natanson's commune actually became members of the combined group. Aleksandra Kornilova, as well as Peter Kropotkin and Sergei Kravchinskii, two male members of the circle, contend that it arose in August 1871, that is, after the men's and women's circle had merged. Aleksandra Kornilova-Moroz, "Perovskaia i osnovanie kruzhka Chaikovtsev," *Katorga i Ssylka*, no. 22 (1926): 23.
3. Everyone in Russia had to carry a passport, and women were registered on their father's until they were twenty-one. If a man refused to give his daughter a separate residence permit, marriage was her only way out. Unconsummated unions, arranged solely to free women, came to be known as fictitious marriages. They were quite common during the 1860s. For an account of one, see *Sonya Kovalevsky, Her Recollections of Childhood* (New York, 1895).
4. Aleksandra Kornilova-Moroz, "Perovskaia."
5. Aleksandra Kornilova-Moroz, "Avtobiografiia," in *Entsiklopedicheskii slovar "Granat,"* vol. 40, pp. 203–204, 207; Kornilova-Moroz, "Perovskaia," pp. 9–10.
6. Russia's estate system meant that people could change their social status only through legal action.
7. E. Koval'skaia, "Avtobiografiia," in *Entsiklopedicheskii slovar "Granat,"* vol. 40, p. 191.
8. E. N. Koval'skaia, "Moi vstrechis S. L. Perovskoi," *Byloe*, no. 16 (1921): 43, or Barbara Engel and Clifford Rosenthal, eds., *Five Sisters: Women Against the Tsar* (New York, 1975), p. 216.
9. Kornilova-Moroz, "Perovskaia," pp. 12–13.
10. Ibid., p. 18.
11. Vasilii L. Perovskii, *Vospominaniia o sestre* (M–L, 1927), p. 51.
12. Ibid., p. 85.
13. See *Five Sisters*, especially the memoir of Olga Liubatovich, for examples of this.
14. Kornilova-Moroz, "Perovskaia," p. 19.
15. Koval'skaia, "Moi vstrechi," pp. 42–43; *Five Sisters*, pp. 212–13.
16. Koval'skaia, p. 43; *Five Sisters*, p. 213.
17. Koval'skaia, p. 43; *Five Sisters*, p. 214.
18. S. F. Kovalevskaia, *Vospominaniia i pis'ma* (Moscow, 1961), p. 141.
19. E. Koval'skaia, "Moi vstrechi s Lazarem Goldenbergom," *Katorga i Ssylka*, no. 3 (1924): 89.
20. A. Iakimova, "Avtobiografiia," in *Entsiklopedicheskii Slovar "Granat,"* vol. 40, pp. 623–24.
21. E. Koval'skaia, "Iz moikh vospominanii," *Katorga i Ssylka*, no. 22 (1926): 30–31.
22. Kornilova-Moroz, *"Granat,"* p. 208.
23. Kornilova-Moroz, "Perovskaia," p. 16.

24. Koval'skaia, "Moi vstrechi s S. L. Perovskoi," p. 44.
25. Kornilova-Moroz, "Perovskaia," p. 19.
26. *Revoliutsionnoe Narodnichestvo*, vol. I, p. 235.
27. Kornilova-Moroz, *"Granat,"* pp. 210–211.
28. Kornilova-Moroz, "Perovskaia," p. 18. In an account of the Chaikovskii circle written around 1880, this proposal is described as follows: "Here Aleksandrov for the first time attempted to propagate his original views on free love. But here, too, he failed. However young the members of the women's circle were, nevertheless they quickly realized that Aleksandrov wanted to lead them into some kind of swamp." *Revoliutsionnoe Narodnichestvo*, vol. I. p. 217.
29. E. Koval'skaia, "Iz moikh vospominanii," *Katorga i Ssylka*, no. 22, p. 33.
30. Kornilova-Moroz, "Perovskaia," p. 22; N. V. Chaikovskii, "Cherez pol'stoletiia," *Golos minuvshego na chuzhoi storone*, no. 3 (1926): 150.
31. Koval'skaia, "Moi vstrechi s Perovskoi," p. 45; *Five Sisters*, p. 217.
32. Kornilova-Moroz, *"Granat,"* p. 207.
33. I. E. Deniker, "Vospominaniia," *Katorga i Ssylka*, no. 11 (1924): 27.
34. *Protsess 193–kh* (Moscow, 1906), p. 6; L. Tikhomirov, *Zagovorshchiki i politsii* (Moscow, 1930), p. 28.
35. Nikolai A. Charushin, *O dalekom proshlom* (Moscow, 1926), p. 105; Sergei Sinegub, *Zapiski Chaikovtsa* (Moscow, 1929), p. 19.
36. See pp. 18–82 of Sinegub, *Zapiski Chaikovtsa* for one of the more detailed accounts of a fictitious marriage that turned into a charming love story. For a sarcastic commentary on it, see [L. Tikhomirov] *V Pod'pol'e* (SPb, 1907).
37. Chaikovskii, pp. 180–181.
38. Kornilova-Moroz, *"Granat,"* p. 213.
39. *Revoliutsionnoe Narodnichestvo*, vol. I, p. 220.
40. Skvortsova dropped out because of family pressures; we do not know why the men did.
41. E. A. Pavliuchenko, *Sof'ia Perovskaia* (Moscow, 1959), pp. 24–26.
42. Peter Kropotkin, *Memoirs of a Revolutionist* (New York, 1970), p. 304.
43. P. L. Lavrov, *Narodniki-Propagandisty, 1873–8 godov* (Leningrad, 1925), p. 69.
44. V. Bogucharskii [Vasilii Iakovlev] *Aktivnoe narodnichestvo 70–kh godov* (Moscow, 1912), p. 153.
45. N. Asheshov, *Sof'ia Perovskaia* (Petersburg, 1921), p. 19.
46. "Starik," "Dvizhenie semidesiatykh godov po Bol'shomu protsessu," *Byloe*, no. 12 (1906): 70.

4 • Socialism Faces Feminism: The Failure of Synthesis in France, 1879-1914

• Marilyn J. Boxer

After languishing under the censorship of Louis Napoleon's Second Empire, the causes of women and the working class reemerged in the Paris Commune of 1871. Whatever the patriotic, personal, political, or economic goals that motivated the Communards, women fought and died in the violent struggle to create a new society. In the continuing debate that preceded and followed the formation of the Third Republic, republican journalists, educated artisans, leisured ladies, and working women offered presciptions that presumed the unity of socialism and feminism. By the 1890s, numerous socialist and feminist organizations existed, centered around rival individual leaders and periodical publications. The first group to champion a union of women with working-class interests had been the French Workers' party (P.O.F.), which at its founding congress in 1879 had called for the complete equality of the sexes in public as well as private life. Under the leadership of the Marxist Jules Guesde, it never failed to include women's rights in its rhetoric. But the first effort to organize women as socialist feminists came twenty years later when Elisabeth Renaud and Louise Saumoneau, two working-class women, founded a Socialist Feminist Group in Paris's Latin Quarter; they won no support from any of the socialist parties. French socialism rejected both the indigenous utopian socialist heritage and the imported Marxist rationale that embraced feminism. Were there no effective feminist leaders in the French left? Was the failure, as Saumoneau suggested, due to the "torment preceding the realization of socialist unity" (in 1905)?

Were there peculiarly French conditions that made feminism appear an "anti-French disease?" What happened to socialist feminism in the land of its birth?

In the last years of France's authoritarian Second Empire, long-repressed conflicts over the "social question" reappeared in public forums and were echoed in renewed debates over the role of women in a changing world. The foundation of the Ligue française pour le Droit des Femmes (French League for the Rights of Women) in 1869, however, awakened no great interest in a nation increasingly concerned with the threat of a fast-growing German Empire on its borders. During the Franco-Prussian War, the Paris Commune, and the protracted competition for political and economic ascendancy that characterized the emergence of the Third Republic in 1875, women's issues remained submerged. Despite the participation of thousands of women in the Commune and the heroic defense of accused Communards by the "Red Virgin," Louise Michel,[1] only a few Frenchmen of any class envisioned a major role for women in the new public life.

In economic life, however, women's presence was undeniable. By 1866, they constituted 30 percent of the industrial labor force, a proportion which increased gradually to 38 percent by 1911.[2] The continuing movement of women from country to city and home to workshop evoked negative responses from both middle-class moralists and working-class traditionalists. In 1860, the eminent historian Michelet had declared *ouvrière* (working woman) an "impious, sordid word."[3] When working men assembled in congresses in 1876, 1878, and 1879 for the first time since the repression of the Commune, they showed their concern for the presence of women in the growing capitalist economy by placing the "woman question" at the head of each agenda. Moving toward reassertion of revolutionary socialist principles on the question of class conflict, they struggled also to resolve differing views about the place of women in both capitalist and socialist society.

French working men of the 1870s had inherited several traditions, two indigenous and one imported, with widely different implications for women. From Fourier and the Saint-Simonians, as seen in Chapter II, came a commitment to elevation of women's status. If Flora Tristan's "utopian synthesis" of socialism and feminism remained largely unknown, her belief that working-class men had a special obligation toward women was widely shared by participants in working-class assemblies. Many, perhaps even most workers, however, understood their charge in the manner outlined for them by the artisan anarchist Proudhon: "equality" defined as "equivalence" of the sexes in fundamentally separate spheres of life. Only the socialism of the Germans, Marx and Engels, clearly implied resolution of the woman question through redefinition of age-old relations between the sexes. Whatever the origins of their socialism, most men of the left in nineteenth-century France (and Europe) understood their persuasion as a call for revolution in political and economic structures, having little to do with private life.[4]

"Equality for women," however, meant to some radical women in the late nineteenth century emancipation from traditional sex roles and revision of discriminatory economic practices and legal codes that had institutionalized female inferiority. Several early feminist organizations in France, hearing working men discuss new roles for women, sent delegates to the socialist workers' congresses.[5] The strongest encouragement to their hopes came in 1879, when the founding congress of the French Workers' party (Parti ouvrier français, P.O.F.) at Marseille passed a resolution that called for the complete equality of the sexes in public and private life. Rejecting the precedent of earlier Proudhon-inspired congresses, which had prescribed only traditional familial roles for women, the delegates at Marseille specifically denied such a limitation: "Considering that a role should reflect the choice of the individual who fulfills it, the Congress does not assign any particular role to woman. She will assume in society the role and the place which her vocation dictates." Henceforth the socialist party would accept members "without distinction of sex."[6]

By adopting this position on the role of women, the Marseille congress matched in revolutionary rhetoric its resolution favoring expropriation of the propertied classes, which was the most radical statement taken by a French workers' congress since the Commune. Subsequently incorporated into the P.O.F. program of 1880[7] and repeated for decades in party manifestos, the call for female equality masked the reality that the majority of this party, a coalition of anarchist, Marxist, and independent socialists, and the subsequent splinter groups which comprised French socialism, remained deeply divided over the woman question. For the next twenty-six years, until the unification of the Section française de l'Internationale ouvrière (French Section of the Workers' International, S.F.I.O.) in 1905, French socialist groups would attract women seeking political expression and feminists searching for allies.

As political conditions in the Third Republic stabilized and it became clear that no revolution was imminent, French socialism opted for parliamentarianism. After the Dreyfus crisis at the turn of the century, some socialists joined bourgeois ministries. On the eve of World War I, the S.F.I.O. counted a million and a half votes and constituted the largest party in the Chamber. In this political game, no women were permitted to play. Lacking the vote they possessed no power at the polls.

Political issues, however, tell only part of the tale. Equality for women in late nineteenth-century France also entailed economic and sex-role conflicts that socialist men preferred to avoid. By espousing working women's right to relief from economic exploitation, and supporting "protective" legislation that restricted women's work in industry, they might relieve women of a double burden, return them to their homes, and hopefully raise men's wages. French family life might again fulfill its purpose: the bourgeois ideal, promoted by Proudhon and his followers within the French working class, of home as the basis of civilization and, no less, necessary retreat from its stresses. Women, therefore, who tried to translate revolutionary rhetoric into programs to reform the reality of women's oppression met stubborn resistance.[8]

After 1879 the French Workers' Party, the several smaller

French socialist parties, and eventually the unified S.F.I.O. opened their ranks to women. If relatively few joined—probably no more than one thousand, constituting at most 3 percent of the membership—nevertheless, a handful of exceptional women played a significant role in attempting to unite the causes of women and the working class. In the early 1880s two propagandists, Léonie Rouzade and Paule Mink, advocating feminist and socialist goals, participated in the foundation of rival socialist parties. During the 1890s, the decade of mass organization for both socialist and feminist groups, Aline Valette served as secretary to both the P.O.F. and a coalition of French feminist groups. Between 1899 and 1905, in the struggles for socialist unification, Elisabeth Renaud and Louise Saumoneau tried to organize and win recognition for a separate group for socialist women. From 1906 until the outbreak of World War 1, while the S.F.I.O. wrestled to resolve tensions among its reformist and revolutionary factions and to gain some share of governmental power, Dr. Madeleine Pelletier won membership on the party executive and waged a virtual one-woman war to insinuate radical feminism into mainstream socialism. All tried to accommodate in their lives a dual commitment to women's rights and to working-class liberation. They considered feminism and socialism inextricably linked. For them no separation of the woman question from the social question was possible. Examination of their careers, however, shows that the tie between feminism and socialism was a marriage of convenience between unequal allies. Only women who in practice subordinated their feminism to their socialism could remain within the party; and one, Valette, brought into the P.O.F. a new theoretical justification for the relationship of inequality.

The first woman to test the new public role advocated by the Congress of 1879 was Rouzade (Louise-Léonie Camusat, 1839–1916), who wrote a novel, *The World Turned Upside Down*, and decided in 1880 actually to challenge established order by presenting herself as a candidate for the municipal council of Paris. While she won approval from one socialist faction, the leader of the dominant group at Marseille, the Marxist Jules Guesde, and his party rejected her candidacy as "an encumbering thing" for socialists seeking new members. Faced with her challenge to its principles, the party, she later declared, "played deaf and dumb." Caught in the rivalry between socialist groups, her only solid support came from the Union des Femmes (Women's Union) she herself had formed, a small, short-lived group of bourgeois women whose demands included communal responsibility for child rearing.[9]

Four years before, however, Guesde had strongly attacked a congress of Proudhon-inspired working men for prescribing a purely domestic life for women. With considerable eloquence he had protested their wish to confine women to traditional sex roles, declaring in his newspaper, "The place for woman is no more at home than anywhere else. Like that of man, it is anywhere and everywhere she may wish to go." Through a long career as the leader of the largest and strongest of French socialist parties, Guesde continued, on occasion, to defend feminist principles. Strongly influenced by Chernyshevsky's novel, *What Is To Be Done?*, Guesde envisioned a new society that allowed absolute self-determination to individuals of both sexes. With economic equality assured all citizens, socialized production of household services, community-supported education and health care, social protection would supersede the functions of the family, and the new and higher form of relationship among individuals, postulated by Marx, would become possible. Guesde was, his granddaughter suggests, a "feminist by instinct"; he was also a Marxist. But his principles faded before expediency and women's rights remained an ideal.[10]

Politically, however, the woman question could be useful. During the 1880s in the critical tasks of consolidating a Marxist party and contesting for power among socialist factions, Guesde and his followers employed the talents of three women, Léonie Rouzade, Louise Michel, and Paule Mink. Rouzade joined another faction, "ran" for office, and soon dropped out of politics. Michel, amnestied in 1880 from banishment to New Caledonia for her role in the Commune, avoided further conflict by self-exile to England. Mink, an impassioned orator, spent five years after the amnesty aiding Guesde and his group to build the new workers' party. As a self-styled *pétroleuse* ("female arsonist";

one of the women accused of putting Paris to the torch in the final days of the Commune), she used her notoriety deliberately to attract audiences and won support for socialism by her tales of the suffering of women laboring for capitalist profits. Her life and long career exemplify the role played by women in the formative period of socialism.

Paule Mink (Pauline Adèle Mekarska, 1839–1901) was born in France of dissident members of the Polish and French nobility.[11] Reared in the revolutionary tradition of 1830, she entered public life in the later years of the Second Empire, quickly demonstrating the superior talent as a speaker with which she would serve the socialist cause. Even a police agent who described her an an ugly, slightly deformed, sloppy woman with a strong mouth, big nose, and missing teeth, admitted that she was "completely metamorphosed when she speaks, for then her face lights up and wit sparkles in her eyes."[12] Gifted with a flair for the dramatic, skillful in manipulating crowds, she won applause even from hostile audiences. The combined careers of socialist agitator and single mother (she bore eight and raised four children, both with and without a husband), often made misery her lot. Never far from destitution, she lived from lecture receipts, subsidies dispensed sporadically by socialist groups, and stratagem. Police reported she ate at restaurants and left without paying, and used pseudonyms and frequent changes of address to cheat landlords. She also sewed, kept books, proofread, gave lessons, and finally, advertised in socialist papers for "any kind of work."[13] Suffering privation herself, however, she spoke to distressed workers with authenticity, and they followed her.

In her campaign against the social order Mink enlisted in the movements against clericalism, against capitalism, and against patriarchy. Her first public act of defiance was interference with a religious procession. Her first publication was an attack on Louis Napoleon's Empire, an article, *Les Mouches et les Araignées* (The Flies and The Spiders), which portrayed the people caught in webs spun by bourgeois masters of government, industry, and church.[14] The first organization she founded was a cooperative society for women workers. She demonstrated her feminist philosophy at the very outset of the organized workers' movement, publicly refuting an assertion by French workers at the Lausanne congress of the First International in 1867, that women belong at home living a completely private life and depending entirely on men for their subsistence. Instead of restricting the access of women to work, organized working men should concentrate on ameliorating the conditions of work for everyone. They should endeavor to establish a more equitable system that would eliminate all nonworking "parasites," reward equal work with equal pay, and, far from fearing competition from women seeking men's jobs, attend to the proper distribution of work along "natural" lines of division. Mink thus subscribed to the "separate spheres" concept, believing men and women predisposed by nature toward complementary roles.[15]

Both sexes, however, could serve the revolution. If men and women, peasants and proletariat, together united and rebelled, they might destroy the capitalist system which oppressed them. Their effort had already commenced with the Commune, during which Mink had founded a club for women, opened a school for poor children, helped create an ambulance corps, and contributed to several journals. As an agent of the Commune, she had also toured the provinces in search of support for Paris. On the pretext of selling small wares, she had distributed propaganda flyers by wrapping merchandise in them. At the end of May 1871, she fled to Switzerland, hidden in a locomotive. When the train crossed the border, she sprang from shelter, waved to a guard on the French frontier, and shouted, "*Vive la Commune!*"[16]

Mink's experience in the provinces engendered a lifelong preoccupation with arousing people outside Paris to rebellion. Returning to France in 1880, she immediately commenced a tour of the provinces. As an "apostle of socialism," she preached revolution to unhappy workers earning only two or three francs for a day's labor, and delighted in provocative gestures against authority. A typical gesture occurred at Elbeuf, a town on the road between Paris and Le Havre, where she found herself speaking in a hall decorated with the tricolor, rather than red, flag displayed.

At that sight my heart rose up and I had that rag, stained with the slime of Sedan and the blood of Paris, removed. I asked them to replace it with the standard of the people and the social revolution. They did it timidly at first, by rolling the blue and white around the stand, leaving only the red showing. But last night, at my second lecture, the room was decorated, at my formal request, with three superb red flags, unfurled and casting their vivid light on the assembly. . . . The reactionaries are astounded and petrified at such audacity.[17]

She soon joined Guesde's campaign and used her oratory to help present sophisticated socialist theory to a working class equipped with only elementary education. The Guesdists welcomed her aid for propaganda purposes and paid her expenses. In the early years, on tour with Guesde, her name took first billing on propaganda flyers. On one occasion, a local council in Paris proposed a meeting "only on condition that Paule Mink is willing to lend her assistance."[18]

Feminist topics vied with socialist ones in Mink's repertory. She spoke on "Social Movements in the Nineteenth Century," "Socialism and Revolution," "Free Thought and Socialism," "Capital and Labor," and "Liberty and Equality," but also on "Woman and Socialism," "Marriage and Divorce," "The History of Women in Society," and "The Emancipation of Women." Recruiting for the P.O.F. and initiating groups based on the 1880 program, she found that some workers balked at the call for the equality of women, "a phenomenal thing for the southerners," she once reported from Montpellier.[19] But she assured them they had nothing to fear; feminist efforts would be sheltered within the workers' movement:

> [What] we convinced women socialists want is the suppression of privilege, of exploitation, the complete liberation of human beings, certain that women will find their place in a society regenerated by suppression of the wage system and all the iniquities which it engenders. . . . We know this will come about only by the union of workers without distinction of sex, race or nationality.[20]

It was up to women to rally round the red flag. While "fancy-talking politicians and old fogey philosophers and bourgeois

83

women are still groping their frightened way, our brothers and workers recognize fully the equal rights of the two beings. . . ." Although she noted the special suffering of women and called for a "republic in the home," she subsumed the woman question within the social question, whose solution lay only in socialist revolution. "The emancipation of labor will liberate humanity, without distinction of sex." The achievement of civil and political rights by women under capitalism would mean nothing. Women legislators would fare no better than their male predecessors. Had queens proved less despotic than kings? Or female employers less oppressive than male? After all, had it not been men who in 1789 had voted equal inheritance rights for girls, free choice of marital partners for women, and control of their children's estates for widows? While she agreed with the resentment of women against their legal status as perpetual minors, she felt that the most insufferable persecution lay in their economic situation.

> Exploited as labor, just as her male companion in misery, instrumental in the reduction of men's wages—for the leaders of industry tell her cruelly that she can use her sex to complement her notoriously inadequate wages—the working woman is also exposed to every kind of obsession and tyranny. 'Chair à travail,' she is also 'chair à plaisir!' ["Beast of burden," "instrument of pleasure"] . . . O woman, poor woman, she is eternally exploited.

The source of the subjugation for Mink lay in the fact that maternity, a form of labor that should bring esteem and reward, instead made woman the "servant of the servant . . . the unhappy whipped dog of the most humble . . . the victim of the victims themselves." Women who raised their voices to protest met ridicule or indifference. Unfortunately the majority lacked the education to locate their true path to liberation. Therefore, she concluded, "It is her companion in suffering who will emancipate her . . . in freeing himself." The first step must be economic liberation, because only when "there are no longer exploiters and exploited" would laws and manners change and realize "absolute equality—but not identity—between the two beings who form the human personality." [21]

Convinced by her experience in the Commune that the bourgeoisie would give no quarter, she insisted on a total solution by revolution. Yet, she also offered a rationale for feminist reform: she called for equal education for women, hoping thereby to release them from the influence of priests, to free prostitutes from the sons of the bourgeoisie, and to encourage female proletarians to support revolutionary action by their men. Male revolutionaries, however, even though they fought for economic and social reform for workers, tended to scorn feminist partial goals. Her descriptions of the suffering endured by working women, low wages, importuning bosses, degradation into prostitution, the double burden of work in the factory followed by work at home, aroused the sympathy of her audiences, but tended to confirm their belief that the immediate solution was total rejection of work outside the home for females. When she cried that the underpaid woman "cannot go into the streets dressed only in her innocence," the men laughed and resolved to keep their women properly at home.[22]

For a few years Mink's passionate speeches paid off, in new members and small study groups formed about the countryside. As the Commune receded into the past, however, and the Third Republic survived, conquest by the ballot became an attractive alternative to the barricade for the Guesdists and most French socialists. In 1893, a decade after Guesde had declared, "Our ballot will be the rifle,"[23] he and thirty-six other socialists were elected to the Chamber of Deputies. These contests for political power and battles for legislative reform required new tactics, less congenial to the old ideologues. And Mink, following Guesde, tried to change styles. When he chose to run for office, she accepted an invitation from the feminist La Solidarité des femmes (Solidarity of Women) to stand as their candidate for municipal council, asking not "Vote for my sex," but "Vote for my program."[24] The feminists hoped for socialist backing, writing Guesde:

It is precisely because the party asks equality for all *without distinction of sex* and race that we make your cause ours, and that we ask the same of you. Our group La Solidarité is preparing to make a female electoral campaign of protest in the 1893 elections and voted unanimously in its last session it would address all French socialist groups to ask them to present a female candidate....[25]

The P.O.F., however, refused to take the illegal candidacies seriously, alternately chiding and laughing at the women.[26]

In the 1890s, as socialists turned toward parliamentarianism and feminists began to demand specific civil and political reforms, the fragile bridge between the two movements collapsed. The major women's issues of the period found them on opposite sides. Feminists wanted political equality. Socialists wanted the votes of men who envisioned no part in public life for women; and they feared, moreover, that women, under clerical influence, would vote for reactionary parties. Feminists called for equal pay for equal work, and beyond, for equal access to employment opportunities. Socialists won votes by supporting legislation that protected women from the worst of working conditions while also restricting them from some of the best (e.g., premium pay for night jobs). Feminist attacks on traditional codes of law and custom threatened workers who argued, correctly, that work for most proletarian women meant long, hard, underpaid labor, not "self-fulfillment"; and questionably, that patriarchal family life served women better than men.

In a decade of practical politics, women played a different role in French socialism. Paule Mink, symbol of the Commune and fiery orator, became superfluous. Unlike her male counterparts, who now began to reap the rewards of long service—seats in the Chamber or on municipal councils or leading positions in the socialist parties—she gained minimal compensation and no power. She continued to serve on minor committees, write for socialist and anticlerical journals, speak at ceremonial gatherings, and inspire younger women. But excluded from the centers of socialist power, in her later years she reached out increasingly to feminist groups, reminding bourgeois women of social problems, as earlier she had told working-class men of women's oppression. The first woman in France to carry the banner of revolt in public after the amnesty, she waved the red flag until May 1, 1901, when in a last spectacular demonstration she lay in state under it in a funeral attended by thousands of socialists and chaperoned by 1,300 "guardians of the peace" (police).

In the 1890s, while Paule Mink lost her place as the leading woman socialist in France, another woman with different talents gained prominence. Despite the fact that she had no heroic history like Michel and Mink, Aline Valette (Alphonsine Caroline Eulalie Goudeman, 1850–1899) in a few years of party membership attained the highest position accorded any socialist woman in prewar France, secretary to the P.O.F. National Council. She also integrated socialism and feminism in her own life better than any other Frenchwoman.[27]

Valette was a pretty, petite, soft-spoken, forty-year-old widow whose rapid rise in the P.O.F. caused police agents, and some of Jules Guesde's colleagues as well as enemies, to assert that she owed her success to amorous relations with the party leader.[28] But she was also an accomplished woman, a lay teacher specializing in vocational training for girls, author of a thoroughly traditional, nonfeminist handbook for homemakers adopted by the Paris school system, and a child labor inspector. Neither inspired nor eloquent like Mink, she was instead conscientious and "very calm, with a grave and serious, almost *male*, temperament," said one Guesdist leader. She was also "modest," "humble," and "remained a woman." Guesde considered her "the only woman who understood socialism."[29] She demonstrated her understanding of socialist goals, and an intimate knowledge of intraparty politics, in a long article on the movement for an eight-hour day published in a socialist review in 1890.[30] In October 1892, she began publication of *L'Harmonie sociale*, a short-lived but outstanding socialist feminist journal with the motto, "The Emancipation of Woman Lies in Emancipated Labor." Covering working-class and women's issues, literature and politics, economic developments and foreign events, Valette campaigned for P.O.F. interests and presented, in *L'Harmonie sociale* and other publications, a new theory that attempted to resolve the tensions between socialism and feminism. It was termed "sexualism," and appeared, variously, under the by-lines of Valette and "Dr. Z," actually a little-known socialist physician, Pierre Bonnier, the brother of Guesde's good friend Charles Bonnier. In a 1914 book, *Sexualisme*, Bonnier claimed authorship for himself.[31] The concept of sexualism represents an all but unique attempt to raise a theoretical structure that houses both socialist and feminist postulates. In Bonnier, the Spencerian hypothesis of a biological "struggle for life" intersects Marxian moralizing over the "industrialization of women" and prevailing French fears about a declining population. Arguing that there was indeed a battle of the sexes, which many socialists denied, he proposed to

> unite and mingle, for the time being, the struggle of classes and the struggle of sexes, the social question and the sexual question, socialist doctrine and sexualist doctrine, to show that by their common ground the two questions are only one, and that it is the economic solution which will establish the absolute conditions of human emancipation in its social form and its sexual form.[32]

He would "graft" the sexual revolution onto the social revolution, and thus complete it.

After setting forth parallels between the condition of workers and of women, Bonnier asserted that working women were oppressed more than men. They were doubly deprived: dispossessed of their product as workers by capitalists, and of their product as mothers by males. While workers were subjugated only economically and politically, women suffered "economic, political, conjugal and maternal servitude." As reproducers of the human species, women contributed a product of greater social value than men. Yet they were despoiled and deprived of their product, children being given by law into the possession of the male sex. "Paternity ... is a capitalization for the profit of men."[33] This injustice stemmed from the same condition that permitted exploitation of workers by owners of capital: individualism. In a society based on unlimited rights of the individual, superiority depended upon individual strength, and the hierarchy of power that followed was: man, woman, child. Progress of the species had been arrested at this stage.

A socialist revolution would usher in a higher form of relations, based on a just relationship between social responsibility and reward. The status of women would reflect their social utility. Since motherhood was more useful than other work, which has only economic value, the new order of preference would become: woman, man, child. Even later, thanks to mechanization, "the great emancipator of woman and of the species," man, would be relegated to his rightful place at the end of the line. The child, the "germ of the species," would be elevated to its proper place at the forefront, leading humanity in its endless evolution. In a sexualist regime, society would be properly organized to support its reproductive resources as well as its productive forces.[34]

According to Bonnier, socialists had a perverse tendency to see woman only in her productive capacity and to identify the working woman's cause with that of the worker, isolating her from nonworking women. They interpreted the "sexual question" as only a woman question, rendering socialism exclusively masculine and sterile. They should, he believed, make no distinction between working women and other women.[35] Sexualism therefore offered Valette a means not only to synthesize socialist and feminist theories, but to reconcile the interests of working and nonworking, proletarian and bourgeois, women. Reconciliation, however, hung on acceptance of maternity as woman's chief function. When Valette, following Bonnier's philosophy, proposed to women that they adopt sexualism as their "true religion," she recast an old idea. Couched in terms of historical and biological science, Bonnier and Valette adopted an argument designed to lift woman back onto the pedestal and into the home. In the sexualist world, women would be "free" because supported by the community rather than by individual men. But they would be free only to fulfill their traditional role without the burdens imposed by capitalist society. "If women today seem to evade their primary purpose, maternity, it is," Valette asserted, "in order to return to it more surely, with independence, serenity, and dignity assured."[36]

As a solution to the problem of sex-role conflict, sexualism also had much to offer. Its tenets, expressive of several nineteenth-century ideas, later appeared in better known works by such women as Charlotte Perkins Gilman, an American feminist and socialist sympathizer, Ellen Key, a Swedish proponent of the cult of motherhood, and Margaret Sanger, who sought to regenerate the human "race" through birth control and eugenics.[37] Women would, in this new world, pose no threat to men. Despite altered economic relations, traditional sex roles would prevail. Meanwhile, according to Valette and Bonnier, a "socialist women's party," latent but powerful, should "march in step with the socialist revolution and the immense force of the workers; and even before its birth, the sexualist party [will] triumph in every victory of the proletariat."[38]

Thus resolving all potential conflicts in theory, Valette offered the P.O.F. a way to embrace feminism while postponing practical change for women until after the socialist revolution. Guesde made campaign speeches lamenting that the industrialization of women meant "the race comprised, attacked at its source, right in the maternal womb,"[39] and elevated Valette to eminence in the party. He also allowed her to cross class lines and work with bourgeois feminists. Representing a needleworkers' union, she attended the first annual convention of the Fédération française des sociétés féministes, where she was elected secretary and chosen to write a brochure it commissioned, the *Cahier des doléances Féminines* (Notebook of Women's Grievances).[40] Active in syndicates of women teachers and women journalists, she contributed a series on working women to Marguerite Durand's all-woman daily *La Fronde*, and encouraged the wealthy, eminently bourgeois feminist publisher to organize women in printing. "They distrust bourgeois women, the poor things!" Valette wrote Durand. "I am sure to obtain their confidence. *La Fronde* will succeed also."[41]

Paraphrasing Marx, "Working women of the world unite," and adopting a slogan that made syndicated labor the first step to women's liberation, Valette built a case for socialist feminism. Predicating her work on the assumption that in a free society women would choose maternity as their primary goal, she created a brand of feminist socialism which did not threaten antifeminist socialists of either sex. By example as well as carefully constructed argument, Valette convinced some women and some workers that their causes belonged together. Unlike some socialists, who considered themselves proponents of women's emancipation, she saw women whole. They were more than workers. They must participate not just as class-conscious workers but as self-conscious women. Entrance into the "struggle for life" was the "ransom of their future freedom." Women must "do it themselves." [42] Unfortunately Valette failed to see that, lacking both education and economic independence, the women of her day could not do it themselves, least of all working-class women.

Her success at integrating her commitments in her own life allowed the socialist party to idealize her and a later French socialist woman to assert that Valette's "influence was not unrelated to the great place given to women in the P.O.F." [43] She was a good organization woman and represented the party on innumerable, usually ceremonial, occasions. But she rarely spoke at Council meetings, unfailingly voted with Guesde, and when she tried to buck the leadership, calling for addition of a "women's platform" to the party program, she failed. Both party theoretician Paul Lafargue (son-in-law of Marx who wrote on the woman question), declaring men and women already equal within the party, and Guesde, asserting they must first attract the masses, reneged on their promises. [44] When she died, the party erected a monument above her grave, and Guesde himself traveled south to dedicate it. It read:

Le Parti ouvrier français

à Aline Valette

1850–1899

"The Emancipation of Woman
Lies in Emancipated Labor"
(L'Harmonie sociale)
ALINE VALETTE [45]

Valette died in 1899, Mink in 1901. Mink had continued to invoke the Commune thirty years after its death and Valette had obscured the reality of conflicting political, economic, and social interests with ideal constructs about women's mission. Both had attained eminence as individuals, but neither had succeeded in bringing socialist women together or in winning support from the existing parties for organizational work among women.

At the turn of the century, four million French women worked outside their homes in nonagricultural labor, constituting more than one-third of the labor force. In working-class organizations, however, the participation of women lagged far behind. In 1900 they constituted 5 percent or less of syndicated workers in the *départements* where unions were most successful, and averaged about the same overall. In political parties that purported to represent the working class, they numbered even fewer, and at least half of these were wives and daughters of members. In the fifty *départements* of metropolitan France, there were eighteen women's unions.[46] But there was no socialist group for women exclusively until 1899, when two working-class women personally launched a campaign to educate the "women of the people" in politics and to enlist them in the socialist movement.

In July 1899 with notices placed in the socialist press, Elisabeth Renaud, a teacher, and Louise Saumoneau, a seamstress, along with two other needleworkers, announced the formation of a Groupe féministe socialiste (Feminist Socialist Group, G.F.S.). Noting the presence of the bourgeois feminist movement, they declared their intention to create a new movement on the ground of class differences. While "recognizing the legitimacy of feminist claims for equal rights," they declared such reforms inadequate to relieve the double oppression of working women. Believing that feminist unity rested on spurious grounds, they had decided to expose the truth to women of the people, and to undertake "the first attempt made in [France] to tear socialist and proletarian women away from feminist confusionism." Unlike bourgeois feminists, they intended to give women's demands a "scientific basis conforming to historical materialism." Women of the working class must attack not male workers, already embattled against the machine, but bourgeois feminists who demanded equal rights because they already had everything else.[47]

The leaders of the new movement, Renaud (1845–1932) and Saumoneau (1875–1949), were both daughters of artisans, a watchmaker and a carpenter respectively.[48] The elder woman was a widow at whose boarding house in the Latin Quarter young socialist students from all over Europe congregated for tea and talk. It was, according to Marx's grandson, Jean Longuet, a "veritable foyer of propaganda and socialist controversy."[49] For a period of years in middle age she enlisted in the socialist movement, publishing articles in various party journals, attending congresses, lecturing and helping to found several socialist women's groups. Perhaps her chief claim to fame is the tribute she earned as candidate for office under S.F.I.O. auspices in 1910, when she won 2,813 votes, far more than any other woman in any of the extralegal campaigns.[50]

The younger partner, Saumoneau, entered the socialist movement early and devoted her life to it. Radical convictions came naturally; her mother was so well known for militant ideas that neighbors called her "Louise Michel." Saumoneau's conviction that bourgeois feminism offered little to working women reflects the experience of her father, who worked twelve or more hours a day from the age of ten, and lived a "life without joy." As a working woman, she wanted more than equal right to such an existence.[51] Where Aline Valette had tended to minimize the differences between women of different classes, Saumoneau used them to create a raison d'être for socialist feminism. For fifty years she continued, often single-handedly and vainly, trying to awaken working-class women to political consciousness and socialist men to the necessity of enlisting female support. Serving periodically in minor party posts, earning her living by sewing at home, she was a lonely, courageous woman who during World War 1 led resistance to the "sacred union" in which socialists subordinated their principles of international working-class solidarity to patriotism. By dedication, dogged persistence, and longevity, she, more than any other woman, put her stamp on French socialist feminism.

While it is impossible to report how many women responded to Renaud's and Saumoneau's first appeal, within a year several groups of women socialists had been founded in Paris. The first

G.F.S., formed in the Latin Quarter, was succeeded by two groups in other areas of the city, as well as by a union of needleworkers under Saumoneau's leadership. In 1901 the groups formed a coalition, the Union of Socialist Women of the Seine, perhaps the greatest success of their organizational efforts. But their difficulties in attracting women can be inferred from the periodic reappearance in the socialist press, unchanged, of the original appeal.

Women socialists, few as they were, found themselves divided by affiliation with the different splinter groups which characterized French socialism before 1905. But the two main problems faced by Renaud and Saumoneau in organizing socialist women were the disinterest of most male socialists and the difficulty of dealing with bourgeois feminism. Taking their cues from Clara Zetkin of German Social Democracy, they tried to convince socialist leaders that women's support was indispensable to the movement; and they denied the problem of sex-role conflict, attributing it to bourgeois feminism. On the masthead of *La Femme socialiste* (Socialist Woman), a journal they inaugurated in 1901, they stated, "There need be no antagonism between men and women of the proletarian class." By support for striking workers, censure of women who acted as strikebreakers, defense of the Millerand–Colliard act of 1900 for standardization of the working day at eleven hours (though this meant a setback for women, previously granted a ten-hour day), and applause for Belgian socialist women who in 1901 suspended their demand for the vote in the superior interests of universal male suffrage, Renaud and Saumoneau intended to emphasize that proletarian women could achieve emancipation only along with their men. Working women must join the class struggle, not the bourgeois feminist movement. Bourgeois women were their "natural adversaries."[52]

Yet in 1900, bourgeois feminism, commencing a decade of successful, if minor, reform, might easily have attracted working-class women. Beginning with two feminist congresses in 1889, the bourgeois women's movement had grown rapidly, the result of the expansion of women's education and professional activity in the 1890s, as well as increasing contacts with American and British feminists. Doctoral theses and other publications devoted to the woman question multiplied. Proposals for moderate reform, including the rights of married women to control their own earnings and to testify in civil suits, as well as legal inquiry into the paternity of "illegitimate" children, won considerable support from a large proportion of middle- and upper-class French women, and several parties in the Chamber of Deputies. By 1900, when the fourth international congress on women's rights met in Paris, feminism had become "fashionable" among the educated bourgeoisie. Some women had begun to advance more radical demands, including woman suffrage.[53]

To the founders of the socialist women's group, bourgeois feminism represented a lure away from their true interests. While they might support some feminist claims, such as civil equality, others, especially those related to property rights, they considered irrelevant for working-class women, and they showed little interest in the vote. Unlike the German socialist women, Renaud and Saumoneau opposed exceptional laws to "protect" women workers on grounds they perpetuated female inferiority. But ultimately, Saumoneau wrote, economic interests "break the very fragile thread that, in the eyes of some persons, unites women of the bourgeois class and those of the proletarian class." The first act of bourgeois women awakened to political consciousness would be to defend their property. Besides, she declared, the bourgeois feminist program, insofar as it affected workers, was already inscribed in the program of the socialist party.[54]

At the International Congress on the Condition and Rights of Women, which met in Paris in September 1900, Elisabeth Renaud and a few other socialist women interceded in debate to emphasize the realities of working-class life. When delegates discussed the extension of protective legislation to domestic workers, Renaud, who had worked as a domestic herself, pointed out that many feminists themselves exploited their maids. In debate on a proposal for divorce by mutual consent, she reminded the delegates of the greater vulnerability of women without property. She chided them for suggesting a mandatory postpartum rest of one month for unwed mothers which, while laudable in intention, might in fact mean starvation for poor women. Her frequent insertion of economic issues to expose the inadequacies of bourgeois feminism brought censure from the president of the Congress, who charged the socialist delegates with seeking to erect a "wall of hate" between bourgeois and working women.[55]

In ensuing years, Renaud, who broke with Saumoneau and left the group in 1902, supported a number of feminist efforts, though she continued to believe in socialism as a necessary prerequisite to the emancipation of women. But Saumoneau regarded bourgeois feminism with increasing hostility, displaying open enmity to overtures toward "sisterhood." After the Congress of 1900 she used class hostility as her primary argument for the mobilization of proletarian women.

During 1901 and 1902, the Union of Socialist Women responded with increasing stridency to bourgeois feminists. When a group of "ladies" sponsored by a clerical, nationalist party, announced their forthcoming participation in an electoral campaign, the socialist women declared a state of emergency and challenged them to a series of public debates between "nationalist feminism" and "socialist feminism." The tone of the invitation probably assured a negative response: "Members of the bourgeois class and thus beneficiaries of the present social order which guarantees your privileges... you have come forth to defend the right to parasitism which society affords you. ...." None showed up, despite repeated appeals. The "nationalist" women had proved "mediocre Joans of Arc."[56]

But the proletarian women responded little better. If the gates were, in a formal sense, open, few ventured through. The original 1899 group attained its zenith in 1902, lingering on until 1905, when it requested from the newly unified party admission on the same basis as student and youth groups. In August 1905 the executive committee for the Paris area, suggesting that the women be assimilated into other groups, referred the question to its next congress. Ultimately the party refused to admit the women's organization. According to Saumoneau, it "perished during the torment preceding the realization of socialist unity," at least partly because "our male comrades ... did not understand the utility of the movement."[57]

Some of the responsibility, however, belongs to Saumoneau. She once wrote that bourgeois feminists needed to "enlarge their brains to the size of their hearts. And if their sentimentalism should thereby be lessened, humanity would lose nothing." Saumoneau herself failed as a leader of women because she lacked sensitivity to women's issues. She repeatedly misinterpreted the goals of the women whom she saw as "natural adversaries" pursuing only "individual interests." "I personally refuse the right to *masculine "liberties,"* and I would never help transform young girls into the boys of today. This would in my opinion, constitute a crime against humanity." She refused to concede that bourgeois feminism might also represent a struggle for human freedom.[58] Moreover, she failed in her overtures toward working-class women because, like male socialists, she did not broach specific issues of direct interest to women. Following their pattern, she proposed no ameliorative action beyond supporting the socialist program, addressed audiences of women in abstract terms, and deferred their hopes to a future world. Perhaps she was not, as defined in Chapter I, a feminist.[59] When, in 1913, she became active in forming a new group it would be called not the Feminist Socialist Group but the Group of Women Socialists, and limited to card-carrying members of the party.

While the G.F.S., excluded from party organization, died during the period of socialist unification, bourgeois feminists were winning a number of reforms. Thanks to the leadership of Radical and Radical-Socialist (middle-class, anticlerical) legislators and the voting support of socialist deputies, single women won rights to tesify in court, to vote for judges in commercial tribunes, and to exercise the legal profession. In 1907, mothers were accorded joint authority with fathers over their children, and mothers of "illegitimate" children the right to exercise "paternal powers." The same year married women won full title to their own earnings, and the tiny electoral franchise was extended to councils of arbitration. But most socialist feminists, looking toward revolution, dismissed the women's movement as "reformism" that constituted a deviation from socialist principles.

When once again, a few years after unification, a socialist woman with a feminist consciousness made her way into the party bureaucracy, she failed to advance women's rights within the movement. The career of Dr. Madeleine Pelletier exemplifies the conflict of a class-conscious woman seeking to reconcile commitments to socialism and to feminism. Between the Commune of 1871 and the movement of French socialism to communism in 1920, Madeleine (née Anne) Pelletier (1876–1939) was the most outstanding woman to associate herself with the leftist movement in France.[60]

Born in a greengrocer's shop, daughter of a woman who was ignorant, "illegitimate" (and *literally branded* with a mark of her shame), and fanatically religious, Pelletier fought not only to overcome for herself but to eradicate the handicaps imposed by society on proletarian women. Reared in squalor, she raised herself by her bootstraps to membership in two male preserves, the medical profession and the administration of the S.F.I.O. Struggling to elevate herself above the level of her mother, with common looks and no dowry but intelligence and determination, she suffered from sexual discrimination as well as poverty. Despite careful suppression of her sensitivity in the laboratory, she had to endure taunts from both medical students and professors. Her severely functional dress, short hair, hat, tie, collar, and vest, with only a skirt as concession to fashion, elicited insult from political allies and enemies alike. Termed a "hybrid being," she became an uncompromising feminist. Her medical work, treating exhausted wives of workers, "administered first a blow and then a baby" by drunken husbands they were legally powerless to resist, confirmed her views. Growing up in proletarian Paris, she suffered deprivation and witnessed brutality, and she sought justice in the left-wing movement. But she insisted on equal justice for women. She tried socialism, moving to the extreme left of the unified party, later turned to anarchism, and finally abandoned collective solutions altogether to devote herself to individual direct action, the practice of abortion. For that reason, in 1939 she was incarcerated in a mental institution, where she soon died.[61]

MADELEINE PELLETIER. Courtesy Bibliothèque Marguerite Durand, Paris.

Beyond the tragic aspect of her death lies an element of irony. Dr. Pelletier first won public attention when she dared to contend for a place as resident in a Parisian mental hospital, previously a male monopoly. She was refused, nominally because of a rule that required applicants to possess full political and civil rights. When she protested she was told, "Go win your rights and then return." Instead she carried her story to the feminist press, and the following year won her position.[62]

In her early career she proved her talent by publishing a number of studies in biological, anthropological, and medical journals, gaining in the process knowledge useful in combating arguments that alleged female inferiority. She also wrote for the Free Masons, calling on this "enlightened oligarchy" to open its ranks to all intelligent persons, including women and the poor. She urged that they preempt the socialists, who suggested proposals but did not produce anything of benefit to the oppressed sex. Skeptical about the promises of the left wing, she noted that

> certain women, disdaining feminism by a childish inconsistency, swell the ranks of socialism, hoping naively that its triumph will be theirs. How they will be deceived if this triumph ever occurs! The socialist worker has a conception of women no more elevated than the religious worker. Even the fraction called the most advanced, the anarchists, have in general nothing for women but mistrust. In the society envisioned by Kropotkin, women do not work. They have only to be mothers of families.... [63]

Nevertheless, in 1906, she began writing on both feminism and socialism in the socialist press and other radical journals, including after 1908, her own *La Suffragiste*. For two years she waged a virtual one-woman campaign to persuade the S.F.I.O. to adopt a forceful position, more than a "platonic wish," she insisted, on woman suffrage. Her resolution, calling for "urgent" action and charging socialist deputies with presentation of a bill in the Chamber of Deputies "this year if possible," was placed on the agenda for the party's national congress at Limoges in 1906.[64]

Writing to Guesde in support of her motion, she acknowledged she need not convince him of her arguments:

You know them better than I. I know that every time that you have alluded to the woman question in your work, you have resolved it in the direction of women's emancipation, even in the present society. Unhappily, in our Party, they are always satisfied to express wishes on the question, and I do not believe that one action has ever been undertaken. . . .

She hoped that now the party would charge one of its deputies with bringing a specific proposal before the Chamber. If complete political equality was asking too much, perhaps they would sponsor a vote limited to municipal affairs or restricted to spinsters and widows. She later stated that she had expected no success from her venture, but wanted to force the socialists to reveal their hypocrisy. Nothing of the kind happened. They passed the resolution at Limoges, confirmed it the following year at Nancy, and ignored it, or, more exactly, repeatedly promised to follow through, "after a brief delay." Another "platonic wish" lengthened the list of socialist good words on the woman question.[65]

The socialist position on women, Dr. Pelletier pointed out, was an inheritance from the formative period when the party was "more ideological than political." Later, "in its preoccupation with assuring an electoral clientele it dropped the cause of those who necessarily could not bring the party votes." Party leaders, "nourished on Marx, Guesde and Lafargue," could not entirely avoid the woman question, but used it as "a parenthesis, very quickly closed, in order to return to more vital questions." Occasionally, between campaigns, the militants reminded each other, "Oh yes, there's also the woman question . . . and after all we've done for women, they haven't come to the Party."[66]

Since there was, at this period, no organization of women socialists, the most radical women's group in France was the Solidarité des femmes, spiritual sisters of the British suffragettes, who advocated direct action. Its president, Caroline Kauffmann, had launched feminist leaflets from the Chamber gallery onto the heads of deputies who remembered the bomb thrown by the anarchist Auguste Vaillant, and scrambled under their seats at the paper assault. In 1904 she publicly burned the Napoleonic Code, and interrupted solemn centennial ceremonies at the Sorbonne by releasing balloons inscribed, "The Code crushes women!" Kauffmann personally enlisted Dr. Pelletier to succeed her in office. Together they posted flyers about the city declaring "Universal suffrage, not unisexual suffrage.'[67]

One month after the Limoges Congress, Dr. Pelletier brought one hundred "suffragettes of Paris" to exert pressure on the deputies. The popular reform socialist Jean Jaurès and others promised they would fulfill their pledge "in the very near future." Guesde's lieutenant Bracke even declared on the front page of *L'Humanité*, "Women Must Vote." But the party was divided. Three days later another contributor to *L'Humanité* responded with an article entitled "Officious Feminism," declaring that suffragists "set women in a state of disloyal competition with men, and against their own interest." Only success of the workers' movement could improve their lives. Another comrade attacked Bracke for attempting to ally with a group which was "nonsocialist and even bourgeois . . . and proclaims the solidarity of women, as elsewhere people have tried to affirm the solidarity of classes." Bracke replied, recalling that in 1905 the federation had rejected the socialist women's group. Now they must meet women where they were, in feminist groups.[68]

Dr. Pelletier contended that her campaign for woman suffrage represented no deviation from socialist principles, but only a means to arouse proletarian women from passivity, and to link the feminist and socialist movements. After Nancy in 1907, she carried her arguments to the Second International Congress held at Stuttgart a few days later. But wherever she turned, if there was relatively little overt resistance, there was considerable inertia. "Suffrage for women, yes! But later, when they are educated." To Dr. Pelletier herself the party offered only nominal acceptance. In theory women were accepted as equals. "In practice," she concluded, "only the woman who comes to double her husband, father or brother is received without objection. But they always find obstacles against admitting a woman who comes on her own account." An examination of women delegates to the congresses substantiates her charge; almost all accompanied a man of the same name.[69]

At the beginning of her socialist activity, Dr. Pelletier had gravitated toward the Guesdist faction, seeing them, in contrast to the moderate Jaurèssians, as the "real socialists, these men of doctrine, who put first the struggle of the proletariat as a class against the bourgeoisie." Later she drifted leftward toward the insurrectionist Hervéism, attacking Guesde in Hervé's *La Guerre sociale. (Social Warfare)*. With this faction she hoped to organize a new revolutionary elite drawn from socialist, anarchist, and syndicalist sources. But even here, she found that a woman was treated like a "Jew in the Middle Ages." Hervé himself criticized her unmodish dress. While he agreed with her on some radical feminist demands, including the right to abortion in capitalist society, he opposed woman suffrage out of disdain for parliamentarianism. To Dr. Pelletier this was the most crucial of claims, for the ballot represented both the symbol of and the key to power. Still, in 1909 the Hervéist connection won her a seat on the central administrative committee of the S.F.I.O. In three years of militant action, she had gained access to the upper reaches of French socialism, bringing feminism further into the socialist inner sanctum than any woman since Aline Valette. If unlike Valette who "remained a woman," she never gained its love, she did win its nominal support for candidacy for elective office. Running under S.F.I.O. auspices, in 1910 she drew 340 votes, 77 more than the previous socialist candidate, in a very reactionary district, and in 1912 she gathered 250 in another.[70]

Between reform and revolutionary socialists, Dr. Pelletier found herself in a double bind. The socialist establishment refused to risk its vote count by actively supporting feminist reform. Only revolutionary enthusiasm might move the stolid working class. But an immediate revolution that transferred power to the workers might, she feared, enshrine the traditional restrictions under a new name. "The working class," she predicted, "will be the last to accept feminism. The ignorant respect nothing but brute force." To most working men, feminism constituted the crime of *"lèse-masculinité."*[71]

Disappointed with both Guesdists and Hervéists, she mingled with the anarchists. In their journal, *Le Libertaire*, she discussed many of her ideas, including the most radical, her demands for legal abortion and equal conscription. The anarchists loved an argument and enjoyed baiting her with such questions as, "Would it represent an advance for women if they became hangmen?" to which she resolutely answered, "Yes."[72]

By the outbreak of the war, Dr. Pelletier had sadly concluded that the left wing offered nothing to women. Socialists continued to honor "woman" only with platitudinous phrases based on the principles embalmed in their platform. Unlike reforms attractive to male voters (including "protective" legislation that restricted the right of women to work), they dismissed reforms proposed by feminists as bourgeois, or premature. Equality for women, they said, must await the revolution. In the end, Dr. Pelletier concluded she must preach feminism first. Repeating the words of Aline Valette, in 1914 she declared, "Women, do it yourselves."[73]

At the end of her journey through the leftmost regions of the political realm, Pelletier advocated founding a vast feminist organization and penetrating all existing parties. She continued to practice medicine, to spread feminist propaganda, and—despite herself—having followed the road to Moscow in 1920, to call for Communist revolution. Believing morality a mere social convention and law necessary primarily to prevent a tyranny of manners, she performed abortions. In the spring of 1939 she was arrested as a *"faiseur d'anges"* ("maker of angels," or abortionist), and committed to a mental institution as "totally irresponsible." Patient instead of practitioner, she lived only six months in the asylum. The friend who settled her estate wrote Marguerite Durand that she "feared the sisters and company might have dragged from a weakened Madeleine Pelletier some promise which would have been the negation of her entire life. But nothing of the kind happened." To her death, she refused to patronize those whom she called "merchants of illusions"; she had not taken the last rites.[74]

Through her intellect and her spirit, Dr. Pelletier won access to a man's education and succeeded in overcoming the disadvantages of class and poverty. She could not, however, transcend the handicap imposed by her sex. She tried, by promoting feminism within the socialist movement, to work for the emancipation of women and of all workers. Had not Guesde and Lafargue proclaimed that socialism must work toward emancipation of women even in capitalist society? Perhaps the repugnance felt by socialists, she once said, was not for "feminism" but for "feminists." But she was as disdainful as they of feminist ladies afraid to venture into the street without a carriage; and she herself took to the streets on foot, promising to "glue them to the wall alongside antifeminists of the same class" on revolution day.[75] Nonetheless, she was treated *en bourgeoise*. It was not a question of distinguishing between bourgeois feminism and socialist feminism, as socialists pretended. To be a practicing feminist, in the eyes of French socialists after the turn of the century, was to be bourgeois. It meant to be a class enemy. Even though socialist politicians themselves made alliances with bourgeois parties, women could practice socialism only by rejecting feminist association.

Like Paule Mink they could serve as agitators and moralize about the condition of women under capitalism. They could enjoy the accolades of power, like Aline Valette, as long as they ceded its substance. They could, like Louise Saumoneau, serve the party as workers "without distinction of sex," ignoring the antifeminism that survived within the movement. But they had to subscribe to the policy that equality for women lay over the horizon in another world. First must come the revolution. If the French socialist party in practice yielded to reformism, becoming before World War I merely the "avant-garde of democracy,"[76] it refused to concede in one area, women's rights. Rather than jeopardize their tenuous hold on the working class by threatening tradition, socialists gave only sporadic, verbal support to women. They called Madeleine Pelletier "no Marxist," because of her feminism. In truth, it was they who denied their Marxist heritage by refusing to accept the new relationship between the sexes latent in the industrialization of women.

Between 1879 and 1914, the women who tried to engage French socialism in the movement for equality of the sexes won little support. Despite some degree of personal achievement, they remained leaders without followers, unable to build a constituency for feminism among working-class women or men. The expectations first raised by the "prophets of the left" during the July Monarchy, rekindled in the social upheaval of the early Third Republic, proved illusory. Long after significant numbers of women entered the industrial labor force, French workers retained traditional views of women's roles. To the extent that feminism entered French socialism with Marxism, it remained a superficial accoutrement, grafted onto a socialist program concerned essentially with economic issues. As economic determinists, most Marxists paid scant attention to the functions of women that could not be reduced to economic terms.

Waiting for the revolution, most socialists failed to deal with issues of immediate concern to women. Assurances of societal support of women and children in a far off socialist community offered less to working-class women than the measures advocated by the middle-class feminists, whom, especially after the turn of the century, they regularly attacked as class enemies. For the principles of the right to work and a living wage, women might have been able to mobilize across class lines. But since this would have encouraged competition in the marketplace and redefinition of sex roles, French socialists left this to the bourgeois feminists.[77] Practical politics dictated that instead male socialists support legislation that restricted the work opportunities open to women.

In a historical situation, moreover, in which the socialist party chose in practice to support the bourgeois state, there was no chance that it would work for radical change in the lives of women who, through their role in the family, were seen to be the sinews which held the body politic together. The French socialist party in essence became reformist. To the extent, in theory and rhetoric, that it maintained its commitment to revolution, it defined its position narrowly in economic and political terms.[78] Failing to see the struggle for freedom as a total revolution encompassing personal as well as political, sexual as well as economic, and private as well as public, dimensions of human experience, it would not truly incorporate feminist goals.

Feminism, in order to achieve a fully functional equality between the sexes, would require revolutionary change in all aspects of society. Therefore the "synthesis" of socialism and feminism in France, begun by the "utopian socialists," remained an ideal and an illusion.

N O T E S

1. See Edith Thomas, *The Women Incendiaries*, trans. James and Starr Atkinson (New York, 1966).
2. Madeleine Guilbert, *Les Femmes et l'organisation syndicale* (Paris, 1966), p. 14.
3. *La Femme* (Paris, 1860), cited by Evelyne Sullerot, *Histoire et sociologie du travail féminin* (Paris, 1968), p. 41.
4. For Tristan's "Utopian Synthesis," see Chapter II. Proudhon's attitude toward women is summarized in my article, "Foyer or Factory: Working-Class Women in Nineteenth Century France," in Brison D. Gooch, ed., *Proceedings of the Second Annual Meeting*, Western Society for French History (College Station, Tex.: Texas A & M University Press, 1975), pp. 193–203.
5. A thorough study of the early organizational efforts of French socialist women is available in the dissertation of Charles Sowerwine, "Women and Socialism in France, 1871–1921: Socialist Women's Groups from Léonie Rouzade to Louise Saumoneau" (University of Wisconsin, 1973).
6. *Séances du Congrès ouvrier socialiste de France tenue à Marseille du 20 au 31 octobre 1879, 3ᵉ session* (Marseille, 1880), pp. 802–805.
7. Jules Guesde et Paul Lafargue, *Le Programme du Parti ouvrier, son histoire, ses considérants, ses articles*, 1st ed. (Paris, [1883]), p. 2.
8. The socialist response to the "woman question" and to the growth of feminism, especially within the working-class movement, is the subject of my dissertation, "Socialism Faces Feminism in France: 1879–1913" (University of California, Riverside, 1975).
9. See "Biographies: Nos Militantes" in *L'Equité*, 15 Jan. 1914; on rejection of candidacy, also *Le Clairon*, 27 Sept. 1882, *La Bataille*, 29 Sept. 1882.
10. *Les Droits de l'Homme*, 16 Oct. and 18 Oct. 1876; *Le Socialiste*, 9 Oct. 1898. Claude Willard, *Les Guesdistes: le mouvement socialiste en France: 1893–1905* (Paris, 1965), p. 13, mentions the influence of the Chernyshevsky book. It was translated into French by Guesde's wife, *Le Socialiste*, 8 July 1900. Guesde predicted that social services would supersede the family in an undated, unpublished manuscript, *"Sur la Famille,"* which is in the Guesde archive at the International Institute for Social History (IISG)

at Amsterdam, 547/4. See also his *Essai de catéchisme socialiste* (Brussels, 1878), 78–79; and "Le Collectivisme et la famille," *Le Socialiste*, 9 Apr. 1893, also in Suzanne Lacore, *Jules Guesde: Textes choisis* (Paris, 1946), 135–39; letter to author from Mme. S. Benoist-Guesde, 29 July 1973.

11. Archives de la Préfecture de police (APP), dossier Ba/1178 includes extensive biographical information. Dossiers Ba/1482, Ba/1484, Ba/38 cover political activity in early 1880s. Bibliothèque Marguerite Durand (BMD), dossier 091 MIN includes several letters from late 1890s. Brief accounts appear in Jean Maitron, *Dictionnaire biographique du mouvement ouvrier français*, pt. 2, VII (Paris, 1970), pp. 369–70; Compère-Morel, *Grand Dictionnaire socialiste* (Paris, 1924), p. 543; Léon Osmin, *Figures du jadis* (Paris, 1934), pp. 71–73; Charles Vérecque, in *La Femme socialiste*, Nov. 1932.

12. APP, Ba/1178, pt. 1: Report to Ministry of Interior, 20 June 1872.

13. APP, Ba/1178, pt. 1, and Ba/39 reports dated 24 Sept. 1882; APP, Ba/1178, pt. 2, report dated 12 May 1896; *La Petite République*, 4 April, 2 July, 22 August 1895, 28 August 1897.

14. Paule Mink, "*Etudes sociales. Les mouches et les araignées. Une heroine populaire*" (Marseille, 1880). This article, said to have been originally published by Mink under the Second Empire, was reprinted in Moscow in 1972 and attributed to the cofounder of German Social Democracy, Wilhelm Liebknecht.

15. Mme. Paul [sic] Mink, *Le Travail des femmes, Discours prononcé par Mme. Paul Mink à la réunion publique du Vauxhall le 13 juillet 1868* (Paris, n.d.).

16. Hélène Gosset, "Les Polonais dans la Commune de Paris," *Europe*, nos. 64–65, Apr.–May, 1951; also Albert Goullé, *L'Aurore*, 1 May 1901.

17. APP, Ba/1178, pt. 1, copy of letter to Louise Michel, dated 14 Dec. 1880.

18. APP, Ba/1178, pt. 1, reports dated 24 Mar., 5 Apr., 17 Apr., 24 Oct., 14 Dec., 17 Dec. 1883; 9 Mar., 9 Apr., 19 Apr. 1884. APP, Ba/1482, reports dated 29 Dec. 1882, 13 Jan. 1883, 14 June 1884; also flyers announcing their appearances.

19. *Le Socialiste*, 24 Feb. 1892.

20. Guesde archive, IISG, 607/18, letter dated 17 July 1889.

21. *Le Cri du peuple*, 25 Dec. 1883; "L'Emancipation de la femme et le socialisme," *La Question sociale*, 1 Oct., 1 Nov., 1891.

22. Quoted by Charles Longuet, *Le Justice*, 23 Nov. 1880.

23. *Le Cri du peuple*, 17 Aug. 1885.

24. Guesde archive, IISG, 564/12, copy of Mink letter to *Solidarité des femmes* dated [Jan.–Mar.] 1893; *L'Eclair*, 17 Aug. 1893.

25. Guesde archive, IISG, 219/2, letter dated 13 Oct. 1892.

26. *L'Harmonie sociale*, 25 Feb. 1893; APP, Ba/1483, report dated 6 Apr. 1893.

27. See APP, Dossiers Ba/1290 and Ba/1651; BMD, dossier VAL; Osmin, *Figures du jadis*, 84–87; Charles Vérecque in *La Femme socialiste*, Dec. 1932; Marie Bonnevial in *La Revue socialiste*, I(1899): 491–94 for biographical data.

28. Police agents, referring to Valette as Guesde's "mistress," assumed that she owed her position to his desire to facilitate their amorous relations. The first such report, dated shortly after her appointment as council secretary, sug-

gests that the assignment created dissension among Guesde's colleagues. The last, dated shortly before her death, dismisses her fatal illness, and a concurrent one of Guesde's, as mere excuses for the pair to escape to the south together. For a fuller discussion of Valette's influence, see Boxer, "Socialism Faces Feminism," pp. 139–56. For police reports: Archives Nationales (AN), F7, 13966, report dated 22 Feb. 1899, 29 Jan. 1896; F7, 12886, same report dated 22 Feb. 1899. APP, Ba/1484 report dated 21 Dec. 1893; Ba/1290 report dated 9 April 1896.

29. Ferdinand Roussel, cited in obituary, *Le Socialiste*, 2 Apr. 1899, his italics; Osmin, *Figures du Jadis*, 85; Bracke in Suzanne Lacore, *Femmes socialistes* (Paris, 1936) p. 5; Guesde quoted by Vérecque, *La Femme socialiste*, Dec. 1932.
30. "Une Journée historique: le 1er mai en France," *La Revue socialiste*, II (1890): 129–55, 433–48.
31. Pierre Bonnier, *Sexualisme* (Paris, 1914).
32. Aline Valette and Dr. Z., *Socialisme et sexualisme* (Paris, 1893), p. 15.
33. Bonnier, letter dated 13 Apr. 1896 to A. Zévaès, in *Sexualisme*, p. 88.
34. Valette and Dr. Z., *Socialisme et sexualisme*; also in *L'Harmonie sociale*, 29 April 1893.
35. "Mise au point," *L'Harmonie sociale*, 11 Feb. 1893.
36. "Point d'arrêt," *L'Harmonie sociale*, 4 Mar. 1893.
37. Charlotte Perkins Gilman, *Women and Economics* (New York, 1966; orig. 1898); Ellen Key, *The Century of the Child* (New York, 1972, orig. c. 1909); Margaret Sanger, *Woman and the New Race* (New York, 1920).
38. Bonnier, *Sexualisme*, p. 72; *L'Harmonie sociale*, 29 April 1893.
39. Guesde archives, IISG, 200/4 speech in Brussels, 7 July 1891.
40. APP, Ba/1651, report [1893] on *Congrès général des sociétés féministes*; *L'Harmonie sociale*, 25 Mar. 1893, 1 Apr. 1893.
41. *La Fronde*, Dec. 1897–Sept. 1898; BMD, dossier 091/VAL letter dated 16 April 1898.
42. "Aux Travailleuses," in *Almanach du Parti ouvrier pour 1896* (Lille, 1895), 72; "Une Première Etape," in *Le Socialiste*, 26 May 1895.
43. Marthe Louise-Lévy quoted by Vérecque, *La Femme socialiste*, Dec. 1932.
44. AN, F7, 12888, reports on 15th national congress of P.O.F., dated 16 July, 26 July 1897; for resolution proposing to study role of woman in order to determine if there were grounds for a women's program, see *La Petite République*, 15 July 1897.
45. *Le Socialiste*, 11 Feb. 1900.
46. M. Guilbert, *Les Femmes*, pp. 30–33; Willard, *Les Guesdistes*, p. 362.
47. *La Petite République*, 3 July 1899; Louise Saumoneau, *Principes et action féministes socialistes* (Paris, n.d.); *La Femme socialiste*, Oct. 1930.
48. For Saumoneau, see AN, F7 13266, "La Campagne féministe en faveur de la paix," 58-page report dated 27 Oct. 1915; also *La Femme socialiste*, esp. later series. For Renaud, see obit. in *Le Populaire*, 17 Oct. 1932. On both, Chas. Sowerwine, "Le Groupe féministe socialiste," *Le Mouvement social*, 90 (1975): 87–120.
49. Jean Longuet, "Elisabeth Renaud," in *Le Populaire*, 17 Oct. 1932.
50. *L'Humanité*, 23 April 1910; BMD, dossier REN; *Le Siècle*, 18 May 1910, gives figure of 2721.

51. Personal communication dated 2 July 1973 from Saumoneau's niece, Mme. F.A. Fourtoy of Clermont-Ferrand.

52. *La Femme socialiste*, Nov. 1901, 1 May 1914, Oct.–Nov. 1914 (in later series, Saumoneau recounted many of her earlier activities).

53. For an excellent discussion of French feminism in this period, see Karen Offen, "The Woman Question As a Social Issue in Republican France Before 1914," unpublished paper (Woodside, California, 1973); on reforms passed by the Chamber, Offen, pp. 65–66 or Boxer, "Socialism Faces Feminism," p. 221.

54. *La Femme socialiste*, Mar. 1901, May 1902, Feb.–Mar. 1932. *Le Parti ouvrier*, 19 Oct. 1901.

55. *Congrès international de la Condition et des Droits des femmes, 5, 6, 7 et 8 Septembre 1900* (Paris, 1901), 43–44, 47, 50, 73, 75, 83, 86–87, 113–14, 235, 290–91; *La Petite République*, 14 Sept., 18 Sept., 1900.

56. *La Petite République*, 22 Jan., 16 Feb., 28 Mar., 10 Apr., 24 June, 3 Sept., 18 Sept. 1902; *Le Parti ouvrier*, 16 May, 1902; *La Femme socialiste*, Oct. 1927, Jan. 1934.

57. *L'Humanité*, 21 Aug., 4 Oct., 22 Dec. 1905; *La Femme socialiste*, Jan. 1924; *Continuité et l'action féminine socialiste* (Paris, 1947). Eight years later others constituted a group limited to party women in the S.F.I.O. The earlier effort was so completely forgotten that a report to the first International Congress of Socialist Women at Stuttgart in 1907 declared that "nothing had yet been attempted toward organization of socialist women in France," until a tiny group formed in the 13th section of Paris that year. *Rapport de la Commission féminine de la 13ᵉ section du Parti socialiste de France* (Paris, 1907), p. 29.

58. *Principes et action féministes socialistes*, p. 12; *La Femme socialiste*, 20 July, 1 Oct. 1913.

59. This conclusion represents the opinion also of Saumoneau's niece, Mme. F.A. Fourtoy; see note 51.

60. The best biographical source is Pelletier's own work, especially her autobiography "Anne dite Madeleine Pelletier," dictated shortly before she died, BMD, Dossier PEL. (Ms. in hand of Hélène Brion.)

61. BMD, Dossier PEL; see articles dated 9 Apr. 1910, Apr., June, July 1939; *La Guerre sociale*, 12 Apr. 1907.

62. *La Fronde*, 2 Dec., 4 Dec., 7 Dec., 21 Dec. 1902, 1 Jan. 1904; *La Petite République*, 3 Dec., 19 Dec. 1902.

63. "Admission des femmes dans la franc-maçonnerie," *L'Acacia*, May 1905.

64. *L'Humanité*, 2 July 1906; *Le Socialiste*, 21 July, 8 Sept., 29 Sept. 1906.

65. Guesde archive, IISG, 306/3, letter dated 3 Oct. 1906; "Ma Candidature à la députation," *Documents du progrès*, July 1910, 11–16; *Le Socialiste*, 3 Nov. 1906, *L'Humanité*, 2 Nov., 4 Nov. 1906. Examples of "brief delay" promises: L. Dubreuilh in *L'Humanité*, 23 Dec. 1906; Bracke in *L'Humanité*, 13 July 1912, 10 Aug. 1913. In 1908, to protest the failure to act, Dr. Pelletier threw stones into parliamentary windows on election day, *Le Matin*, 17 July 1908.

66. *Le Socialiste*, 13 Oct. 1906.

67. *Le Gaulois*, 15 May 1906, "Le Féminisme et ses *militantes*," *Documents du progrès*, July 1909; *La Fronde*, 17 Aug., 25 Dec. 1926.

110

68. *L'Humanité*, 22 Dec., 23 Dec. 1906, 23 Mar., 26 Mar., 29 Mar. 1907.

69. *L'Humanité*, 6 Sept. 1907; Pelletier, *La Femme en lutte pour ses droits* (Paris, 1908), p. 60.

70. Pelletier's movement leftward can be traced in *La Suffragiste*, June 1910, July 1919; *La Guerre Sociale*, 14 Aug. 1907; "Ma Candidature," *Documents du progrès*, July 1910. For her attacks on Guesde see *La Guerre sociale*, 14 Aug., 4 Sept., 25 Sept., 4 Dec. 1907, 16 Sept. 1908; her seat on CAP: *L'Humanité*, 13 Apr., 15 Apr., 29 Nov. 1909, 10 Feb. 1910; her candidacies: *L'-Humanité*, 19 Apr., 22 Apr., 23 Apr., 25 Apr., 1910, *Le Matin*, 1 April 1910, *Le Socialiste*, 17 April, 24 April, 1 May 1919, 12 May 1912, "Ma Candidature," *Documents du progrès*, July 1910, *La Suffragiste*, June 1912; also "Discours prononcé par Madeleine Pelletier ds. le Préau r. de Florence samedi 23 avril 1910 (élections législatives)" in BMD, dossier PEL.

71. *La Revue socialiste* I (1908): 51; Pelletier, *L'Etat éducateur* (Paris, 1931), p. 12; "La Classe ouvrière et le féminisme," *La Suffragiste*, July 1912; "Déviations," *La Guerre sociale*, 4 Dec. 1907.

72. *Le Libertaire*, 24 May, 1 Nov. 1908, 17 Jan. 1909.

73. *La Suffragiste*, Feb. 1914; APP, Ba/1651 report dated 30 Mar. 1914.

74. Pelletier, *Mon voyage aventureux en Russie communiste* (Paris, 1922); BMD, dossier PEL, articles dated 26 April, 6 June, June, July, 1939; letter, A. Hamel-Jankov to Marguerite Durand, 29 Dec. 1939; Pelletier, *L'Individualisme* (Paris, 1919), p. 92.

75. *Le Socialiste*, 5 May 1907.

76. Aaron Noland, *Founding of the French Socialist Party 1893–1905* (Cambridge, Mass. 1956), p. 207.

77. In 1913, bourgeois feminists organized a major campaign in support of the right of Emma Couriau, a working-class woman, to work. Couriau was a veteran typographer working for union wages at a union shop. Following the decision of her trade syndicate to admit women, she applied for membership, only to be refused, and her typographer husband ejected, by the local section. Only feminist groups came to her defense. The socialist women in Paris refused, fearing, according to Saumoneau, to take "antimasculinist" action. See Guilbert, *Les Femmes*, pp. 63–64, 409–412 and Boxer, "Foyer or Factory," pp. 199–200.

78. Recent efforts to broaden the theoretical basis of socialism to include feminist analysis include Juliet Mitchell, "The Longest Revolution," *New Left Review* (Nov.–Dec. 1966), pp. 11–37; Herbert Marcuse, "Marxism and Feminism," in *City Lights Journal*, no. 3 (1974), pp. 34-41; Barbara Ehrenreich, speech at National Conference on Socialist Feminism, in *Socialist Revolution*, V, 4 no. 26, (Oct-Dec. 1975), pp. 85–92; and Renate Bridenthal, "The Dialectics of Production and Reproduction in History," *Radical America*, 10 (Mar.–Apr. 1976) pp. 3–11.

111

5 • Unequal Partners in an Uneasy Alliance: Women and The Working Class in Imperial Germany[1]

• Jean H. Quataert

German Social Democracy was the pride of the Second International. As the largest, best organized, most disciplined and class-conscious party, it was hailed as the model for others. Its prestige and influence carried over to the German socialist women's movement, which provided leadership in the women's International and inspiration and guidelines for the nascent socialist women's movements emerging on the continent after 1890. Beyond their leadership role, German socialist women distinguished themselves in several respects. First, unlike their French counterparts, their movement reflected greater unanimity on socialist and feminist issues. The explanation lies less in the divisions of French socialism into several competing parties and positions than in the role of leader. After Lenin, no one can deny the importance of leadership in revolutionary movements, and German socialist women had their Lenin. Clara Zetkin, an orthodox Marxist, provided continuity of leadership (1891–1917), an iron discipline and, more importantly, clear theoretical stances and corresponding strategies on the host of issues facing socialist women. The role of ideology in conditioning positions on the women's question comes clearly to light in her debates with the revisionist Lily Braun. Second, unlike the Italian experience discussed in the next essay, the German socialist movement contained a dynamic feminist component and incorporated broad-based feminist reforms into its overall program for change. Encased in a class

CLARA ZETKIN. From Archiv der sozialen Demokratie (Friedrich-Ebert-Stiftung), Bonn.

framework, feminism appeared less threatening to socialists in Germany than elsewhere. Perhaps the strength of the German socialist subculture permitted it to accommodate a variety of causes promoting the accepted goal of socialism. Yet even German socialist women had to soft-pedal their feminism. In what ways did feminism conflict with socialism? How was the priority question solved in Germany?

___

In her political awakening during the 1880s, the German working-class woman faced an identity question. Would she join forces with her bourgeois sisters in a broad feminist struggle against patriarchy; or would she unite with her male counterpart and fight the class struggle for socialism? In short, would she be loyal to her sex or her class?

The choice was not quite hers alone. Powerful currents in the German body politic as well as social and economic changes associated with industrialization helped determine courses of action. Industrialization, by creating a new class structure, accentuated distinctions among women according to work and domestic life.[2] The feminist slogans of "right to work" and "equal pay for equal labor" had different meaning for proletarian women and ladies of the middle class. In the political arena the antisocialist laws (1878–1890) heightened class antagonisms and left a legacy of fear and bitterness on both sides. Thus, in Germany, a powerful ingredient of political hatred was added to the class barriers that dissected the female population.

The working-class woman's solution to her quest for political identity was seemingly simple yet fraught with difficulty. She chose loyalty to class *and* to sex by allying feminism with socialism. This meant she stood apart from the bourgeois women working in feminist movements for better educational and employment opportunities, jobs in municipal services, or a "new morality." The symbol of her choice was the Social Democratic women's movement (*Frauenbewegung*) which, by the outbreak of World War I, had nearly 175,000 members. The adherents were rebels in a double sense, fighting both the social and the sexual prejudices of their society. As such, they worked doubly

114

hard in the movement: with men for the general cause and together for the goals of feminism. They saw themselves as an integral part of the socialist workers' movement.

In socialist conceptions, feminism was both a means and an end. In the short run, equality with men under capitalism would help the working-class woman withstand capitalist exploitation, so she could join more easily the proletarian liberation struggle. This effort to emancipate women in order to hasten the revolution contrasted with bourgeois designs to assimilate females into the capitalist state as equal and responsible citizens. For the long run, the end goal of feminism was equated with socialism: the future society would introduce a new era in human relations and accord women and men an equally dignified existence.

Much worked in favor of the alliance. In Imperial Germany, the socialist subculture provided the most supportive milieu for women seeking to improve their economic, social, and political position. Sex equality was an integral part of Marxist ideology, and the socialist platform embraced such crucial feminist demands as equality in education and employment as well as in political and family life. After 1890, both the political and trade union wings of German Social Democracy—the Social Democratic party (SPD) and Free Trade Unions—incorporated into their structures committees dealing with women's issues and staffed by women well versed in the life experiences of their female constituency. Through socialist efforts the working-class female—disenfranchised and poorly organized—found her interests being championed in parliamentary debates and during labor disputes.

Yet a latent tension, unperceived by most participants, was part of the historic union. Since socialism alone promised true sexual liberation, the first priority was accorded the social revolution. If priorities conflicted, the women's struggle bowed before the class struggle. And the socialist feminist plank incorporated only those demands compatible with the final end of proletarian liberation.

What, then, was the nature of feminism-in-socialism? How far did the feminist vision go? What ideological as well as attitudinal and social barriers to sex equality existed in the socialist subculture? This essay sets out to treat these key issues in an effort to assess the advantages and disadvantages in the linkage of two great social movements in Imperial Germany.

The ideas of Marx, Engels, and Bebel on the women's question were reformulated for the German setting by Clara Zetkin, schoolmistress of the socialist women's movement and self-proclaimed "inveterate Marxist."[3] The theory remained true to its ideological fathers by welding the women's question securely to the larger social question and viewing the female sex together with the proletariat as victims of capitalism. Class not sex ultimately was seen to determine a woman's existence—her status, rights, and consciousness—although German socialist feminism came to recognize non-work-related influences (such as family and the schools) on the social world of women. Work was hailed as the great prerequisite for female liberation as it freed women from economic dependency on husbands or fathers. However, Zetkin showed her socialist seasoning by carefully noting that in gainful employment the working-class woman, unlike her upper- or middle-class counterpart, merely exchanged one dependency for another: the husband for the capitalist employer.[4] Zetkin's theoretical formulation and her subsequent political activity emphasized the inexorable conflict between bourgeois and socialist feminists. Although she admitted that parallel action was possible, she was quick to point out that such collaboration in Germany would be "a retrogression" for socialists. German middle-class women's righters, she judged, were so "muddle-headed, wishy-washy, weak" that they feared presenting forcefully either their feminist or their reform proposals.[5]

Mobilization efforts for German socialists remained restricted to working-class females and centered on creating proletarian consciousness and promoting the class struggle. Within this goal, women leaders sought to mold a new working-class woman who would step into the socialist society aware of her rights and willing to assume responsibilities in public life. The feminist component reflected the deep commitment to women's equality as well as the need to devise slogans and tactics that would reach working-class women as women. Embedded in the writings of the leaders, then, was a view of life for women inherently different from that prescribed by traditions and customs. This feminist vision is ambiguous and often inconsistent because the proponents failed to pose specific questions relating to ways women could find fulfillment. Rather, in articles and speeches on a host of diverse topics such as the eight-hour day or protective labor laws they offered implicit answers. Nevertheless, these socialists were pioneers in women's struggle for equality, pathfinders in analyzing the reasons for and proposing solutions to women's inferior status. Among the first to challenge age-old assumptions, they advanced radical reforms; at the same time, they unconsciously internalized certain traditional attitudes.

The feminist vision as part of the values of the socialist subculture can be analyzed in two complementary ways. One involves the more traditional historical method of dissecting the women's writings and speeches to ascertain the aspiration for change. The other, less customary, approach for the historian derives from an analysis of the personal experiences of several leaders that accounted for their political awakening. As noted in the introduction, working-class history usually neglects the politicization process. The paucity of biographical information has focused the historians' attention either on the ideology or the larger class context. This part of the essay seeks to shift the emphasis away from an abstract discussion of class to a more specific examination of the lives of several prominent socialist feminists. By supplementing the writings of the movement's leaders with biographical materials, one can obtain insights into their hopes for the female sex that are more penetrating than an analysis of the written word alone. Their perception of women's place at home and in society as well as their blueprint for change could not but mirror their own stage of consciousness based on personal experiences.

From biographical materials, it is clear that an important motive in sustaining female membership was the perception of the SPD as the most consistent champion of women's equality in Imperial Germany. The German middle class, socialists agreed, had compromised its historic role to complete the bourgeois revolution and failed to champion meaningful feminist causes.

117

Consequently, the proletariat alone had taken up the women's struggle. Lily Braun succinctly crystallized the sentiments of her socialist colleagues when she hailed the SPD as "the sole bearer of the social movement pertaining to women."[6]

No typical pattern emerges in the politicization process. Several leaders such as Lily Braun, born an aristocrat, and Emma Ihrer, of lower-middle-class origin, moved from bourgeois feminism to socialism once they became convinced that middle-class reforms offered no effective solution to the women's question. Their hope for a better world for women triggered concern with the social question. In other cases the reverse process occurred. Two leaders of middle-class origin, Clara Zetkin and Marie Juchacz, were attracted to the movement by the ideas of socialism and gradually turned to consideration of women's issues. Others such as Luise Zietz and Ottilie Baader, both from the working class, became politically active after they perceived their second-class status as both women and working-class members. Helene Grünberg and Gertrud Hanna, to mention two union leaders of working-class origin, experienced oppression as female workers. These unionists seethed under social limitations that prevented women from acquiring skilled jobs in the labor market. The trade union movement offered them a chance to improve their economic position and satisfied their emotional and material needs as well. All the eight personages reviewed here expressed great emotional satisfaction at the feeling of belonging to the socialist movement and collaborating with like-minded individuals.

Several examples document the fact that membership fulfilled personal needs, an important requirement for organizational vitality that social scientists have recognized.[7] Baader failed to marry, and only when she turned to the socialist world view and found another content to life did she accept spinsterhood.[8] In Juchacz's case, her move to socialism filled a void created by the dissolution of her marriage. She reminisced back to 1903, the year she had joined the movement:

It was a very decisive time for me. Economic worries and responsibilities and personal ... hardships were hard to bear. ... Entering the socialist world of ideas helped me accept my fate.... I learned many things ... but above all I learned to think and view things as part of the whole not just from a personal perspective or that of my immediate surroundings.[9]

Participation offered Braun the chance to satisfy her overwhelming desire to be active.[10] Hanna was inclined toward melancholy and seclusion, according to Juchacz. "Her work brought her into contact with many persons and prevented her from sinking into isolation."[11]

The women's movement had an added meaning. It offered an alternative route to social integration, especially for those who rejected the paths to fulfillment offered by the dominant society. Luise Zietz, for example, found camaraderie and a milieu in which she could follow her ideals.[12] Participation, in short, gave women not only the chance to dream about alternatives for women's existence but the opportunity to act out their vision in the present.

The memoirs of Baader and Braun indicate some other reasons why women became socialists. Both works record a growing sense of frustration at societal and familial constraints on their ability to develop freely—a frustration widely shared by women activists. Consciousness of a dependent status, the low valuation of females as "only women," and opposition to parental expectations catalyzed their political awakening.

Baader, born in 1847, portrayed her father as a worker and radical democrat who held traditional ideas on women's place in the family. He taught her reading and writing and at ten years sent her to a Catholic institution (*Mittelschule*) considered "a good school." That meant, she explained, that "Girls were trained there mostly in 'good manners.' To be soft, tender, and gentle was the woman's idea of this time."[13] At thirteen years, economic necessity forced Ottilie to work. She wrote in terms applicable to her working-class sisters that "it was unnecessary to hold a big family council to select the right occupation because at that time there was not much of a choice for girls."[14] She became a seamstress, a typical job for young working-class women. Since she never married, she ended up

119

supporting herself and also her father for twenty years, a major source of frustration for her. Baader described her feelings of resentment.

> I experienced myself the great dependency of women, even working women, on the male member of the family. . . . Even though I had been for a long time the sole supporter of our small household I remained for my father 'the daughter' who does not need to have an opinion of her own and who has to adjust to him without any question.[15]

During the anti-Socialist laws she and her father observed discrimination against ordinary workers and read up on socialism. "My father read and we discussed the works while I sewed."[16] Bebel's "Frau" (as *Woman under Socialism* was affectionately called) proved decisive. She experienced an almost "religious" rebirth. Baader best describes its impact.

> Life's bitter needs, overwork, and bourgeois family morality had destroyed all joy in me. I lived resigned and without hope. . . . News came of a wonderful book that . . . Bebel . . . had written. Although I was not a Social Democrat I had friends who belonged to the party. Through them I got the precious work. I read it nights through. It was my own fate and that of thousands of my sisters. Neither in the family nor in public life had I ever heard of all the pain the woman must endure. One ignored her life. Bebel's book courageously broke with the old secretiveness. . . . I read the book not once but ten times. Because everything was so new, it took considerable effort to come to grips with Bebel's views. I had to break with so many things that I had previously regarded as correct.[17]

The book, she recalled, brought "hope and joy to live and fight."

Baader's penetration into the socialist world view at the late age of forty transformed her whole life. By confronting for the first time reasons for her subordinate position as a member of the female sex and the working class she felt rejuvenated and willing to face the present and work for a better future. A similar transformation occurred in Braun who, at the age of twenty-seven, wrote to a cousin about her new political commitments. "I have the future for myself . . . and I feel the strength in me to make each year one of progress. . . ."[18] Less explicit but similar expressions of faith in progress, courage, and hope accompanied the political awakening of other prominent personalities in the socialist women's movement.

For Baader, the decision to embrace socialism meant final independence from her father, which she said "was not so easy." He had helped her understand the socialist world view, and as they read the literature she learned to form her own opinions. He prevented her from going to meetings alone until she put her foot down and challenged him. "This burst of energy must have taken my father by surprise. He remained completely silent and did not object any more to my going out alone."[19] The influence of men in the politicization of socialist women appears typical. Many women were aided in their political maturation by husbands, brothers, or male friends, a reflection of the broader educational and political opportunities available to men.

Lily Braun's case was unique. As a member of the upper class, she received explicit instructions and training for her deportment and future role in life. Familial designs were clear: she would grow up to be a lady and marry an aristocrat. In her memoirs Braun depicts continuous pressure to mold her into an acceptable member of the upper class. Norms such as "the female's task [is] to please" or "we women simply do not belong to ourselves" filled her childhood and early adolescence.[20] At sixteen years, her parents sent her to Augsburg to visit an old aunt who reinforced the socialization process by speaking constantly of her future husband and home. By then, she wrote, she had become truly a "young lady" and internalized the values of her family.[21]

Several experiences shattered the mold. Conflicts arose over her relations with the opposite sex and her growing desire to do something meaningful in life. On one occasion after her parents forbade her to talk to a young man of a lower social class because he might get "ideas," she wrote angrily to her cousin. "Can't you see how disgusting this is: what a grave offense against our sex? Female dogs are not judged differently from us."[22] She began to feel that being bred for mating was a disgrace and that women had more to live for than just catching a man. A determination to work stirred as she perceived the empty, superficial, and boring existence in high society. In a revealing statement she crystallized her resentments. "I am twenty-three years old, healthy in mind and body, perhaps more able to achieve than many others and not only do I not work, I don't even live; rather my life is being arranged."[23] The passive tense at the end of the sentence symbolized her feelings of being an object in life, unable to control her destiny. Life was passing her by, her fate had been decided at birth because society ruled that gender defined a person's expectations and opportunities.

From the working class echoed a similar feeling of resentment at being an object in life. Grünberg described women in the labor force as "playthings" bantered about by forces beyond their control. Reflecting a common grievance, she complained that society inadequately trained them for employment since their "true" profession was seen anchored in the home. Women were unprepared for work and had no possibility of making life easier and more meaningful through labor.[24] Both Braun and Grünberg believed that women should be free to determine their own course in ways that would allow them to develop and mature. The trade union movement offered Grünberg the chance to control her life and improve the options of other women as well.

Braun could satisfy her personal needs only by rejecting the views of her family and social class. Her memoirs describe the family's attitude that had become intolerable. Explaining to her father her desire to work she heard him argue: "If you had been a man I would certainly have guided you to paths which would guarantee a meaningful content to life—but as things are—you are just a girl, destined for one job only—all others would be nothing but sad stopgaps."[25]

Braun's break with her social class initially led her to the middle-class feminist camp. Contact with socialists and Marxist literature, however, convinced her that bourgeois women engaged in Sisyphean labor. At a public meeting in 1896, she declared that middle-class goals profited small numbers only while they left the "mass of suffering women untouched."[26]

She expressed dismay that bourgeois antipathy toward Social Democracy "had led to stagnation in our bourgeois women's movement," and she criticized middle-class leaders' hesitancy to adopt radical reforms for fear of being identified in the public mind with socialists.[27] In a telling debate with a former colleague, Wilhelm Foerster, president of the German Ethical Culture Society, Braun explained her decision to become a socialist. She wrote that had she compassion only, she would have remained a bourgeois reformer. But deliberate study and personal experience had convinced her that middle-class reformers, no matter how radical, failed to attack the roots of the problem and offered mere palliatives, "bandages for festering wounds."[28] She broke publicly with the bourgeois feminist movement.

Yet Braun's socialism reflected humanitarian concerns, and she emotionally rejected the class bases of the socialist world view. Similarly, she distrusted historical materialism with its claim to scientific objectivity. It was Bernstein's theories, first published in 1898, that struck a receptive cord. She wrote that the "cool, clarity of [his] arguments had a crushing effect," and henceforth it became "a matter of intellectual integrity" to examine Marxist principles critically.[29] Braun became an ethical revisionist, closer on the ideological spectrum to reformers than radicals in German Social Democracy.[30] She shared with the former the belief that practical, immediate reforms of the present society provided preconditions for the emergence of socialism that would banish misery and inequity from the world. But she diverged subtly from them in her approach to the women's question. Braun proved unrelenting in her critique of sex discrimination and offered novel solutions to the problem of women's oppression. In contrast, reformist women, bereft of ideological tools, restricted women's roles in the party and in public life basically to social work at the municipal level.[31] Yet Braun had warned time and again that "social welfare of all types had nothing to do with the women's question."[32] Her reading in scientific socialism deepened her perspective on the women's question even though she rejected basic assumptions of historical materialism. In Braun's own case, feminist consciousness matured as class consciousness waned.

The biographical sketches show that activists in the women's movement of Social Democracy were feminists in that, at a minimum, they were conscious of being female. This becomes clear also from their speeches and writings—the other source of information on German socialist feminism. Sex consciousness distinguished them from women socialists such as the fiery radical Rosa Luxemburg who "regarded her sex as irrelevant."[33] Luxemburg held that women's oppression was an ephemeral capitalist misery that would disappear in the socialist society. All energies, she prescribed, had to be directed toward promoting the revolution. The leaders of the socialist women's movement, too, saw in socialism the only way to true emancipation of the female sex but deviated from Luxemburg over strategies for the revolution. They were bent on mobilizing working-class women as a special group. Furthermore, they did not deny their womanhood. Rather, they believed that women were capable of performing what society defined as men's tasks without aping men. A clear indication of their redefinition of femininity to subsume traditional male roles is found both in the obituaries and in the short characterizations of one another they wrote on birthdays or other occasions. Pride in their "womanly nature" or "motherly way" complemented praise for public activity. Zetkin's obituary for Ihrer typifies their ideal.

> The implacable foe of all prejudice . . . was an utterly good woman, a womanly nature through and through. Life truly did not spare Emma Ihrer bitterness but it did not wither her . . . sensitivity. . . . Enthusiastic studies broadened and secured her . . . socialist knowledge, yet her service remained always a matter of the heart.
> So in our memory, she is perfect proof that the woman . . . can be a true fighter without giving up being a woman. . . .[34]

Socialist ideology saw customs, morality, and values mirroring stages of economic development. Most activists drew the logical conclusion that women's role in social life including assumed "feminine" characteristics had been socially conditioned. They scornfully rejected assumptions about women's mild, pliant, or weak nature, and they fought stereotyping at every turn. Ihrer, for example, judged that women's double burden at home and work had made them "mild," and she chal-

124

lenged the pseudoscientists who "proved" women's inferiority by the size of their brain: "If one hears that only the largest brains are suitable for intellectual capabilities, one could then send whales to the university," she mocked at a meeting in 1890. Ihrer concluded that women had been "intellectually crippled" by the schools and the character of education they received as well as by their dependency in the home, factory, and workshop.[35]

The *bêtes noires* for socialist women were the prevailing ideals that "women belong in the home" and "men provide for the family." Grünberg represented the sentiments of her colleagues when she disdainfully rejected both platitudes "since . . . million[s of] working women are torn from their homes and families and work for the capitalist state." She stated that the same employers using female labor "scream bloody murder" when women begin to concern themselves with public life. And Braun, in a similar vein, described as philistines those who cried "how unfeminine" when proletarian women, driven to work, engaged in strikes for higher wages.[36]

Socialists expected that women's gainful employment as well as the economic changes associated with industrialization would offer females broad options in life and provide the basis for new consciousness and unstereotyped roles. To further this process, the women's movement sought to instill new values and promote legal change more in harmony with the ongoing revolutionary transformations. In educational clubs and reading sessions, the leaders propagandized a more favorable view of women's role and talents in society. And they proposed a series of reforms designed to promote women's rights in the capitalist state. The very act of championing women's interests was seen as crucial to revolutionizing their minds—to bringing, in socialist terminology, the subjective side of the battle into harmony with the objective.

The reform proposals of German socialist feminists were decidedly advanced for the times. They advocated women's vote as a social right. With women's increased participation in public life, it had become necessary for them to defend their interests; the foundation for women's suffrage lay in social necessity and represented recognition of their useful functions in society. Bourgeois women, socialists contended, wanted political reform to preserve their society; proletarian women needed the vote not only as a defense against exploitation and for the sake of social justice, but as a weapon to fight the bourgeois class.[37] Unlike their contemporary British and American feminists, German socialist women never overestimated the importance of the vote in and of itself. They were all too aware of the ways in which the effect of universal male suffrage in Germany was diluted by constitutional manipulations and chicanery. But since the class struggle was conceived of as a political struggle, women needed political rights to participate fully in the liberation movement.

Socialists demanded reform of education to provide skills and broaden women's employment opportunities. They proposed that occupational training be included in the curriculum and raised the then scandalous demand for coeducational instruction. Coeducation could help alleviate sexual fears and misconceptions and bridge the artificial gap between the sexes.[38] As a corollary to the working-class woman's professional training and growth, socialists expected a corresponding change in men who no longer would see the employed woman as a wage depressor and resist her attempt to rise professionally.[39]

Leaders of the women's movement came out for legal changes favoring equality in the family and demanded the grounds for divorce be eased. Also, most felt, at least in theory, that a woman should have the right to limit the size of her family—it was her most inherent personal right, the right of self-determination.[40] But the degree of commitment to this radical proposal varied greatly.

In the years before World War I, birth control became an extremely emotional and divisive issue for socialist feminists. The German government unsuccessfully sought to improve the falling birth rate by preventing the sale and use of contraceptives (*Gebärzwang*). During the ensuing controversy, a minority in the socialist camp came to advocate birth control as a "revolutionary weapon" in the class struggle (*Gebärstreik*). It was more important, some intimated, than the parliamentary tactic.[41] The debate reveals important limits in socialist thought to the acceptance of feminist goals.

The question of birth control placed the SPD leadership in an uncomfortable position. According to its official response, limitation of births was a private matter to be discussed in a couple's bedchamber or with a doctor. But the public call for using the subject as a political weapon forced an open debate in the party.

Proponents of the birth strike saw reduction of births as a means of mitigating the present misery in working-class homes. They hoped to ease the burdens on working-class families, improve welfare and educational opportunities of each working-class child, and assure more freedom for the individual woman. As a by-product, the potential for political mobilization among women with fewer children would be greater. Birth control also would deprive the German military of future soldiers.[42]

Opponents of the birth control strike in the socialist camp, most vigorously political radicals, rejected the neo-Malthusian analysis that population was responsible for poverty. The culprit was rather the unequal distribution of goods and services, i.e., capitalist society itself. They feared that concentration on the population issue would divert the masses from the main goal of overthrowing capitalism or, secondarily, of winning from capitalism child care and other municipal services. As Zetkin, the most vocal champion of this position put it, a restructuring of the family might reconcile the individual to existing social conditions. Drawing on her reading of history, she implied that "numbers not quality" guaranteed victory in social struggles. Furthermore, if one struck against the military, the number of soldiers for the revolution would be reduced as well. Quite simply, although birth control might help the individual, it hurt the class. Zetkin also questioned the claim that large numbers of children kept women away from the movement. The relevant criteria were not numbers but the health and intellectual alertness of women. She admitted at one public meeting in Berlin that children added problems, but so did husbands who expected to be catered to by their wives, a statement that produced enthusiastic response from a generally cool audience.[43]

127

The socialist leadership squelched the issue shortly after the outbreak of the war. The executive committee adhered to Zetkin's views and threatened reprisals for those females who continued agitation for birth control. Party leaders—male and female—had decided that individual or family needs in this case were immaterial for the working class as a whole. Birth control might be liberating for individuals, but its inclusion in the party program would be inimical to the collective interests of labor. Thus, party opposition stood in the way of achieving a feminist goal.

Because their ideology conceived of work as the emancipator of the female sex, socialist women rejected traditional role divisions between men and women, although the position of some leaders on the issue of domestic roles was filled with ambiguity. Most believed that women were primarily responsible for domestic tasks but that social changes no longer permitted them to perform these duties adequately. They often proposed radical solutions to ease married women's double burdens without explicitly calling into question the precept that women's primary role lay with the family. The writings of Luise Zietz, for example, clearly reflect such a mixture of traditional and radical ideas. In her view, reforms advocated by socialists, ranging from the eight-hour day to maternity insurance to protective laws, would allow women to perform their domestic duties more effectively. Zietz explicitly stated that women needed protection because "employment did not free [them] from housework," implying that housework was, after all, women's domain.[44]

Beyond these notions went a more revolutionary idea to socialize some traditional domestic functions. Generally, socialist women were well aware that one prequisite for equality was the reduction of home tasks. Institutions were needed to help lower-class working women save time, energy, and money in the performance of domestic duties. Suggestions for municipal programs to be initiated in the capitalist state included communal eating and laundry services, day-care centers, playgrounds, obstetrical wards, and household service for pregnant women.[45] Nevertheless, the writings expressed a certain nostalgia for an idyllic home life beyond the grasp of working-class women. Socialists could hail education of children and administration of the home as "holy duties" while at the same time demand that society perform these functions since a woman could no longer be the "capable *Hausfrau*" of yesteryear.[46]

Yet the movement as a whole was unwilling to countenance too radical a change in life-style for the present society. At the turn of the century, Lily Braun published a short pamphlet entitled *Frauenarbeit und Hauswirtschaft* (*Female Labor and Cooperative Living*, Berlin, 1901), a plea to alleviate women's domestic functions by organizing household cooperatives. She called on the leaders of the women's movement to incorporate the reform in the general propaganda campaign. The fate of her proposal underscores clearly the socialist requirements for adoption of a feminist demand: they had to "raise women to equality" but, perhaps more importantly, "incorporate them into the struggle of their class" as well.[47] In Zetkin's and most leaders' eyes, Braun's proposal only served to diminish women's domestic duties; it deviated from official guidelines by failing to further the class struggle. An examination of this debate sheds further light on the uneasy side of the relationship between socialism and feminism.

Braun based her call for communal household arrangements on the inevitable transformation of the single-family establishment under the impact of economic development. She recognized that industrialization had wrought changes in the family as a production unit and in women's economic functions at home. As early as 1896 she had proclaimed that economic growth would destroy the last bastion of traditional family life, the kitchen, and later she pointed out that the basis of marriage should not be in the kitchen but in common intellectual and emotional ties and experiences.[48] The trend of female employment, Braun believed, necessitated new institutions to reduce women's wifely, motherly, and housekeeping burdens. Cooperatives could become the foundation of women's emancipation; unless they obtained the leisure to develop harmoniously, their liberation would remain chimerical. Home cooperatives, Braun predicted, would encourage feelings of brotherhood within the dominant system and further the preconditions for socialism. She saw cooperatives as an important building block in the future construction of a socialist society. According to Braun, capitalism would not suddenly disappear; she envisioned the gradual disintegration of the capitalist order concomitant with the slow ripening of the socialist system.[49]

As Braun described it in her memoirs, the reaction to her proposal remained cool at best. Some women charged that such agitation for communal households would divert the working class from its main political goals; others claimed she wanted to drive "all women from the intimate family life to the barracks."[50] Quarreling and hatred were predicted if large numbers of families adopted a communal form of living. The only favorable contemporary review came from Helene Bloch in *Sozialistische Monatshefte,* a revisionist organ, who wrote perceptively that even radical comrades supporting women's emancipation refused to apply their principles to their "four walls" and had a "good bourgeois fear" of a revolution in domestic life.[51] But it was Zetkin's uncompromising opposition that destroyed Braun's hope for official adoption of her proposal.

In a letter to Karl Kautsky, theoretician of orthodox Marxism, Zetkin described Braun's brochure as the "latest blossoming of utopianism in its most dangerous, opportunistic form."[52] By implication, she related Braun's proposal to the ongoing revisionist debate involving most party members at the time. Underlying Zetkin's overt hostility was the specter of socialists adopting, from her perspective, the erroneous view that socialism could be realized within the capitalist system, a view she thought was nothing but an "amiable delusion."[53] This would imply, she wrote publicly in *Gleichheit* (Equality), the women's movement's organ, a total rethinking of Social Democracy's concepts and tactics. In reality, Zetkin maintained, socialist goals could not be achieved contemporaneously with the political class struggle and the only crucial tactic was "preaching" socialist ideas to the masses, organizing and educating them for their historic role in opposing the capitalist system.

Zetkin detailed specific objections to Braun's plan. She recognized, as did Braun, that economic change revolutionized the family and that raising the position of working women required an easing of their burdens as wives and mothers. But she questioned Braun's solution, ostensibly because of the proletarians' living condition. First, the major prerequisiste, a secure, regular income, was lacking; employment insecurity characterized the realities of life for most working-class members, and the unemployed could not maintain a smoothly functioning cooperative. Second, only a small percentage of the proletariat, those who were relatively well-off, could benefit from home cooperatives. Statistics showed, Zetkin added, that within this section most women did not work. Third, the psychological preconditions for communal living did not exist among those proletarian "aristocrats"; they prized the single-family establishment. Finally, striking at the heart of the matter, Zetkin believed that cooperatives would acquire revolutionary meaning only after the proletariat obtained political power. Cooperatives depended on radical change in thought, habits, and beliefs which, in turn, was based on transformed production and private property relations.[54] She called cooperatives bourgeois reform work, chastised Braun for not decisively distinguishing socialist from middle-class concerns, and dismissed the proposal as having no relevance for the agitational efforts of women socialists.

Braun's plan would not have hastened the revolution. Yet it came from a deep concern for the position of women and would have eased the lives of those women living in the cooperatives. Her proposal envisioned transformed bases of existence—communal living—and a corresponding change in values and attitudes. Zetkin refused to accept the proposition that cooperatives within the capitalist society could transform the members' bases of existence, presumably because the visualized communes would be solely consumption entities and leave work relations unaltered. Zetkin's preoccupation with the economic preconditions for change, in short, made her unwilling to experiment with alternative life-styles. By rejecting home cooperatives in the name of ideological necessity, Zetkin remained true to the prevailing orthodox interpretation of Marx. At the same time her position narrowed feminist options.

The preoccupation with the goal of economic change meant

that socialist women generally devoted less time to questions of love, marriage, and family relations. It was assumed that the self-aware, economically independent woman would marry solely for love, and that common interests and mutual respect would bind husband and wife. Once in the mid-1890s, in response to an ongoing discussion in the bourgeois feminist camp and to contemporary novels depicting an emancipated woman, both Braun and Zetkin had sketched their "ideal" woman. The attributes of their ideal attest to these socialists' pride in being women. Both felt that the models held up by (bourgeois) feminists and contained in literature were incomplete. Braun criticized authors such as Ibsen for failing to portray a whole woman. She felt his Nora in *A Doll's House*, whom most saw representing "a woman yearning for freedom and chance to develop her personality," in fact symbolized egoism and lacked "heart and femininity."[55] According to Braun, women's one-sided struggle against men in England and Scandinavia had produced truncated literary figures—"abnormal women"—and she pointed to Gerhart Hauptmann's heroine Anna in *Einsame Menschen* as an ideal, a true woman "healthy and strong in spirit and body yet delicate and soft as well."[56] The new woman would be free to develop her individuality, maturing in an occupation that corresponded to her abilities. From youth on, she would be able to socialize with men as innocently as with women, from friendship love would grow, and the emancipated woman would stand at the side of a man as a true comrade.

Zetkin sought to harmonize the traditional view of women that saw them as sexual beings only (*Nur-Geschlechtswesen*) with the feminists' portrayal that depicted them as human to the neglect of their sexuality. She felt that a woman was neither "just a person" (*Nur-Mensch*) nor "totally female" (*Nur-Weib*) but a full human of the female sex (*Weiblicher Vollmensch*) with corresponding duties in the family and in public life. Both sides of women's nature required cultivation. To neglect her humanity would cripple a woman's growth as a female and restrict her influence at home. Conversely, satisfying her needs as a woman saved her from becoming "a superficial copy of man," a mere working *Mannweib*.[57] The capitalist society, however, forced women to choose: work or family. Only socialism would nurture women's dual nature.

The visions of Zetkin and Braun were daring and bold, yet contained sentiments that are distracting to a modern reader. Succinctly stated, neither succeeded in freeing herself from a male-centered standard. Braun described the new woman as man's comrade, partner, and fellow fighter, but unaware of potential contradiction, stated also that "she will belong to the man of her choice." For Zetkin, the fact the men did not bear children did not make them half human; rather, women were true human beings when they worked as hard and well as men did while succoring and mothering. She conjured up a modified bourgeois ideal.

> Rooted and active in the world at large and in the family she can make the man in the home once again comfortable. From her own rich, expansive sphere of activity grows clear understanding for his strivings, struggles, creations. She doesn't stand next to him as an obedient maid ... but as a companion in his struggle, as a comrade in his troubles ... supportive and receptive.[58]

For both, the emancipated woman was still, in part, man's creature even if she freely chose the man.

In 1905, Zetkin, Braun, and Ihrer offered more penetrating analyses of the changing relationship between the sexes, in part to meet a challenge launched within the socialist world against basic assumptions of their movement. That year, *Sozialistische Monatshefte* published an article by Edmund Fischer, reform socialist Reichstag deputy, that sought to prove that women's struggle for emancipation contradicted human nature.[59] Within a socialist framework, Fischer reformulated traditional views of women's place in social life and erected a socialist "wife-mother-housekeeper" model for women in the future society. He questioned how one could free women from their domestic duties when "the first and highest goal in life for the woman, buried deep in her nature, [was] to be mother and live to educate her children." He blandly dismissed the Marxist belief in work as the vehicle for women's emancipation because, in his eyes, women's employment was "unnatural, socially unsound, and a capitalist misery which must disappear when capitalism is destroyed."[60] The women's question would not be solved by liberating women from men, he concluded, but by overthrowing capitalism and returning women to their families.

The reaction among socialist women was swift and biting and highlights a key issue in socialist feminism that had crystallized by the early twentieth century. The major problem now centered on the realization of equality while taking into account differences between the sexes and became acute primarily in the pressing need to reconcile work—the liberator of the female sex—with motherhood. For German socialist feminists like Aline Valette earlier in France (Chapter IV) held implicitly that a woman was not complete unless she was a mother. But unlike Fischer, of course, they stressed as well the key role of gainful employment in rounding out a woman's existence.

Ihrer proved most unconventional in responding to Fischer. She scorned his idolatry of the "home sweet home," calling such expressions of sentimentality "a sickness," and categorically dismissed his view that motherhood and child bearing were the highest goals for women. "To be a mother is as little a life's goal as to be a father. Women can find their life's purpose only in general work areas or in solving social tasks which lie in the interest of all."[61] In balancing motherhood and professional life, Ihrer tilted toward employment; she did feel, however, that society had to be reorganized so that a married woman could work without suppressing her desire to have a family. She described an alternative model for the "new woman." "The woman of the future will choose one occupation according to her capabilities and inclinations; she will be either working woman or educator of children or housekeeper but not all three as today's proletarian woman."[62]

Zetkin took Fischer to task for perpetuating the values of a particular stage of economic development and reminded him that socialists, above all, had no reason to halt historical change.[63] In her immediate response as well as in later articles on related topics, she stressed the dialectical nature of capitalist misery that inevitably pointed toward future resolution. Women under capitalism, she admitted, suffered from the irreconcilable twin roles of workers and mothers. But this was no reason to slight either function in the future socialist society, and she resurrected her ideal of the *Weiblicher Vollmensch*. Within the womb of capitalism, the proletarian class struggle initiated the process of harmonizing work and motherhood; it forced reforms on the ruling classes. The proletariat was fighting for legal protection for the gainfully employed woman, for maternity insurance, and was actively seeking to unionize women. Women's labor, of extreme discomfort to Fischer, was, in fact, revolutionary. It dissolved the old form of marriage, bourgeois monogamy based on the subordination of women to men's desire for legitimate heirs, and spurred its evolution into a higher moral unit. Zetkin expected the marriage of the future to be a monogamous union, but one based on equality between husband and wife and on fidelity as the moral ideal for both sexes.[64] The woman then could become a wife and mother in the highest meaning, not as a "crippled creature," but as a free, strong, and fully developed individual. Fischer's perspective on child education, which said, in essence, "my wife educates my child in my home," provoked her wrath. Only if fathers and mothers jointly raised children, she countered, could boys and girls learn to appreciate sex differences and later work together in life. A more realistic apportionment of home tasks, in turn, would help resolve the conflict between women's professional life and motherly tasks.[65]

With gross overidealization, however, Zetkin asserted that since men and women in the working class had no wealth they rejected men's privileged position in the family. To the extent that wives worked, male privileges disintegrated in working-class homes: "Legal dogmas cannot preserve what life's bursting surge destroys." Zetkin recognized that most proletarian couples clung to the bourgeois form of marriage but felt respect for the institution had waned. "It is a small step from lack of respect for form to noncompliance with form," she predicted, brushing aside inconsistencies apparent in her statements.[66]

Braun was less sanguine than Zetkin that the monogamous marriage would survive in the future, and she questioned the assumption of many reformers who predicted a lasting and successful union between two intellectually equal persons. This view failed to recognize that "the instinct of the sexes [was] not identical with understanding." She feared that the complexity of modern life multiplied possibilities for conflict: men would find in their working wives the same intensity and nervousness as existed in the outside world, and women would experience the external world directly, not through an intermediary.[67] Marital peace, Braun basically believed, required the subordination of women to men. But she also felt that awareness of sexual needs made monogamy problematic and labeled her age a "turning point" in sexual relations. Prevailing Christian morality had made sexual release through prostitution inevitable for men but women could find "love" only in marriage. She boldly stated that marriage destroyed "love." "On the corpse of the martyrs of marriage speaks the priest of the religion of love with the words 'faithful spouse,' " she wrote bitterly.[68] With candor unusual for the times, she admitted that "since the women's movement has loosened our tongues we see that the sexual drive is as strong in women as in men," and she sanctioned premarital sexual relations for both sexes.[69] Braun rejected "universalizing" free love because it alone could not guarantee a woman independence and stated that common-law marriage without economic freedom for women would bind them as tightly to men as the conventional marriage.

Braun's position on the women's question had changed over the years; her solution had become—a child and work. She stated that women's economic independence, which "liberated love," could not be secured through employment only because women had a higher duty than work, a duty to become mothers. To insure a woman independence during pregnancy and the child's early years (Braun strongly felt that children needed their mothers until they went to kindergarten) she advocated universal maternity insurance for all women, paid by a progressive income tax. She left the "form of love"—whether marriages or free relationships—unspecified for the future and stated only that it would correspond to the needs of individuals.[70] Braun's writings betrayed a strange blend of unconventional, radical, often contradictory ideas revolving around one constant: a belief that motherhood was a woman's highest duty in life. Through her own unique route she, too, had arrived at a solution to the basic question raised by socialist women: how to reconcile work and motherhood.

In contrast to Zetkin, Braun felt that members of the working class were unreceptive to changes in family life promoting greater equality for women. She spoke of hearing complaints at meetings that men did not understand women's desires for education or public activity. Furthermore, she did not share the belief of most of her SPD comrades that the presence of men and women working together in public life or standing side by side in the economic struggle would automatically be reflected in more equitable familial relationships. On the contrary, she stated that the proletarian woman had to wrest from the the man her personal rights because "the bourgeois philistine morality was so deeply ingrained in him." And she declared that the socialist women's movement must educate her if she is unable to see this.[71]

Braun alluded to a problem which the socialist women's movement largely neglected in its fight for women's liberation: the tenacity with which the average working-class male and SPD member adhered to traditional family forms. In their official debates, socialist feminists failed to dissect the family and analyze its place in conditioning male and female role divisions or women's subordinate status. When the question of the family was brought up before the women's conferences and SPD congresses in Imperial Germany, it was only in connection with other issues such as education. To a certain extent, socialist feminists generally were victims of their Marxist ideology that posited the *inevitable* evolution of the family to a higher moral unit based on full equality between husband and wife, an evolution that was to begin first in working-class homes. Since such familial equality was seen as the guaranteed by-product of ongoing economic transformations, socialist ideology interfered with a thorough critique of actual family life in the working class.

This is not to say that socialist women were oblivious to the presence of traditional sentiments among family men in the organized working class. They often prescribed that "the duties of good [male] comrades and union members must begin at home."[72] But Ihrer's analysis in 1890 could apply equally well to the state of affairs in 1914, after twenty-four years of efforts by female leaders to raise consciousness. At a meeting she had remarked, "Among men as well as women there reigns a large amount of indifference. . . . When women inquire of men about the position of workers they usually get an answer: you don't understand anything of that. This egoism . . . must disappear."[73]

The extent to which male comrades had retained traditional family notions that reinforced feelings of women's inferiority eluded socialist women. Even August Bebel, chairman of the SPD and staunch champion of women's equality, described his marriage in these terms.

> To the man who fights in public life against a world of enemies it is not unimportant what kind of spirit lives in the wife who stands at his side. . . . I could not have found a more loving, a more dedicated, a more self-sacrificing woman. If I achieved what I accomplished it was primarily possible through her untiring care and assistance.[74]

Despite his clear theoretical and even, in general, practical commitment to the struggle for women's equality, he implicitly praised the virtues of the traditional division of labor between men in public life and women supportive at home. And Karl Kautsky, too, expressed similar sentiments in his eulogy for Julie Bebel: "All that Bebel did as a pioneer and leader we thank him . . . but also the strong support which he found in his wife, the intelligence, untiring dedication with which she kept the small daily worries away from him. . . . Her ambition was to rule over an area which was cut out for her.[75] Although he added that Julie was also Bebel's comrade and advisor, Kautsky stressed how well she had fulfilled the traditional roles assigned to women.

In general, large numbers of male socialists failed to regard their wives as equals or help them grow and mature. Gertrud Bäumer, in the middle-class feminist camp, analyzed a random selection of workers' autobiographies that, she claimed, reflected prevailing ideas. She noted the indifference with which men—particularly the politically active and enlightened—regarded the intellectual life of their female family members. For example, the union leader Bromme's autobiography vividly juxtaposed the exciting intellectual world of a worker to the "emptiness and drudgery of a woman's life." And Karl Fischer, a baker's son, wrote of his mother that "she was for my father his assistant and servant ... his shopping agent ... his housekeeper and babysitter."[76]

It was only after World War I that socialist women clearly began to recognize and lament this gap. In 1921, Grünberg, disillusioned over the political behavior of women in the early Weimar Republic, bitterly charged, "People are criticizing women that they are not using the vote correctly. Big brother scolds little sister. If in the thirty years that we labored ... more practical socialism had been promoted in the family then women would have had more love and understanding for socialism. . . ."[77] But only after World War II did the focus turn to the nuclear family as a key institution preventing women's real emancipation once they had achieved political and legal equality. Juchacz, who returned to Germany after exile during the Third Reich, foreshadowed the growing consciousness among midcentury women of their subordination in the private sphere. At the SPD's 1952 congress she called on men and women comrades to recognize that "the cell of work is in the nuclear family. . . . The position of men to one another, between men and women must be based on real equality. . . . It is true that in the family the man is still a Pasha."[78]

In Imperial Germany, Social Democracy spearheaded efforts to liberate the woman in her public and private life. Socialist women proudly hailed their party as the only consistent advocate of women's equality and chided German liberalism for its equivocating stance. Within socialist ideology, feminism addressed the problem of sex discrimination and sought reforms embracing the whole of social life. Ranging from equal employment and educational opportunities to day-care centers and women's vote, the socialist feminist platform marked an important stage both in confronting women's social, economic, and political subordination and in proposing remedies and novel conceptions that upheld the equal worth of the sexes. Socialist feminism, furthermore, turned to the individual working-class woman and encouraged self-awareness and pride not only to enrich her life but to win her for the class struggle.

Socialist women envisioned a life radically different from that prescribed by the dominant society. Personal experiences and the dictates of ideology conditioned their vision. They sought a new social organization that offered the woman a chance to develop both as a human being and as a female. The "new woman" would find her purpose in life in the society at large and in the family. The transformed family, based on sexual equality, would form the unit within which women could satisfy their needs as women; it would also provide the moral support for their activity in society. This vision remained unrealized, and the failure to remove the barriers the nuclear family placed before women's emancipation, in part, proved the nemesis of the socialist women's movement.

Despite the milieu favorable to feminism, discrepancies between public and private postures in German Social Democracy frustrated socialist women's efforts to create a new consciousness of sex equality. That male social democrats shared assumptions of their age and culture should not detract, however, from their progressive stand on women's liberation nor obscure the gulf between them and the average German philistine clinging doggedly to his belief in women's intellectual and social inferiority. Women leaders themselves felt ambivalent toward family roles. While they recognized that women's triple jobs as workers, wives, and mothers hindered emancipation, they could not divest themselves of the belief that women remained responsible for running the home. Their progressive call for municipal institutions to carry some of the domestic burdens came more from a recognition that industrial change led to widespread female employment away from home than from a considered rejection of the adage that women's essential role lay with the family. Dominant norms filtered through socialist views.

The women's movement of German Social Democracy sought to harmonize class and sex by defining feminism in class terms. Hierarchies existed, however, and class loyalty stood at the apex. Since women activists put their faith in socialism to redress sexual inequalities, the first priority involved furthering the revolution. Thus two feminist proposals—birth control and cooperative living—were never adopted officially and omitted from the propaganda platform because they were seen as inimical to the collective needs of labor. This choice derived from an implicit assumption that sex inequality was a function of prevailing property relations. By socializing the means of production and thereby creating new consciousness, activists envisioned the automatic cessation of sex oppression. The persistence of "traditional gender discrimination" that Marxists recognize in so-called socialist countries today belies this calculation.[79] Male/female role expectations have proven to be remarkably tenacious. But socialist women at the turn of the century lacked the advantages of hindsight. Enveloped in a world view promising victory, they accepted only those reforms that spurred history onwards; those seen as ends in themselves were rejected. Working-class women in Imperial Germany had made their choice and joined up with the socialist movement. This decision promoted their feminist aspirations but subordinated these to the struggle for the socialist society.

NOTES

1. This essay derives from various chapters of my Ph.D. dissertation, "The German Socialist Women's Movement 1890–1918: Issues, Internal Conflicts and the Main Personages" (University of California, Los Angeles, 1974). I dedicate it to the late Robert Wheeler, friend and collaborator. I wish to thank specifically Rose Glickman, Claire LaVigna, and Vera Wheeler for offering comments and criticisms in the initial writing phase; revisions were aided by Hilary Karp and Sharilyn Wood. Responsibility for the final product is, of course, my own.
2. Peter N. Stearns and Patricia Branca Uttrachi, "Modernization of Women in the 19th Century," *Forums in History* (1973). Renate Bridenthal, "The Effects of Women's History on Traditional Historiography with Specific Reference to Twentieth Century Europe" (Paper read at the Berkshire Conference on the History of Women, 27 October 1974).
3. *Protokoll des SPD-Parteitages zu Jena, 17–23 September 1905* (Berlin, 1905), p. 281.

4. "Frauenagitation," *Protokoll des SPD-Parteitages zu Gotha, 11–16 Oktober 1896* (Berlin, 1896), pp. 160–68. Zetkin's analysis here supplements an earlier work that she published on the women's question, "Die Arbeiterinnen-und Frauenfrage der Gegenwart," in Max Schippel, *Berliner-Arbeiter Bibliothek*, Bd. 1, no. 3 (Berlin, 1894).

5. "Proletarische und Bürgerliche Frauenbewegung," *Gleichheit* X, no. 24 (21 November 1900): 186.

6. L. von Gizycki (Braun), *Zur Beurteilung der Frauenbewegung in England und Deutschland* (Berlin, 1896), p. 35.

7. See, Steven R. Brown and John D. Ellithorp, "Emotional Experiences in Political Groups: The Case of the McCarthy Phenomenon," *The American Political Science Review* LXIV, no. 2 (June, 1970): 349–66. Also, Cecil A. Gibb, "Leadership," in *International Encyclopedia of the Social Sciences*, ed. David L. Sills, IX (New York, 1968): 91–99.

8. O. Baader, *Ein steiniger Weg: Lebenserinnerungen* (Berlin, 1921), p. 15. M. Kuhnert, "Ottilie Baader," *Gleichheit*, XIII, no. 8 (August 1950): 262.

9. Friederich Ebert Stiftung (hereafter referred to as FES), Personen-Sammlung, Marie Juchacz. Clipping of *Neues Beginnen*, "Marie Juchacz' Kindheit, Jugend und erste politische Tätigkeit," p. 66.

10. L. Braun, *Memoiren einer Sozialistin: Lehrjahre* (Munich, 1909), p. 515. Julie Vogelstein, "Lily Braun: Ein Lebensbild," in *Lily Braun: Gesammelte Werke*, Vol. I (Berlin, n.d.) pp. xxxii, xxxvii.

11. FES. NL Marie Juchacz, D. 3. "Frauen ihrer-Jahrhunderts" (unpublished manuscript).

12. F. Osterroth, *Biographisches Lexikon des Sozialismus*, vol. I (Hannover, 1960), p. 342.

13. Baader, *Lebenserinnerungen*, pp. 9–10.

14. Ibid., p. 9.

15. Ibid., p. 19.

16. Ibid., p. 20.

17. "Was Bebel den Proletarierinnen gab," *Gleichheit* XX, no. 10 (14 February 1910): 150–51.

18. J. Vogelstein, "Lily Braun," p. xxxv.

19. Baader, *Lebenserinnerungen*, p. 25.

20. L. Braun, *Lehrjahre*, pp. 37, 41, 175.

21. Ibid., pp. 179–80.

22. Ibid., p. 246.

23. Ibid., pp. 370–71.

24. 20. *Jahresbericht Arbeiter-Sekretariat Nürnberg: Geschäftsjahre 1914–1920*. Ortsausschuss Nürnberg des Allgemeinen Deutschen Gewerkschaftsbunds (Nürnberg, 1921), pp. 42, 44.

25. L. Braun, *Lehrjahre*, p. 374.

26. L. Braun-Gizycki, *Frauenfrage und Sozialdemokratie: Reden anlässlich des Internationalen Frauenkongresses* (Berlin, 1896), p. 3.

27. L.v. Gizycki, "Nach rechts und links," *Die Frauenbewegung*, I, no. 7 (1 April 1895): 51.

28. "Herrn Foerster zur Erwiderung," *Gleichheit* IX, no. 22 (25 October 1899): 174.

29. L. Braun, *Memoiren einer Sozialistin: Kampfjahre* (Munich, 1911), pp. 245–46. In 1898 Bernstein created a storm by publishing *Evolutionary Social-*

ism, an ideological challenge to the prevailing socialist interpretation of Marx. He had observed that capitalism, contrary to the Marxian analysis, betrayed rejuvenative powers, and he moved socialism from the realm of necessity (inevitability) to the realm of ethics (choice). Socialism, he argued, would result from the determined actions of the trade unions, cooperative societies, and party in exerting pressure for reforms within the capitalist system. By implication, he dismissed the need for revolutionary action, questioned the reality of the class conflict, and destroyed the intricate connection between means in the service of the final end, the socialist revolution. Debate in German Social Democracy quickly gathered momentum and engulfed the socialist world for five years until the SPD Dresden Congress in 1903 officially rejected "in the most decisive fashion revisionist efforts to change the victorious tactics we have hitherto followed based on the class struggle...." Quoted in English in James Joll, *The Second International 1889–1914* (New York, 1966), p. 100. Consult also Peter Gay, *The Dilemma of Democratic Socialism* (New York, 1952).

30. P. Gay, *The Dilemma*, pp. 257–60. In his analysis of Bernstein, Gay distinguishes between revisionism and reformism, although he admits that the lines became blurred after the turn of the century. On page 260 he writes: "Revisionism, then, may be separated from general reformism through its emphasis on intellectual criticism of Marxism and its attempts to establish an ethical Social Democratic world view."

31. The shift occurred after reformist women inherited the women's movement in 1917 when German Social Democracy split into two hostile camps under the strains of war and prewar ideological tensions. For more on Majority Socialist women (reformers) see my dissertation, pp. 359–71.

32. L.'Braun, "Die Interessen der Arbeiterinnen und der Internationale Frauenkongress," *Correspondenzblatt* XIV, no. 26 (2 July 1904): 420. Also, L. von Gizycki (Braun), *Zur Beurteilung*, p. 25.

33. A. J. Nettl, *Rosa Luxemburg*, abr. ed (Oxford, 1969), p. 88.

34. "Emma Ihrer," *Gleichheit* (16 January 1911).

35. Staatsarchiv Hamburg (Hereafter referred to as StAH). S 1926, "Versammlungsbericht," 6 September 1890.

36. Stadtarchiv Nürnberg. 2923. Clipping of *Fränkische Tagespost* (10 April 1909). L. v. Gizycki (Braun), *Die Stellung der Frau in der Gegenwart* (Berlin, 1895), pp. 11–12.

37. *Protokoll des SPD-Parteitages zu Mannheim, 23–29 September 1906 mit Bericht der 4. Frauenkonferenz* (Berlin, 1906), pp. 445–46.

38. *Protokoll des SPD-Parteitages zu Bremen, 18–24 September 1904 mit Bericht der 3. Frauenkonferenz* (Berlin, 1904), pp. 363, 365. Also StAH. Clipping of *Reform* (27 March 1890).

39. *Protokoll über die Verhandlungen des 9. Kongresses der Gewerkschaften Deutschlands, München 22–27 Juni 1914* (Berlin, 1914), p. 197. L. Zietz, *Gewinnung und Schulung der Frau für die politische Betätigung* (Berlin, 1914), p. 4.

40. C. Zetkin, "Die Ehescheidung im Entwurf eines neuen Bürgerlichen Gesetzbuches und vor der Kommission zur Vorberathung desselben," *Gleichheit* VI, no. 12 (10 June 1896): 90. The following articles in *Gleichheit* deal with the question of divorce: "Warum fordern wir Reformen in neuen Bürgerlichen Gesetzbuch?" (7 August 1895), p. 123; "Die eheherrliche Vogtei

des Mannes über die Frau im neuen bürgerlichen Recht," (24 June 1896), pp. 105–106. On the right of women to limit the number of children: Vorstand des Sozialdemokratie Deutschlands, *Material zur Geburtenfragen* (Berlin, 1918); L. Zietz, *Gegen den staatlicher Gebärzwang* (Hannover, 1914); articles in *Gleichheit,* 1 October 1913, 1 April 1914, 13 May 1914, and 10 June 1914.

41. Stadtsarchiv Potsdam, Pr. Br. Rep. 30, Berlin C. Tit. 95, Sek. 7, Nr. 15856, Bl. 33–45.
42. Ibid., Bl. 11, 40–45, 55–56, 78.
43. Ibid., Bl. 7–8. Marx had not dealt with birth control *per se;* he had, however, related the question of population to the surplus labor problem and to wage levels. During the debate, neither side brought out these issues.
44. *Zur Frage des Mutter-und Säuglingsschutzes* (Leipzig, 1911), p. 25. Also, "Der Achtstundentag und die Gewerkschaftliche Agitation und Organisation," *Gleichheit* XIV (20 April 1904); *Die Frau und der politische Kampf* (Berlin, 1912), p. 9.
45. "Notwendige Ergänzung," *Gleicheit* XI (30 January 1901): 17–18.
46. StAH. S 1926. Clipping of *Hamburger Echo* (24 October 1899); also S 20627. Polizeibehörde Abt. IV, 13817.
47. "Bahn frei," *Gleichheit* XIV (20 April 1904).
48. L. Braun-Gizycki, *Frauenfrage und Sozialdemokratie*, p. 14. "Die Ehe auf der Anklagebank," *Die Neue Gesellschaft* III, Bd. 5 (10 July 1907), p. 55.
49. *Frauenarbeit und Hauswirtschaft*, pp. 27, 30–31.
50. *Kampfjahre*, pp. 394–97. Also, "Zur Frage der Wirtschaftsgenossenschaften," *Gleichheit* XI (25 September 1901), pp. 155–56.
51. *Sozialistische Monatshefte* Bd. 1, no. 6 (June, 1901), pp. 469–71.
52. International Institute of Social History. NL Kautsky. D XXIII, 339. Stuttgart (16 May 1901).
53. "Die Entgegnung zur Antwort," *Gleichheit* XI (28 August 1901): 144.
54. Consult the following articles in *Gleichheit:* "Die Wirtschaftsgenossenschaft" I–IV (19 June 1901): 97; (3 June 1901): 105–106; (17 July 1901): 113 –14; (31 July 1901): 121–22.
55. L. v. Gizycki (Braun), "Die Frau in der Dichtung," *Neue Zeit* XIV, Bd. 2 (1895/1896), p. 297.
56. Ibid., pp. 302–303.
57. "Nicht Haussklavin, Nicht Mannweib, weiblicher Vollmensch," *Gleichheit* VIII (19 January 1898): 9–10.
58. Ibid., p. 9.
59. "Die Frauenfrage," *Sozialistische Monatshefte* XI, 3 (March, 1905): 258–66.
60. Ibid., p. 258.
61. "Die Proletarische Frau und die Berufstätigkeit," *Sozialistische Monatschefte*, XI, Bd. 1 (May, 1905): 448.
62. Ibid., p. 446.
63. "Aus Krähwinkel," *Gleichheit* XV (22 March 1905): 31–32.
64. "Ehe und Sittlichkeit" Part II, *Gleichheit*, XVI (16 May 1906): 64; Part V (8 August 1906): 105.
65. "Aus Krähwinkel," pp. 31–32.
66. "Ehe und Sittlichkeit," Part V, *Gleichheit* XVI (5 September 1906): 119.
67. "Das Problem der Ehe," *Die Neue Gesellschaft*, Bd. 1, no. 10 (7 June 1905): 114–16.

68. "Die Enthronung der Liebe," *Die Neue Gesellschaft* I, no. 20 (16 August 1905): 239.

69. Ibid., p. 238. Also, "Die Ehe auf der Anklagebank," *Die Neue Gesellschaft* III, Bd. 5 (10 July 1907): 56.

70. "Die Befreiung der Liebe," *Die Neue Gesellschaft*, Bd. 1, no. 21 (30 August 1905): 260–63. For her position on maternity insurance see, Braun, *Die Mutterschafts-Versicherung* (Berlin, 1906).

71. "Die 'unterdruckte' Frau," *Die Neue Gesellschaft* II, no. 29 (18 July 1906): 348.

72. C. Zetkin, "Dringende Aufgaben," *Gleichheit* XIV (9 October 1904). Also, *Protokoll des SPD-Parteitages zu Nürnberg, 13–19 September 1908 mit Bericht des 5. Frauenkonferenz* (Berlin, 1908), p. 530.

73. StAH. S 1926 "Versammlungsbericht," 6 September 1890.

74. August Bebel, *Aus Meinem Leben*, vol. I (Stuttgart, 1914), p. 186. Also, Barbara Stolterfaht's review of Werner Thönnessen, *Frauenemanzipation* in the *Internationale Wissenschaftliche Korrespondenz*, 11/12 (April 1971), pp. 93–94.

75. "Julie Bebel," *Neue Zeit* XXIX, Bd. 1 (2 December 1910): 276–77.

76. Gertrud Bäumer, *Die Frau in Volkswirtschaft und Staatsleben der Gegenwart* (Berlin, 1914), pp. 22–23. Fischer was not a member of the Social Democratic Party.

77. *Protokoll des SPD-Parteitages zu Görlitz, 18–24 September 1921* (Berlin, 1921), p. 186.

78. FES. Personen-Sammlung. Marie Juchacz, "Parteitag 1952."

79. Harriet Holter, "Sex Roles and Social Change," in *Towards a Sociology of Women*, ed. Constantina Safilios-Rothschild (Massachusetts, 1972), p. 333. Also, for example, Inge Hieblinger, *Frauen in Unserem Staat* (Berlin [Ost], 1967), and Gerda Weber, "Um eine ganze Epoche voraus? 25 Jahre DFD," *Deutschland Archiv: Zeitschrift für Fragen der DDR und der Deutschlandspolitik* V, no. 4 (April 1972): 410–16.

6 • The Marxist Ambivalence Toward Women: Between Socialism and Feminism in the Italian Socialist Party

• Claire LaVigna

In Italy, socialism and feminism remained basically two parallel rather than intersecting movements. Because the country was slow to industrialize, the working class was rather weak and the emergence of the Socialist Party in the early 1890s represented the imposition of Marxism on a predominantly conservative labor movement. The party was plagued by doctrinal and tactical controversies revolving around the question of parliamentary activity and alliances with nonsocialist parties. Reformists who, unlike the Germans of a similar name, balanced the twin goals of reform and revolution and revolutionaries—staunch noncollaborationists and believers in direct action—coexisted uneasily until shortly before World War I when the latter expelled the former. In this context of transformation and controversy, feminism was seen as divisive. First, the new commitment to class made feminism suspect. As LaVigna argues, "Utopian and other forms of socialism that stress class cooperation rather than class conflict are at least in theory more compatible with multiclass feminism than is Marxism." Second, the precarious party unity was maintained only by tabling potentially disruptive issues and feminism was a victim. The career of Anna Kuliscioff exemplifies these themes. Why did she choose the proletariat over women? What,

ANNA KULISCIOFF. From Alessandro Schiavi, *Anna Kuliscioff*. Rome: Editoriale Opere Nuove, 1955.

then, was her attitude toward proletarian women? What did bourgeois feminism have to offer in terms of ideas, organization and a social base? What issues most clearly divided bourgeois feminist from Italian socialist?

Anna Kuliscioff (1854–1925), cofounder of the Italian Socialist party and staunch advocate of women's liberation, can serve as a clear prism through which the strengths as well as the weaknesses of the European Marxists' position on women in the late nineteenth and early twentieth centuries can be seen, separated, and analyzed. Not only does her theoretical outlook offer a faithful adaptation of that of Marx, Engels, and Bebel, but her practical work on behalf of her sex places before us an instructive example of European socialist activity for the cause of women. Kuliscioff, a woman and onetime feminist, was sincerely concerned about female emancipation, and her leadership within the Italian Socialist party gave her real power to act for women. But, at the same time, she firmly believed in the socialist cause and bore responsibility for the whole party. Accordingly, when action to benefit women appeared to threaten the success of the party at large, she wavered. Because her vacillation lays bare the problem at the very core of the relationship between women and socialism, Kuliscioff can serve so well as the focus for this study, which is aimed at better understanding the roots, the manifestations, and the consequences of the Marxist ambivalence toward women.

Central to the analysis of her Marxist ambivalence toward women is Kuliscioff's 1897 declaration of independence from the existing feminist movement, which she wrote midway in her political career. This divorce from the feminists did not, of course, mean that Kuliscioff broke with all women. She continued to be the Italian socialist most active on behalf of working-class women. Thus she boldly defended her break from the feminists in Marxist terms, contending that

the present feminism of the middle class is merely a reproduction of the revolutionary movement of the male middle class a century

ago. Freedom for woman, conquered during the period of its economic monopoly, can only be freedom for the middle-class
woman.... Socialism and feminism, if they can be parallel social
currents, cannot be one sole cause.[1]

In an attempt to get at the roots of Kuliscioff's ambivalence,
her 1897 rupture with feminism is of double significance—first
because it justified the tendency, apparent in her political activities throughout the 1890s, to give precedence to socialism
over feminism, and second because it removed all doubt about
the primary allegiance of this woman, who until that decade,
had been more or less equally identified with both movements:
feminism and socialism.

On the one hand, the Anna Kuliscioff poised primly upon her
green velvet divan, sipping espresso coffee from dainty cups
while she presided over salon gatherings in her apartment atop
the elegant Galleria of Milan, baffled her contemporaries by not
physically conforming to the nineteenth-century stereotype of
either the feminist or the Marxist. On the other hand, her consciously defiant actions, which cut across her personal and political life, went far to nullify the salon portrait of soft femininity
and etched instead in the mind of her contemporaries the portrait of a woman strongly and equally committed to both feminism and socialism.[2]

Her roots as a feminist were indeed deep. At age sixteen,
finding herself barred because of her sex from entrance into the
university program of her choice in her native Russia, she went
to Zurich to begin the study of engineering. A few years later,
while in exile in Lugano, Switzerland, following a brief appren-
ticeship in the Russian populist movement, Kuliscioff flaunted
convention again to live unmarried with the Italian anarchist
Andrea Costa and to have a child by him. When, after seven
years, the relationship had become burdensome to them both,
Costa, by then a respectable member of parliament, preferred to
maintain the facade of a union for the sake of appearances. She,
however, insisted on an honest and complete break. In fact, she
had already begun to carve out a new independent life for herself and her daughter. Returning to university after a ten-year

absence, Kuliscioff earned a degree in medicine and set up practice in the working-class district of Milan, where she specialized in gynecology.

In the more public sphere, almost from the moment of her entrance into Italy in 1879, Kuliscioff was placed in the spotlight as a feminist symbol. An article in *La Plebe* attributed the significance of her conspiracy trial in Florence to her proud and courageous conduct on the witness stand, which would surely inspire other women in Italy to abandon the kitchen for the concerns of the outside world.[3] Again in 1890, after a decade of relative political dormancy, Kuliscioff, the feminist, resurfaced boldly to read a paper with the challenging title, *The Monopoly of the Male,* before that male bastion, the Philological Society of Milan.[4]

Further dramatic confirmation of the image of Kuliscioff, the feminist, was found in her penchant for smoking cigarettes in public, a most brazen action for a woman in the 1870s,[5] and also in a brief but revealing exchange in 1893 between her and a flustered neophyte in the Italian Socialist party. He addressed the already famous Kuliscioff as *"la signora di Turati"* (Turati's wife), only to meet her instantaneous reproach. "I am not the *signora* of anyone," she told him. "I am simply Anna Kuliscioff."[6] Indeed, many of the major actions of her personal and political life as well as these symbolic gestures made her appear a walking advertisement for feminism.

At the same time, her commitment to socialism was as deep, as strong, and as long-standing as her fidelity to feminism. Initiated into the socialist movement in her late teens while a student in Zurich, Kuliscioff opened her political career as a Bakuninist anarchist. Upon leaving behind her native Russia in 1877 for a life of exile, she also abandoned Bakuninism in favor of evolutionary socialism, since she deemed the destructive tactics of anarchism better suited to conditions under czarism than to the more liberal atmosphere of the West. A reading of the works of Marx and Engels in the light of her practical political experience in Russia and in Western Europe led to her conversion to Marxism sometime between 1880 and 1885, and until her death in 1925 she never deviated from that creed. Kuliscioff, the avid Marxist, was cofounder with Filippo Turati of the Italian Socialist party (PSI), coeditor with him of the socialist review, the *Critica Sociale* (Social Critic) and in the eyes of many the "Nymph Egeria" of the reformist faction of the PSI for more than forty years. So forcefully was her presence felt within the Italian socialist movement that the opinion that she was "the most intelligent man in Italian Socialism,"[7] has become a cliché.

Utopian and other forms of socialism that stress class cooperation rather than class conflict are at least in theory more compatible with multiclass feminism than is Marxism. For example, before her turn to Marxism, the Malonian-style eclectic socialism Kuliscioff espoused around 1880 seemed to permit socialism and feminism to be "one sole cause." The harmonious union of these two movements is revealed in the program of the *Rivista internazionale del socialismo* (International Review of Socialism) of May 15, 1880, wherein, in collaboration with Andrea Costa, she declared that

> socialism for us is not a system, but the most ample expression of the perfectibility of man.
>
> Understanding it thus, it is natural that we turn ourselves not to one class alone but to all those, whatever may be the class to which they belong, whom the present order of things compromises materially or morally—to workers, youth and women.
>
> We say women, not for empty gallantry, but because it is important that they participate in social activity.... We cannot fail to include women in the work of renewal to which the times and our convictions call us, if we wish that not only the exterior and apparent conditions of life but also personal and family relationships be transformed, and that Socialism insinuate itself into everyday life to change for the better habits and customs—in short the whole human being.[8]

However, after 1885, the two lines of Kuliscioff's commitments—feminism and Marxism—were set upon a collision course as a result of the latent antagonism between the membership of each movement. Women, the sex defended by the feminists, cut vertically through society and thus included female capitalists, the exploiters of proletarian men and women.

The proletariat, the class championed by the Marxists, cut horizontally across society and therefore included men, the exploiters of women. Why then did this conflict of interests not strike Kuliscioff until the mid 1890s?[9] And when she faced the critical moment of decision, why did she choose the proletariat over women?

The seeds of this tension were already present in Kuliscioff's 1890 *Monopoly of the Male* paper, which attempted to be at the same time both feminist and Marxist. On the one hand, the approach was markedly feminist, as the title so clearly suggests, in that she appealed to and for all women, regardless of social class since all, in various ways, were the victims of male oppression at home and at work.[10]

On the other hand, her lecture on the male monopoly was also Marxist. First, it did not deviate from the spirit as much as it expanded upon the content of Frederick Engels's anthropological study, *The Origin of the Family, Private Property and the State*.[11] Like Engels, Kuliscioff went back through history, in an attempt to understand the roots of what she termed the "long martyrdom" of women, but she concentrated on those periods in which Engels was most sketchy, that is the position of women in medieval and in modern society. She began where Engels had left off in another sense as well, and in so doing, her study ironically became more truly Marxist than his. For Engels, in the last few years of his life, was much disturbed "that the younger people sometimes lay more stress on the economic side than is due to it."[12] He admitted that he and Marx were "partly to blame," and indeed his essay *The Family*, which treats the woman question as exclusively an economic problem in its origins and in its solutions, lent itself to just such an oversimplification. So, in keeping with Engels's advice that "[t]he economic situation is the basis, but the various elements of the super-structure . . . also exercise their influence upon the course of the historical struggles and in many cases preponderate in determining their *form*,"[13] Kuliscioff's analysis gained from the inclusion of the ethical and psychological dimensions. She discussed not only the economic dependence of woman, but also the origins and effects of woman's loss of "personality" in a socialization process that made her a "moral parasite,"[14] the role of the "sentiment of motherhood" and of female education in shaping the "conservative" and "patient" character of woman,[15] and the controversial physiological debate on the size of the brain as a determinant of intelligence.[16] Because of the breadth of her discussion, Kuliscioff in *The Monopoly* was better able to plumb the many layers of the complex woman question.[17]

Second, the stamp of Marxism is perhaps even more visible in Kuliscioff's complete acceptance in *The Monopoly* of "the economic situation" as the "basis . . . of the historical struggles." Considering work outside the home to be the nucleus of the woman question, Kuliscioff chose to address herself principally, though not exclusively, to the "struggle for existence." As a feminist she did not ignore the prejudice encountered by professional women, and made brief mention as well of women employed as teachers, clerks, and writers. Nevertheless, Kuliscioff, as befitted a Marxist, focused her attention upon the plight of the proletarian women. In her analysis of the "evils" of capitalist industrialism, she demonstrated statistically that even though more women were employed in industry than men, the strength of their numbers was not felt due to their conservatism and lack of organization. As a result, women in sweat shops were working longer hours than men and receiving lower wages for jobs that they handled as well as and often better than their male counterparts. Consequently, Kuliscioff judged that woman in industry "is doubly a slave: on the one hand of her husband, on the other hand of the capitalist."[18]

However, Kuliscioff did not stop there. She incorporated a third and final Marxist strain into her study of the male monopoly—the dual nature of capitalist industrialism; despite its short-term evils, capitalism, in the long run, is a useful historical stage. With the advent of machines to replace muscle, women could do a job equal to men in the factory. Such remunerative labor, which required little or no training, could thus provide the opportunity for masses of women to break out of their prison in the home and take the first step toward abolishing their "moral parasitism." Nor surprisingly then, Kuliscioff deemed "woman worker—redeeming words."[19]

Despite the presence of both feminist and Marxist elements

in *The Monopoly of the Male,* a dramatic clash between the principles in latent conflict—sex and class—is sidestepped; first because the discursive style of the essay permits contradictory elements to coexist in isolation, and second, and most important, because Kuliscioff did not yet attempt to frame a coherent program of action aimed at breaking the male monopoly, concluding as she did, on the vapid note, "I wish for the triumph of the cause of my sex only a little less intolerance from men and a little more solidarity among women."[20]

But Kuliscioff soon had to move from the realm of thought to the arena of action, since she was an active leader in the Marxist-oriented Italian Socialist party, formed two years later, and nothing if not a political being. Then she could no longer postpone the moment of decision. She had to resolve the conflict by choosing to act either in the name of all women or in the name of all the proletariat; by concentrating either upon the problem of the exploited sex or upon that of the exploited class. And in the 1890s, her priorities were clearly manifested. Kuliscioff the socialist triumphed decisively over Kuliscioff the feminist. The blatant antagonism between socialism and women outside the party was thereby resolved. But the more subtle ambivalence between socialism and the working women inside the party was only beginning.

An example of this subtle ambivalence appears as early as the inaugural congress of the Italian Socialist party at Genoa in 1892. Kuliscioff was a member of the small group that determined the course of the new party. Had she desired that special attention be paid to the female proletariat, which she had only two years earlier designated as doubly enslaved in contrast to their singly enslaved male cohorts, the matter would have been at least discussed. However, no special treatment was even suggested for women. Proletarian women were simply united with the men of their class in a single and undifferentiated struggle against capitalism, as can be seen in the only cursory allusion to women in the party's Program, which read:

Considering
  that in the present order of human society men are forced to live

in two classes: on the one hand exploited workers, on the other capitalists, receivers and monopolizers of the riches of society;

that the wage-earners of both sexes, of every trade and rank, form by virtue of their economic dependence, the proletariat, compelled to a state of misery, inferiority, and oppression; . . .

recognizing . . .

that the workers can only become free through the socialization of the means of production and industrial management;

holding

that this final goal can only be reached through the action of the proletariat, organized into a *Class Party* independent of all other parties[21]

In 1893, at the Zurich Congress of the Second International, women did receive some special attention. A multinational group presented a motion calling for agitation in each nation for factory legislation and stipulating that "woman, considered as a worker, be the first to enjoy this protection."[22] In this favorable environment, Kuliscioff's old loyalties to her sex could emerge, and she moved an amendment to that motion to include the "principle: for equal labor equal salary between the two sexes."[23] When one month later at the Reggio Emilia Congress of her own party the delegation from Mantua proposed that an amendment on women, in keeping with the Zurich proposal, be added to the party program, Kuliscioff voted with the majority for tabling in order to avoid any contentious discussion that might threaten party unity.[24] The Kuliscioff "equal pay for equal work" amendment was not even introduced into the discussion. Kuliscioff, who in Zurich in August had shone brightly as the champion of her sex, on home soil in September failed even to shed a faint glimmer of light upon the woman question.

The key to understanding Kuliscioff's silence on women in Italy was provided by an article she wrote in response to a request that the socialists introduce, and her *Critica Sociale* support, legislation calling for revision of the marriage contract.[25] In it she said:

The *Critica Sociale* could and should concern itself with all these questions [relating to women's liberation and changes in the family]. But, unfortunately, battles in their beginning can only be partial.

155

> Honest, educated and reasonable people are already alarmed at so
> many heresies of the *Critica* and believe, among other things, that
> the class struggle was invented by this periodical. Imagine, there-
> fore . . . if, to the provocation of hatred between the classes, the de-
> struction of the family were also added![26]

This statement is an accurate indication of the priorities of Kuliscioff—the class struggle of the Socialist party came first;
women would have to wait. During those years of silence on
the woman question, Kuliscioff was involved in the delicate operation of transforming the conservative, trade-unionist-
oriented Italian workers' movement into a Marxist party. Her
strategy in that, her major project, was to make the changeover
seem as nonradical as possible. Potentially dangerous or divisive issues, such as women's liberation, which might alarm the
leaders of the workers' movement, whom she was carefully
courting, had at least to be postponed.

In spite of the lower priority that she assigned to women, she
did not entirely overlook them. In fact, for the sake of the all-es-
sential proletarian unity, working women could not be ignored.
The three major forms that her propaganda and organizational
activities among women assumed all clearly demonstrated that
her intention was primarily to have women work for the good
of the party of the proletariat and only secondarily to have the
party of the proletariat work for women. Yet, Italian women
reaped much profit as a by-product of her work.

First, beginning in 1892, the very same year in which the
PSI was established, Kuliscioff went to the factories in and
around Milan and spoke to the workers of both sexes in order
to convince them of the necessity of having women enroll in
the resistance groups under the aegis of the Chamber of Labor,
groups that in turn formed the basic membership units of the
PSI. In painstakingly simple terms she pointed out to these
working women that joining a union benefited their own self-
interest, as this appeal to the "Seamstresses on Corso Magenta"
on the method of obtaining a ten-hour day illustrates:

> Suppose that your society in a year should amass 500 members who
> pay 20 centesimi a week. In a year you would have a capital of 4 to

5 thousand lire. Choose a season when there is a great deal of work, ... and at that moment when your employers earn thousands of lire with your hands, stop working. Having money in the treasury of your society, you can resist for weeks. And under these conditions, just see if your employers do not surrender.[27]

She introduced something of the feminist spirit into her speeches when she attacked the ingrained conservatism of the women and the chauvinism of the men, which together served to perpetuate the lower pay scales and the inferior working conditions of the female workers. In her *"Genio e Lavoro"* (Talent and Work) speech in 1892, she began by pointing out what she regarded as the erroneous conception of both sexes that since "woman is the appendage of man, the emancipation of the male worker will of necessity bring the improvement of the situation of the woman. But this is the reasoning of the men—that is the same reasoning as your employers."[28] And she demanded that the women get out and help themselves, warning that "the emancipation of the proletariat will not occur except through the efforts of the workers of both sexes. But the emancipation of the woman will not come about except through the efforts of woman herself."[29]

Nevertheless, the ringing climax in all of her speeches was decidedly more socialist than feminist, stressing the benefits that would accrue to the proletariat as a whole. For example, to the men in the audience, she asserted

the class struggle will never take effect if those thousands and millions of women who compete with the men in a backwards race, lowering even the male salaries, do not join in. All you working men must convince yourselves that as long as the women remain alone and isolated from the general movement, all your hopes to improve your position will fail.[30]

And to the women she implored, "We must organize, make common cause with our male comrades and form one single party, the Italian Socialist party."[31]

For her second major activity that involved women, Kuliscioff worked tirelessly throughout the 1890s to have a law passed regulating the work of woman and children in factories. This

157

was the purpose of her keynote address at the 1894 International Congress on Injuries on the Job, her speeches at the 1897 regional congress of the PSI at Lodi, the 1897 national party congress at Bologna, and the one at Rome three years later, her organization of women to work in the election campaign of 1897, and her organization finally of three hundred meetings throughout Italy in 1902 for the purpose of discussing the question directly with the proletariat.

Why all of this energy for a piece of factory legislation for women and children? As with unionization, Kuliscioff again pointed out that such a law would benefit the individual woman concerned, this time in terms of improved health. But once more she emphasized that the entire proletariat stood to benefit from legislation that set limits upon the exploitation of women and children, since men would no longer have to submit to the worse conditions that the women endured in order to compete for and hold onto a job.[32] Again, looking beyond the mere benefit to her sex, Kuliscioff, the doctor, continually cited the biological danger to the entire human species if the seeds of future generations, mothers and children, were chronically weakened by overwork.[33]

Perhaps the most telling words in Kuliscioff's campaign for a law to guarantee better working conditions for women are found in the "Call" which she, together with the Female Socialist Group of Milan, prepared for the *Lotta di classe* (Class Struggle). In this paragraph, which bears the unmistakable stamp of Kuliscioff, she explained to the proletariat:

> We are presenting a draft bill to you in order that you, workingmen and workingwomen, may discuss it in your Associations and Sections, may amend it if necessary, and in the end make it your own. Armed with the vote of all the Chambers of Labor and all the principal Workers' Associations in Italy, it will be transmitted to the deputies who represent the interests of the proletariat and by them presented in the Chamber [parliament]. Supported by harmonious agitation by the laboring class, it will become the basis of a law which will signal a notable step on the road to your emancipation.[34]

For Kuliscioff this law served as the paradigm for all socialist legislation, since through these articles and the three hundred

discussion meetings the proletariat had been taught to understand, desire, and defend it. This was to develop into the main
argument of Kuliscioff in the succeeding years of the Giolittian
period (1903–1914) when she repeatedly chided Turati and the
other socialists in the Italian Chamber of Deputies for working
too much in isolation from the proletariat whom they represented.[35] Thus, even in her moment of triumph, when in 1902
parliament finally did pass a woman and child labor law, she
was more interested in the lesson it taught her party than in
what it had gained for women.

And third, in the early twentieth century, when in open conflict with her partner of forty years, Filippo Turati, Kuliscioff
championed the cause of women's suffrage, her socialist sympa-
thies once more overshadowed her feminist. In her polemic
with Turati, which blazed across three consecutive issues of the
Critica Sociale in 1910,[36] Kuliscioff defended her position, not
shared by Turati, that the ideal of truly universal suffrage could
serve as a means "to breathe new youth" into their party, which
she feared "suffers from premature old age."[37] Unable to convince her partner Turati of the value to their party of women's
suffrage, Kuliscioff had to abandon her usual method of working in the party through him. Instead, she prepared her own report on universal suffrage for both sexes, which she presented
at the October 1910 Milan Congress of the PSI. Her lengthy report, backed by statistics pertaining to the large numbers of
women in Italian industry and the extent to which they were
being exploited, warmly exhorted the delegates to consider
"agitation for the vote for women, not as a luxury nor a waste
of time, but as an altogether indispensable, utilitarian and idealistic necessity *to the life and development of the party.*"[38]

Kuliscioff's attitude toward the suffrage question always remained intimately tied to the fortunes of the PSI. After the 1910
party congress, she grew increasingly dubious that her "great
reform" program, which included the suffrage, was adequate
any longer to prevent the leadership of her party from falling
into the clutches of the rival revolutionary faction, captained by
the young firebrand Benito Mussolini. Indeed, her fears mate-
rialized in 1912 at the Reggio Emilia Congress, when her reformist faction did lose control of the PSI. Throughout the pe-

159

riod 1910 to 1912, Kuliscioff continued to press relentlessly for female suffrage, accepting in 1911 the position of editor of the *Difesa delle lavoratrici* (Defense of the Woman Workers), the bimonthly supplement to the party newspaper *Avanti!* (Forward), aimed at the female socialist reader. During her brief term as editor from January to November 1912,[39] she used the *Difesa* chiefly as a vehicle to propagandize in favor of women's suffrage. However, as she discerned effective control of her party slowly slipping from her grasp, she adopted a subtle but significant change in tone that is clearly visible from the very first of her *Difesa* editorials in January 1912. No longer was she defending the vote for women as the idealistic means toward a renascence of the PSI. Instead, she began to demand the vote simply as an essential tool for the women themselves, arguing that

> no economic conquest is strong if it is not strengthened by political rights. The value of labor and the material conditions of the worker are strictly dependent upon his capacity as a citizen. Therefore, even proletarian women, who work on a par with and often harder than men, must share with them the honors and the duties [of a citizen] and need to have their vital interests protected by laws. Even for them, the possession of the ballot is today absolutely necessary.[40]

This new marked attention toward women in and for themselves should perhaps be viewed in the light of the philosophy which Kuliscioff expressed to Turati to console him on their forced semiretirement from politics following the Reggio Emilia Congress. On November 30, 1912, she advised her partner to keep on working, even if on small unimportant concerns, in order to maintain at least "the illusion of doing something in this world."[41] In short, it appears that if she could no longer direct the campaign she considered of the most vital importance —the class struggle in Italy—this woman, who craved involvement in the political world, could at least place her mind and energies at the disposal of a lesser, though still not unworthy movement—the female cause. Accordingly, only in 1912 did Kuliscioff agree to become, albeit briefly, the Clara Zetkin of Italian socialism and lead the women's auxiliary of the PSI.

During the recess between the sessions of the Reggio Emilia Congress, the Unione Nazionale Socialista Femminile (National Union of Female Socialists) was organized with Kuliscioff as the guiding light of the three-woman executive committee.[42]

Clearly there can be little doubt that in her deeds—working for unionization, factory legislation, the suffrage—as well as in her words, Kuliscioff was a socialist first and a feminist only secondarily. What led her to choose socialism over feminism must be more a matter of conjecture, although sufficient evidence is available to permit some solid inferences to be drawn regarding her motives.

Although Kuliscioff's personal predilections influenced her choice, they probably acted more as reinforcement for a decision arrived at on other grounds than as the real determinant. Italian socialists, including Kuliscioff herself, worked more closely with other bourgeois leaders in parliament, in editorial offices, or in party congresses than with the working class they represented. Being insulated from the flesh-and-blood masses and merely seeing them from across the podium during an occasional speech, it was not difficult to maintain belief in the abstraction *proletariat* as a lovely ideal. On the other hand, Kuliscioff was in almost daily working contact with other middle-class women who belonged to the socialist movement. Her frustration in working with these women almost invariably led Kuliscioff to paroxysms of anger, which found their way into her daily letters to Turàti. Women clearly were not an abstraction or an unsullied ideal for Kuliscioff. Devotion to the cause of the pure ideal, the proletariat, was doubtless easier than devotion to the women with whom she worked and whom she deemed chatty, unreliable, and empty-headed.[43]

The real determinant of Kuliscioff's priorities, however, was most likely more intellectual than emotional. In fact, she found a ready-made rationalization for her choice in the introduction to August Bebel's *Woman under Socialism,* in which he set forth the premises that

the mass of the female sex suffers in two respects: On the one side woman suffers from economic and social dependence upon man....

161

On the other side, woman suffers from the economic dependence that woman in general, the workingwoman in particular, finds herself in, along with the workingman.... Furthermore ... it is the part of the workingwoman to make common cause with the male members of her class and of her lot in the struggle for a radical transformation of society.... The goal, accordingly, is not merely the realization of the equal rights of woman with man within present society, as is aimed at by the bourgeois woman emancipationists. It lies beyond—the removal of all impediments that make man dependent upon man; and, consequently, one sex upon the other. Accordingly, this solution of the Woman Question coincides completely with the solution of the Social Question.[44]

In a 1910 article, commemorating Bebel's contribution to socialism, Kuliscioff acknowledged him as her mentor in the matter of socialist policy toward women, writing:

He promoted an absolutely new phenomenon in history. For the first time, a new and perhaps decisive social force was called up and developed around an organizer—the solidarity within the redemptive proletarian movement of that half of the proletariat at first absent, the solidarity of the working women. If Marx is the ideologist who offers to socialism the scientific basis for disclosure of the avenues and outlets for revolutionary energy which capitalism itself has created, the Marxist ideology is completed by the profound intuition and ardent sentiment of justice with which Bebel, first and perhaps alone among the socialists of Europe, shook the headstrong traditions and lashed out at and defied the Philistinism of the socialists of the stronger sex. He called into battle and threw into the struggle the proletarian woman, three times the slave—in the workshop, in the family, and in society.[45]

And the arguments that run through all of Kuliscioff's speeches and articles on women do closely parallel those of Bebel. Nevertheless, even independently of Bebel, Kuliscioff, who had of course read the works of Marx and Engels, might easily have arrived at the same conclusions. The two key notions found in *Woman under Socialism*—the first that the total emancipation of women could only come about through the proletarian revolution when all of society would be transformed, and the second that that revolution would only occur through the unity of both sexes of the working class—are quite simply the logical

162

consequence of the rationale behind the most basic of Marxist dictums—"Proletariat of the world unite!"

Kuliscioff's decision to resolve the conflict of interest between feminism and socialism in favor of socialism appears then to have been basically guided by ideology. And in the nineteenth century, the socialist found in Marxist philosophy a fairly coherent ideology that purported to be a scientifically valid explanation of the past, a key to mankind's future progress, and the justification for a program of action in the present. Unlike many European socialists at the turn of the century, Kuliscioff remained a steadfastly orthodox Marxist, rejecting alike both the Bernsteinian revisionism of the right and the Leninism of the left. Even when in 1911 after leading the Marxist PSI for twenty years, Turati's faith in that doctrine began to weaken, Kuliscioff's Marxist loyalties did not waver. In response to her partner's doubts, expressed to her in a private letter, she angrily shot back the confident reply that

> your great error, and the error of everyone who does not believe any longer in socialism and is no longer convinced of it, is in thinking that Marxism is done for and lacks the basis for reconstructing a socialist party with the criteria and the ideals on which the socialist parties of all Europe are based.[46]

In contrast, when Kuliscioff, convinced by the writings of Marx that the revolution of the proletariat was the route to the emancipation of *all*, turned to the existing feminist literature, no such grandiose world historical ideology confronted her that was capable of competing with the theoretical totality of Marx's revolution of the proletariat. While defenses of women, which claimed a scientific basis, did exist, none of these presented a convincing argument for women as *the* revolutionary vanguard, and none of the feminist ideologies gained such a wide European following as did that of Marx.[47] John Stuart Mill's *The Subjection of Women*, published in English in 1869, translated into Italian one year later, and perhaps the most authoritative volume on women to appear in Europe in the nineteenth century, presented a strong case for the unjustly inferior legal position of women in the family and in society as an anomaly amid an otherwise liberal trend. He demanded redress for the sake of the moral and material benefits that would accrue to both men and women if women were granted liberty commensurate with men.[48] Nevertheless, unlike the proletariat in Marx's socialist movement, women for Mill were certainly not the essential motive force for all liberal progress.[49]

In the Italy of Kuliscioff's era, feminist ideology was particularly retrograde. The leading theorists of the great Italian movement for national revitalization, the Risorgimento, showed little or no inclination to revive in the nineteenth century the active role Italian women had played in the Renaissance. As Eugenio Garin has noted, even those who during and immediately after Unification looked favorably upon women's liberation—Melchiorre Gioia, Giuseppe Mazzini, Salvatore Morelli—leaned more toward "empty rhetoric" than toward a profound discussion of the woman question.[50] Others, especially those of a neo-Guelph (Papal) persuasion—Antonio Rosmini, Caterina Franceschi-Ferrucci, Vincenzo Gioberti—were decidedly opposed to equality between the sexes.[51] Gioberti even concluded, "In short, in a sense, a woman in relation to a man is like a vegetable in relation to an animal or like a parasitic plant in relation to one which is self-sustaining."[52] Likewise, the feminist movement in post-Risorgimento Italy could expect little intellectual guidance from its two dominant philosophical schools—the positivists and the Crocean idealists. The positivist criminologist Cesare Lombrose cited women's small head and lack of beard as positive indicators that the female was merely an underdeveloped male; *ergo* inferior to him in body and mind. Women's limited mental capacity, though precluding genius in every field, had, however, one positive aspect for him; women lacked the necessary intellect to be as criminal as men.[53] Benedetto Croce, unlike Lombroso, recognized the significant contribution that women had made to Italian culture.[54] Notwithstanding this sympathy, Croce was hardly a candidate for the position of Italian philosopher of feminism. Early in his distinguished career, Croce denied the very validity of the woman question, asserting in response to a survey on feminism that "feminism is a movement which to me seems to stand condemned by its very name. It is a feminine idea in the bad sense of the word. Even males have their particular problems, but they have not yet invented masculinism."[55] Not surprisingly therefore, when Kuliscioff, who was a political activist and not a philosopher, sought an ideological guide for her life's work,[56] the more developed Marxism held more attraction than the still embryonic feminism.

Kuliscioff's decision to "Marxianize" the woman question had far-reaching consequences, both beneficial and detrimental, for Italian women. It is certainly not my intention to admonish Kuliscioff or any of her socialist contemporaries, now long dead, with what they should have done. It must be understood that to the extent that they, as Marxists, were rigorously following their creed, they could not have acted otherwise toward women.

Kuliscioff's determination to subordinate the woman question to the social question above all permitted her to act in the name of and with the backing of both the men and the women of the Italian Socialist party. As has been demonstrated, she used the party's national organization, its national newspaper, and its representatives in parliament to organize working women into unions and to secure for them higher wages and better working conditions through strikes and factory legislation. Then in 1897, when Italy was in the grip of a severe economic depression, Kuliscioff recognized that "It is here that the economic class struggle comes up against the necessity of using the political arm because the resistance groups alone are not enough to obtain the essential improvements for all women and in all industries."[57] "The political arm" did not allude to women's suffrage, which Kuliscioff regarded as yet premature,[58] but to female participation in the election campaigns of socialist candidates. She produced a pamphlet for the Gruppo delle donne socialiste milanese (Group of Milanese Socialist Women), that was distributed prior to the national election of March 1897, calling upon women to

become involved in this task. Let us lend ourselves, if necessary, to the humblest of tasks. Let us distribute the ballots, push our men to the voting urns, propagandize in the factories and among our neighbors at home. Let us persuade the most reluctant that it is in their best interests to make the candidates of the proletariat triumph.[59]

The "candidates of the proletariat" she made clear were those from the Socialist party, "the only one on whose banner is written *economic, political, and juridical equality for women and for men.*"[60] These words implied the Socialist party's commitment to the eventual total emancipation of women, and Kuliscioff was quick to remind her party of its obligation to honor these electoral promises.[61] Of even greater immediate consequence, these activities for and especially by women, which Kuliscioff stimulated, served not only to increase the economic independence of Italian working women from husband and father but also provided the opportunity for women to become less dependent upon home and husband for their sole source of identity.[62] In brief, Kuliscioff shared in the greatest asset of Marxism, its possession of a ready-made program of action and the strong call to united action to change the world, so well expressed by the young Marx in the ringing conclusions of the *Communist Manifesto* and in his *Theses on Feuerbach.*[63]

Not only in the ideological realm but in that of concrete accomplishments as well, "the feminists of the middle class" from whom Kuliscioff had chosen to separate herself in 1897 were several steps behind. The career of Anna Maria Mozzoni (1837–1920),[64] Italy's foremost feminist in the nineteenth century provides an excellent study in contrast to that of Anna Kuliscioff. Mozzoni appreciated the importance of the social question, but unlike Kuliscioff, her primary allegiance was to feminism rather than to any other political party or social movement. Mozzoni entered the feminist movement in 1864 with her book, *La donna e i suoi rapporti sociali* (Woman and her Social Relationships). It was she who translated Mill's *Subjection of Women* into Italian. For more than forty years she never ceased her steady production of feminist pamphlets and was a tireless contributor of articles to the feminist periodical press. Mozzoni might thus be credited with having performed that essential function that has been termed "consciousness raising." However, given the low literacy rate, especially among women, in the Italy of the last century,[65] there is some question of the extent to which her writings reached the masses of Italian women. Through the vast network of female leagues and resistance groups established by the socialists, the spoken word of Kuliscioff and other socialists concerned with working women could reach a much wider audience.

Furthermore, when it was time to translate awareness of the woman question into some concrete action to resolve it, Mozzoni was severely hampered by the weakness of feminist organization in Italy. A series of local leagues had been established in the 1890s in the major cities of Italy. But only loosely federated, these small groups were left largely to deal with local issues.[66] The first national congress of Italian feminists was held in Rome only in 1908. There, Kuliscioff's earlier evaluation that even when the feminists were sincere, they were weak and utopistic, lacking a concrete program and an effective organization,[67] seemed to be borne out. In the introduction to a summary of the Rome proceedings, the Catholic feminist journal, *Pensiero e azione* (Thought and Action), applauded the decision to omit discussion of principles in favor of dealing immediately with questions of practical action.[68] But as long as there was no agreement on a feminist creed to unite them, and rival Catholic, liberal, and socialist creeds existed among the delegates to divide them, those present were hampered even in coming to agreement on a practical program. The collision of principles was presaged in the opening remarks of the chairman, the Countess Spalletti, who addressed her audience, sprinkled with Marxists, calling "for union among the classes."[69] The most resounding clash of principles occurred over the education issue. The socialist schoolteacher Linda Malnati presented a motion calling for the laicization of the schools that received the approval of the majority.[70] Subsequently in *Pensiero e azione*, the editor insisted that that majority at the Rome congress did not really represent the majority of Italian women, and therefore she called upon her readers to write letters of protest in an effort to annul the Malnati motion.[71] Clearly as late as 1908, after Anna Maria Mozzoni had dedicated her tremendous energies and intelligence for forty-four years to a campaign to unite Italian women, there was as much competition as there was cooperation among the various feminist groups gathered at Rome.

Consequently, in an effort to compensate for the organizational weakness of feminism, Mozzoni allied herself in turn with a variety of political and social groups in Italy whose programs appeared to offer hope of redress to women—the Mazzinian Republicans, the Radicals, the worker's movement, and the Socialist party. Again, unlike Kuliscioff, who early committed herself to the socialist cause and used her talents to rise to a position of leadership in that movement, Mozzoni was never totally committed to any of these causes except feminism. Willy-nilly, her intransigent feminism led Mozzoni to remain on the outer fringes of each of these groups to which she temporarily adhered.[72] Due to her aloofness and dissension, Mozzoni was never able to harness their organizational resources to the service of women as Kuliscioff was able to do with those of socialism. One such case of Mozzoni's dissension in the name of feminism that is perhaps most relevant to this discussion pertains to Kuliscioff's woman and child labor law. While Kuliscioff desired true equality between the sexes, she recognized that under the prevailing conditions of the "male monopoly" some special protection for the female worker, exploited at home and in the factory, was expedient. For Mozzoni, such special protection betokened the acceptance and perpetuation of the very principle of the inequality of the sexes that she was combating. In defiance of almost all of the feminist groups in Italy and abroad who supported Kuliscioff's bill, Mozzoni opposed it.[73] Ironically, in the eyes of most women's groups, the socialist Kuliscioff was thereby doing more for women than the feminist Mozzoni.

This example of factory legislation can also serve to illustrate in a more general sense the difference between the level of development of the two movements—socialism and feminism. Seven of the nine issues of the Milanese feminist journal *Unione Femminile* (Female Union) for 1901, its first year of publication, devoted extensive space to evoking the maternal sentiment of its readers in support of some kind of protection for the poor working child. Yet when it was a question of converting sympathy into positive action, the *Unione Femminile*, being a small journalistic group of women with no voice of its own in parliament, was incapable of acting independently and could only urge its readers to support the socialist women and child labor law, Kuliscioff's project, already before the Chamber of Deputies.[74]

Such endorsement is truly not incongruous, since as Kuliscioff pointed out, feminism and socialism were "parallel" not opposing social movements, and the cross section of Italian feminists did include socialists as well as women of other political persuasions. What is startling, however, is the Catholic feminist support for the Kuliscioff bill. The Christian Democratic feminist movement had sprung up as an indirect response to the sanction given by Pope Leo XIII in his 1891 encyclical *Rerum Novarum* for the establishment of Catholic social organizations. The expressed purpose of these Catholic unions was to oppose those of the socialists, which were out to destroy the family and religion, and thereby to wean workers away from Marxism back to Christianity.[75] In order to rationalize its support of the "Kuliciof-Turati [*sic*] project," the Catholic feminist journal *La Donna del Popolo* argued that the bill was "Socialist . . . only in its label but Christian, profoundly Christian, in its substance" since it reflected more the sentiments expressed in *Rerum Novarum* than those found in Marx's *Capital*.[76] Leaving aside any discussion of the semimystical thesis implied here of Kuliscioff as the unwitting instrument of the Pope, one is still left with the conclusion that the Catholic feminist organizations were not strong enough to carry out the program of *Rerum Novarum* alone; they had to have recourse to the aid of their archenemy. In short, the superior organization of the socialists in relation to the feminists in Italy permitted the socialists to attempt more on behalf of women.

Another positive aspect of Kuliscioff's Marxist orientation on the woman question related directly to the point of view of the reformists, that faction of the Italian Socialist party to which she adhered. Kuliscioff concentrated on a minimum program of reforms, aimed at preparing the conditions that would permit the proletarian revolution in the future. Unlike the Bernsteinian revisionists, she never abandoned the ideal of revolution to work for reforms *per se*. As concerns women, this policy meant that although her chief work was in the area of gradual reforms —unionization, voting rights, factory legislation, concrete gains in the present—she kept alive the idea, an inspiration for future generations, that the final goal for women must be the radical transformation of society in which even the present family structure would disappear. True to her master Karl Marx, Kuliscioff avoided drawing up a utopian blueprint for the family after the revolution, but she did make clear in *The Monopoly* that

> certainly all this [the family structure] will undergo profound modifications which are *not yet able to be defined precisely*.... During the evolution of the family, the former domestic relationships based on male domination and on the nuclear family home will be dissolved and a more elevated form of the family, founded upon spontaneity and equality will be prepared.[77]

Near the close of 1890, Celestina Bertolini wrote to Kuliscioff, taking issue with the above prognostication, since it would destroy the "sanctity of the family." In a reply shrouded in moderation, Kuliscioff stressed that such a collective society would occur as the result of a slow outgrowth, analogous to and as acceptable as the change by which woman, once identified with the tasks of knitting and spinning the family garments, began to purchase machine-made wearing apparel for her family. She went on to defend honest, free, dissolvable marriages of the future over the present hypocrisy of extramarital relationships, prostitution, and commercial marriages. Lastly, she pointed out that even the practice of having children brought up by the community would be only the slow and natural evolutionary outgrowth of the already existing schools and day-care centers that aided in the education of the young. The shrewd Kuliscioff did not judge it politic to arouse fears of the immediate destruction of the existing family structure, especially as she realized all too well that such profound changes could not be accomplished overnight.[78] But, for all the soothing words she lavished upon the scandalized Turinese schoolteacher, Kuliscioff never repudiated the substance of her *Monopoly* statement.

Kuliscioff's radical outlook in favor of the dissolution of the family contrasted sharply not only with the view of the Catholic feminists but also with that of those middle-class feminists in Italy whose voice was the journal *Unione Femminile*. Apparently Turati, a devoted son throughout his mother's long lifetime, had committed the error of waxing enthusiastic over a poem of Ada Negri entitled *"La Maternità"* (Motherhood), for Kuliscioff was most emphatic when informing him that she was "not moved" by it.[79] Instead, she saw in Negri's work merely the poetic reflection of *Unione Femminile's* main theme that "the happy mother, the pitiful mother, the martyred mother, the mother of Mariuccia, etc., etc., is the basis, the *leit motiv*, of a new social order,"[80] and Kuliscioff had only a smile of derision for that refrain.

If the Italian middle-class feminists were thus involved in a semiconservative attempt to effect a harmonious compromise between the two permanent roles of women—as mother within the home and as worker or career woman outside the home— the Catholic feminists were unwilling even to accept this dualism. For them, the only permanent role for women was motherhood. As long as present economic conditions forced working-class women to work outside the home to help support their families, the Christian Democratic feminists were prepared temporarily to recognize that present necessity and frame a social program for the amelioration of the working conditions of those women. But unlike Kuliscioff, who saw work outside the home as having forever "emancipated women from the pots and pans,"[81] the Catholics looked forward to the day when male salaries would be sufficient to permit women to return to the domestic hearth.[82]

In the realm of practical accomplishments and ideals of equality there were definite advantages to the Marxist position on women. On the other hand, Kuliscioff's Marxist leanings had some detrimental or conservative effects on the women's movement in Italy. A survey of women employed in industry in the Common Market countries in the 1960s, conducted by the French sociologist Evelyne Sullerot, has related the level of female salaries to the degree to which women, rather than holding "feminized" jobs, have entered into jobs traditionally held by men. The same study also found Italy to have "the worst record in dealing with the whole question of women at work."[83] Looking back upon the work of Anna Kuliscioff in this light, we note that the Italian socialists were so concerned with proletarian unity in the major fight against capitalism that they dared not divide their force and dissipate their strength by encouraging the working women to conduct a minor war against their male counterparts through competing for the better-paying jobs monopolized by the men. In fact, Kuliscioff denied the very existence of the problem of inequality of jobs between the sexes of the proletariat, insisting rather that while the middle-class women "are forced into vital competition to conquer the professions monopolized by the masculine sex, the woman worker had already conquered, or rather for a long time had endured the right to be exploited on a par with the male worker."[84] On this point at least one is led almost to doubt the sincerity of Kuliscioff, who never revised this view even though Giovanni Montemartini presented evidence to the contrary. Montemartini, in an article in the *Unione Femminile*, a journal Kuliscioff did read, cited a number of British investigations and one Italian study of the salary differential between the sexes, and he underscored the primary conclusion of the 1897 Report of the Commissioner of Labour in Britain that rarely indeed were women in manual labor performing the same jobs as men.[85] Certainly then, if women did not hold the same jobs as men and were not encouraged to compete with men for the better-paying jobs, Kuliscioff's "equal pay for equal work" resolution was reduced to an empty phrase. Of course, there is always the rationalization of an orthodox Marxist, which Kuliscioff was, that the aim of the future proletarian revolution was to abolish the wage system altogether; thus the male-female salary disparity was only a transitory problem. But as long as the date of the proletarian revolution was at best uncertain, and as long as she was working to ameliorate female working conditions in other less delicate areas, this rationale would seem virtually indistinguishable from the "Philistinism of the ... socialists of the stronger sex,"[86] which she condemned.

A further limitation of Kuliscioff's Marxist bias relates to the almost exclusively economic orientation it often assumed. Although in her *Monopoly of the Male* address, Kuliscioff was concerned for the ethical aspect of the woman question, two years later she seemed to be reducing it to "purely an economic question."[87] Anna Maria Mozzoni in a speech before a group of working women in Alessandria condemned what she interpreted as too narrow an orientation, saying:

> the *Critica Sociale* believes that the woman question basically is an exclusively economic question and that it [the woman question] will just resolve itself along with its [the economic question's] resolution. I do not merely doubt this; I believe it to be absolutely erroneous.[88]

In fairness to Kuliscioff, her statement must be read within its proper context where it is somewhat more subtle than Mozzoni would have it appear. This whole question of the socialist orientation arose in May 1892 when Anna Kuliscioff replied in the *Critica* to a letter from Armando Angelucci. In his letter, Angelucci requested the editor's opinion of his panacea for the "feminine question," which he deemed "of the social problems the simplest to solve." Angelucci felt that free love was the ultimate solution, but to "win over the prejudices built up through centuries of servility and superstition" it was necessary to use "a prudent tactic." Therefore, he asked that the socialists introduce a marriage reform bill based upon the idea of marriage contracts of limited duration, renewable every five years.[89] Anna Kuliscioff brusquely dismissed Angelucci's most simple of solutions to the woman question, which she described as a "question so complex that it is even more intricate than the very question of the proletariat," and she went on to write that

> while woman remained closed within her domestic walls ... how could the consciousness have arisen in her that she possessed social value, that she, too, was a creator of social wealth?
> The machine, the great revolutionary force of industry, has revolutionized even woman. First of all it has emancipated her from the pots and pans and placed her in the condition of the struggle for existence on a par with man. It has made her equal to him in misery and in the aspiration to shake off the yoke of capitalism. ...
> The woman question is not therefore a question of ethics nor of this or that form of marriage, but it is purely an economic ques-

tion; . . . When woman will be able to be self-sufficient and will not need to be maintained in a legitimate or an illegitimate manner, then the form of the relationships between man and woman will become a simple accessory. They will cohabit without marriage, . . .

To sustain and encourage free union between the two sexes now would be a sterile or a dangerous action because the legal contract of marriage is for now a guarantee for the weak, that is for the woman and children, . . . Given the low standard of the female's salaries and stipends and the lack of professional training among the women of the middle class, it [free union] would only increase prostitution and institutions for wayward youth.[90]

In effect, Kuliscioff here was not so much repudiating the ethical side of the woman question as much as she was postponing dealing with it until the economic side had been settled satisfactorily, or in Marxist terms dealing first with the structure and then with the superstructure of society. Anxious, perhaps overanxious, to stress what she believed to be the "scientific" Marxist materialist approach to history against such "sentimental" solutions as Angelucci's, Kuliscioff, not unlike Marx and Engels themselves,[91] was guilty here of overstressing the economic elements for didactic purposes.

As a believer in Marxism, Kuliscioff's attention to economics first is understandable; to the non-Marxist it may appear nonetheless an erroneous ordering of priorities. Kuliscioff insisted upon equalizing salaries first, then attacking customs. It might be argued instead that salaries can never be equalized between the sexes until basic attitudes are changed so that woman is regarded as the equal of man. Otherwise, men, believing their sex to be superior, will find loopholes in any "equal pay for equal work" law that would allow them to receive the higher salaries commensurate with their greater value.[92] However, any attempt to draw an overriding conclusion concerning the relative merits of Marxist versus non-Marxist approaches to the woman question would be beyond the scope of this paper.

On the basis of the evidence we can conclude, in short, that Kuliscioff's break with feminism in favor of Marxism did indeed set definite limits upon her achievements on behalf of her sex. As we have seen, these limitations were the direct result of her commitment to the Marxist ideology, which, in turn induced her to place the needs of the Socialist party above the needs of women. At the same time, however, her campaign for women in the context of socialism enabled her to achieve more, secondarily but no less concretely for all that, than did the weaker groups in Italy that acknowledged feminism as their primary allegiance.

N O T E S

1. Anna Kuliscioff, "Il Feminismo," *Critica Sociale* VII (June 16, 1897): 187.
2. See *Critica Sociale* XXXVI (1–31 January 1926): 1–28; the entire issue dedicated "In Memory of Anna Kuliscioff" includes impressions of her contemporaries. These were reprinted in *Anna Kuliscioff: In Memoria* (Milan, 1926).
3. Andrea Costa, "Le Donne dinnanzi ai giurati," *La Plebe,* December 7, 1879, pp. 1–2. In 1878, Kuliscioff was arrested along with fifteen others and later charged with conspiracy against the state. These arrests were part of the government's crackdown on the Anarchist International in Italy. After suffering fourteen months of preventive imprisonment, Kuliscioff and her codefendants were tried and acquitted.
4. Women were barred from membership in the Philological Society. However a few exceptional women were invited to speak. See Franca Pieroni Bortolotti, *Alle origini del movimento femminile in Italia, 1848–1892* (Turin, 1963), p. 232.
5. *Archives de la Préfecture de Police.* Paris. Carton: B A/43y. Document n. 424, as reprinted in Gianni Bosio and Franco Della Peruta, "La 'Svolta' di A. Costa con documenti sul soggiorno in Francia," *Movimento operaio* IV (March–April 1952): 297.
6. Angiolo Cabrini, "Ricordando," *Critica Sociale* XXXVI (January 1–31, 1926): 15.
7. See Turati to Kuliscioff, February 20, 1908, Carteggio Turati-Kuliscioff, Einaudi Ms., Turin, where Turati attributes the original remark that Kuliscioff was "il solo *uomo* politico del partito socialsta italiano" (the only states*man* in the PSI) to Carlo Tanzi, Milanese socialist.
8. See La Redazione, "Programma," *Rivista internazionale del socialismo* (May 15, 1880), p. 3. Although the program bears the by-line, "Editorial Staff," it is safe to assume that the concern for women in the published program of the *Rivista* is the work of Kuliscioff, who at that time was in close collaboration with the editor Andrea Costa on the journal. The assumption of her authorship or instigation is reinforced by the fact that later in her life, Kuliscioff restated this concern for women in these very same terms, whereas the argument was not taken up again by Costa.
9. A clear statement of this conflict of interest is found in Anna Kuliscioff, "Il Feminismo," p. 186.
10. Anna Kuliscioff, *Il Monopolio dell'uomo* (Milan, 1894).

11. See F. Engels, *The Origin of the Family, Private Property and the State* in Karl Marx and Frederick Engels, *Selected Works,* vol. III (Moscow, 1970), pp. 204–334.
12. See "Engels to J. Bloch in Königsberg, September 21[-22], 1890," as quoted in Marx and Engels, *Selected Works,* vol. III, p. 488.
13. Ibid., p. 487.
14. Kuliscioff, *Monopolio,* 18–19.
15. Ibid., 10, 19–22, 31–32, 44–49.
16. Ibid., 38–41.
17. See "Il Monopolio dell'uomo," *Cuore e critica* IV (April 30, 1890): 103, for evidence of the appreciation of her contemporaries for the breadth of her approach. That review in *Cuore e critica,* written by democratic friends of Kuliscioff and Turati, lauded her ability in *The Monopoly of the Male,* "to demonstrate with data and positive observations and not with metaphysical assumptions how the *present* woman question, the product of economic, physiological and moral necessity, is one social question equal to and joined to others. It [the woman question] is on a par with political questions and the labor question."
18. Kuliscioff, *Monopolio,* p. 25. She here avoids the thorny issue that she faced later that the capitalist can be a woman.
19. Ibid., p. 25; she is here consciously contradicting Michelet's phrase "woman worker—wicked words."
20. Ibid., p. 49.
21. See "Ill Programma e lo Statuto del Partito dei Lavoratori Italiani," *Lotta di Classe,* August 20–21, 1892, p. 3.
22. "Il Congresso Internazionale Operaio Socialista di Zurigo," *Lotta di Classe* (July 29–30, 1893): 2.; and F. Turati, "Il Congresso di Zurigo: le ultime giornate; la chiusura," *Lotta di Classe,* August 19–20, 1893, p. 1.
23. Turati, "Il Congresso di Zurigo," p. 1.
24. "Il Congresso di Reggio Emilia," *Lotta di Classe,* September 16–17, 1893, p. 2.
25. Armando Angelucci, "Questioni femminile, Il matrimonio a termine," *Critica Sociale* II (May 1, 1892): 140–41.
26. Anna Kuliscioff, "Il Sentimentalismo nella questione femminile", *Critica Sociale* II (May 1, 1892): 143.
27. Anna Kuliscioff, "Alle Sarte in Corso Magenta" (n.d.), MS in Internationaal Instituut voor Sociale Geschiedenis, Amsterdam, French-Italian Section, Busta n. 63, Mss. di A. Kuliscioff, 5.
28. Anna Kuliscioff, "Proletariato femminile," *Genio e Lavoro* (1892), MS in Internationaal Instituut voor Sociale Geschiedenis, Amsterdam, French-Italian Section, Busta n. 63, Mss. di A. Kuliscioff, p. 3.
29. Ibid., p. 10.
30. Anna Kuliscioff, "Inaugurazione Bandiera," S. Benedetto Po (1893), MS in International Instituut voor Sociale Geschiedenis, Amsterdam, French-Italian Section, Busta n. 63, Mss. di A. Kuliscioff, p. 6.
31. Ibid., p. 7.
32. See "Congresso Regionale Lombardo: Lodi, 27 giugno 1897," *Lotta di Classe,* July 3–4, 1897, p. 2.
33. See "Discours de Mme. Kuliscioff, Martedì, 2 ottobre 1893," Congresso de-

gli Infortuni del Lavoro, Milan, MS in Biblioteca dell'Umanitaria, Turati Library, Milan.

34. Il Comitato del Gruppo Femminile Socialista, "L'Appello, Lavoratori e Lavoratrici," *Lotta di Classe*, November 20–21, 1897, p. 2.

35. See Kulisciof to Turati, February 27, 1904; Kulisciof to Turati, April 7, 1907; Kulisciof to Turati, May 4, 1907; Kulisciof to Turati, May 25, 1907; Kulisciof to Turati, March 18, 1908; Kulisciof to Turati, December 14, 1908; all letters in Carteggio Turati-Kulisciof, Einaudi MS Turin.

36. See Dott. Anna Kulisciof e Filippo Turati, "Suffragio universale," *Critica Sociale* XX (March 16–April 1, 1910): 83–85; Dott. Anna Kulisciof, Filippo Turati (Postilla), "Ancora del voto alle donne; suffragio universale a scartamento ridotto," *Critica Sociale* XX (April 16, 1910): 113–16; and Dott. Anna Kulisciof, "Per conchiudere sul voto alle donne," *Critica Sociale* XX (May 1, 1910): 130. The three articles were reprinted in pamphlet form later that year; see Filippo Turati, Anna Kulisciof, *Il Voto alle donne, polemica in famiglia per la propaganda del suffragio universale in Italia* (Milan, 1910).

37. Turati, Kulisciof, *Il voto alle donne*, p. 24.

38. Dott. Anna Kulisciof, "Proletariato femminile e Partito Socialista, Relazione al Congresso Socialista, 21–25 ottobre 1910," *Critica Sociale* XX (September 16–October 1, 1910): 277. The report was reprinted in pamphlet form that same year under the same title by the *Critica Sociale*. My italics.

39. The 1911 Congress of the Confederation of Labor had passed unanimously a motion for increased propaganda among proletarian women. Then at the 1911 Modena Congress of the PSI funds were voted for a bimonthly newspaper for women, and Kulisciof was chosen as editor. On August 18, 1912, following the victory of the revolutionary faction at the Reggio Emilia Congress, Kulisciof sent in her resignation. When asked by the party secretary to remain, she temporarily withdrew her resignation. See Il Comitato Esecutivo dell'UNSF, "La solidarietà della Direzione del Partito col movimento femminile socialista," *La Difesa delle lavoratrici*, August 18, 1912, p. 1. But on November 28, 1912, Kulisciof informed Turati that she was finally through with *La Difesa*.

40. La Difesa delle lavoratrici, "Una forza nuova," *La Difesa delle Lavoratrici*, January 7, 1912.

41. Kulisciof to Turati, November 30, 1912, in Carteggio Turati-Kulisciof, Einaudi MS, Turin.

42. In June 1912, Kulisciof convoked the organizational meeting of Socialist women which was held between the sessions of the national congress. Kulisciof was selected to be a member of both the national committee and the executive commission of the National Union of Female Socialists. For the organization and activities of this union see: "Per una Unione Nazionale delle donne socialiste," *La Difesa*, July 7, 1912, p. 1; "Il primo convegno nazionale delle donne socialiste," *La Difesa*, July 21, 1912, p. 3; "Il convegno femminile socialista di Reggio Emilia," *La Difesa*, July 21, 1912, p. 2; "Norma pel funzionamento dell'Unione Nazionale Socialista Femminile," *La Difesa*, August 12, 1912, p. 2; Anna Kulisciof per il Comitato dell'UNFS, "Congresso socialista di Ancona: 2° Convegno Nazionale delle donne socialiste," *La Difesa*, April 5, 1914, p. 1; Per l'Unione Nazio-

nale delle Donne Socialiste: Maria Gioia, Anna Kuliscioff, Ancilla Vare, Carlotta Clerici, "Unione Nazionale delle donne socialiste," *La Difesa*, January 28, 1917, p. 1; and "Convegno Nazionale delle donne socialiste," *La Difesa*, October 4, 1917, p. 3.

43. See for example Kuliscioff's exasperated comments on women in Kuliscioff to Turati, February 27, 1912; Kuliscioff to Turati, November 28, 1912; and Kuliscioff to Turati, December 9, 1912; all letters in Carteggio Turati-Kuliscioff, Einaudi MS, Turin.

44. See August Bebel, *Woman under Socialism*, trans. by Daniel DeLeon (New York, 1904), pp. 4–5.

45. Anna Kuliscioff, "Per Augusto Bebel," *Critica Sociale* XX (February 16, 1910): 51.

46. Kuliscioff to Turati, February 27, 1911, Carteggio Turati-Kuliscioff, Einaudi MS. Turin.

47. Alice S. Rossi, in her introductory chapter, "Sentiment and Intellect: The Story of John Stuart Mill and Harriet Taylor Mill," in *Essays on Sex Equality*, which she edited, cited only one other nineteenth-century work on women of the scope of Mill's, i.e., Charlotte Perkins Gilman, *Woman and Economics*.

48. J.S. Mill, *On the Subjection of Women* (Greenwich, Connecticut, 1971).

49. See Rossi, *Essays on Sex Equality*, p. 5, where she notes that scholars who analyze Mill's works on liberalism either omit entirely the *Subjection of Women* or merely list it among his works.

50. Eugenio Garin, "La questione femminile," *Belfagor*, XVII (January 31, 1962): 19–20 and 26–28.

51. Ibid., pp. 22–24.

52. Vincenzo Gioberti, *Il Gesuita moderno*, vol. VI (Lausanne, 1847), pp. 129–30, as quoted in Garin, p. 23.

53. Garin, p. 29.

54. See Bortolotti, *Alle origini del movimento femminile in Italia*, 19, where she cites Croce's *Nuovo saggi sulla letteratura italiana del '600. Donne letterate nel '600* (Bari, 1931).

55. Risponsta di B. Croce alla *Inchiesta sul femminismo* in *La Nuova antologia*, 1911, p. 221, as quoted in Bortolotti, pp. 132–33n.

56. See La Critica Sociale, "Necessità di un programma practico," *Critica Sociale* XX (August 1, 1892): 228–30, wherein Turati and Kuliscioff wrote: "As for the theoretical foundation [Marxism], by now one can say the positive premises of socialism are scientific dogma. Neither any longer do they have serious adversaries. . . . We find them disseminated everywhere. . . . But the work which remains to be done . . . is the continuation of the theoretical-practical work in a concrete sense, the study of practical applications. . . ."

57. Anna Kuliscioff, "Lavoratrici, professioniste, madre di famiglia!" 1897, MS in Internationaal Instituut voor Sociale Geschiedenis, Amsterdam, French-Italian Section, Busta n. 63, pp. 6–7.

58. In 1892 Kuliscioff had rejected as premature the solution of the Fascio dei Lavoratori (Worker's Group) of Milan that a woman candidate be placed on the voting lists in the administrative elections. See Anna Kuliscioff, "Candidature femminile," *Critica Sociale* II (June 11, 1892): 168. A comment she made in a letter to Turati in 1905 reveals not only her position on the suf-

frage but also her negative opinion of the feminists. She wrote him: "Today I received a letter from Maria Cabrini asking my opinion of her and Malnati's intention to join the campaign for women's suffrage. I will write her that I am opposed to it. Who needs the feminists to create more obstacles in the way of a movement which must be marked by the stately seriousness of a great proletarian conquest?" See Kuliscioff to Turati, November 29 [30], 1905, Einaudi MS, Turin.

59. Anna Kuliscioff, "Alle Donne Italiane (Elezioni politiche 1897)," in *Anna Kuliscioff: In Memoria,* p. 276.

60. Ibid., p. 273.

61. Kuliscioff championed the cause of women in the PSI at both the regional congress of Lombardy at Lodi in June 1897 and the national congress of the PSI at Bologna in September 1897; see "Congresso Regionale Lombardo: 27 giugno 1897," *Lotta di Classe,* July 3–4, 1897, p. 2 and "Il Congresso Nazionale di Bologna: 18, 19 e 20 settembre 1897," *Lotta di Classe,* September 25–26, 1897, p. 2. Shortly thereafter, dissatisfied with the party's inactivity, Kuliscioff accelerated her own efforts on behalf of her sex, contributing as seen above to the campaign of the Committee of the Female Socialist Group in favor of factory legislation and going to the women at the Pirelli rubber plant at lunchtime to help organize them into unions. See "Tribunale di Guerra di Milano, Resoconto stenografico particolare. Il Processo dei giornalisti-L'atto d'accusa," *I Tribunali* (Bolletino Serale), June 16 –17, 1898, p. 4, for her statements during her trial in 1898 at which she was accused of instigating these women to riot a few months later (May 1898); and the police reports of her meetings: Agitazione degli operai addetti all'officina Pirelli e co., Milan, March 13, 1898, ASM. Cartella della Questura, no. 53—1898 (b. scioperi), (Carta no. 140—riservate); Ufficio Telegrafico di Telegramma, March 14, 1898, 11:00 A.M.; 2:00 P.M.; 4:00 P.M., Inspector Annovazzi. ASM. Cartella della Questura, no 53—1898 (b. scioperi); including copies of two invitations to hear her speak: Vittorio Strazze, Segretario della Camera del Lavoro to Operai ed operaie, March 11, 1898. ASM. Cartella della Questura, no. 55—1898 (b. scioperi); and Lega di Miglioramento fra Lavoranti in gomme della Ditta Pirelli, Milano, March 15, 1898. Biglietto personale d'invito alla conferenza che terra la signora Kuliscioff dott. Anna, giovedì, 17 corr., alle ore 12, nel salone del Circolo Cappellini, sul tema "Progetto di legge per la protezione del lavoro delle donne e dei fanciulli." ASM. Cartella della Questura, No. 53—1898 (b. scioperi).

62. It would, of course, be an error to assume that the socialist leagues and unions encompassed the entire 354,732 women in the Italian labor force in 1901. For statistics on working women in Italy see Linda Malnati, "La donna operaia," *Congresso di Attività Practica Femminile, Milano, 24–28, Maggio 1909, Relazioni* (Milan, 1909), p. 58. Indeed in Kuliscioff's report before the Milan Congress of the PSI, she cited statistics from Germany and Austria on the large numbers of women enrolled in the respective socialist parties, and although she did not cite any figures for Italy, she remarked that the proportion of women enrolled in the PSI as compared to the number of women employed in Italy was much lower. She blamed the PSI's flacidity and its growing estrangement from the working masses for the smaller numbers of organized female workers in Italy. See dott. A. Kuli-

scioff, *Proletariato femminile e Partito Socialista* (Milan, 1910), pp. 13–15. Nevertheless, the socialists at that time were speaking to and organizing more women than were the feminists in Italy. Qualitative evidence is even more difficult to obtain than quantitative data to support the inference that women enrolled in labor unions gained a sense of independence. Although it would be risky to generalize from this one example, it is interesting to note the influence Kuliscioff had on at least one working woman for whom some data is available. One of her maids, Signora Sabrina Camerini, reflected in her bearing and recalled in her words how Kuliscioff had imparted to her a sense of the dignity of women and the need to feel and to act always as the equals of men. From an interview with Signora Camerini at Castelnuovo di Farfa (Roma), June 1968.

63. See Karl Marx and Frederick Engels, "Manifesto of the Communist Party," in *Selected Works,* pp. 98–137, originally published in 1848, which concludes, "Let the ruling classes tremble at a Communist revolution. The proletarians have nothing to lose but their chains. They have a world to win. WORKING MEN OF ALL COUNTRIES, UNITE!"; and Karl Marx, "Theses on Feuerbach," in *Selected Works,* pp. 43–45, written in 1845 and first published in 1888, which concludes, "The philosophers have only *interpreted* the world, in various ways; the point, however, is to *change* it."

64. See Bartolotti, *Alle origini del movimento femminile,* which focuses on Mozzoni.

65. In Kuliscioff, *Monopolio dell'Uomo,* p. 32, she cites statistics on literacy from the 1881 census; in Italy 73.51% of the women were illiterate and 61.03% of the men were illiterate.

66. See Franca Pieroni Bortolotti, "Socialismo e Femminismo nell'ultimo ottocento, *Movimento Operaio e Socialista,* XII (April–June 1966): 114; and Bortolotti, *Alle origini del movimento femminile,* p. 191, where she points out that A.M. Mozzoni's League for the Promotion of Female Interests, founded in Milan in 1880 and later subsumed within the socialist party, was among the first of these.

67. See A. Kuliscioff, "Il Feminismo," p. 185.

68. "Il Congresso Femminile di Roma," *Pensiero e azione* IV (May 10-25, 1908): 2.

69. Ibid., p. 4.

70. Ibid., p. 6.

71. Ibid., pp. 3–4.

72. See Bortolotti, *Alle origini del movimento femminile,* especially pp. 16–17, 153 and 203–209.

73. See ibid., 202–203; and F.P. Bortolotti, "Socialismo e Femminismo nell'ultimo ottocento," *Movimento operaio e socialista* XII (July–December, 1966): 194–200.

74. See "Alla Camera," *Unione Femminile* I (June 7, 1901): 48; and likewise the independent feminist organization in Milan that bore the same name as the newspaper, *Unione Femminile,* also urged support of the Kuliscioff bill. See "Attività Femminile," *Unione Femminile* I (November 1901): 122.

75. For some illustrative examples of the anti-socialist propaganda of the Christian Democrats among female workers see: Luigi M. Pessina, "Il socialismo e la donna," *La Donna del Popolo* I (February 16, 1901): 1; and "Alle risaiuole," *La Donna del Popolo* III (May 31, 1903): 2.

76. Dal Fides, "Il lavoro delle donne e dei fanciulli," *La Donna del Popolo* I (February 26, 1901): 3.
77. Kuliscioff, *Il Monopolio,* pp. 45–46.
78. Kuliscioff, "La santità della famiglia: una risposta in retardo," *Critica Sociale* I (January 15, 1891): 9–10.
79. Kuliscioff to Turati, March 17, 1904, Carteggio Turati-Kuliscioff, Einaudi MS, Turin. Turati's letters for this period are not extant.
80. Kuliscioff to Turati, March 19, 1904, Carteggio Turati-Kuliscioff, Einaudi MS, Turin.
81. Kuliscioff, "Il Sentimentalismo nella questione femminile," 142.
82. See Pessina, "Il socialismo e la donna," I; "Nella vita e fra i giornali: Due conferenza femministe," *Pensiero e azione* I (January 20, 1905): 13; and Dell'Ara, "La donna nel Movimento sociale," *Pensiero e azione* I (December 8, 1904): 4.
83. "Women Strictly not for the Birds," *Economist,* January 27-February 2, 1973, p. 50. Mme. Sullerot points out that this is not the sole determinant of the position of women in a nation. The general economic situation of a country also has an effect.
84. Kuliscioff, "Il Feminismo," p. 186.
85. Prof. Giov. Montemartini, "Il Salario delle donne nel lavoro manuale," *Unione Femminile* I (April 7, 1901): 12–13.
86. Kuliscioff, "Per Augusto Bebel," p. 51.
87. Kuliscioff, "Il Sentimentalismo nella questione femminile," p. 143.
88. A.M. Mozzoni, *I Socialisti e l'emancipazione della donna* (Allessandria, 1892), p. 4, as quoted in Garin, p. 27n.
89. Angelucci, "Questioni femminili," pp. 140–41.
90. Kuliscioff, "Il Sentimentalismo nella questione femminile," pp. 142–43.
91. See "Engels to J. Bloch," p. 488.
92. See Evelyne Sullerot, *Woman, Society and Change* (New York, 1971), pp. 122–33, for some examples of such loopholes that permit wage discrimination to continue after the passage of "equal pay for equal work" legislation.

7 • Bolshevism, the Woman Question, and Aleksandra Kollontai

• *Beatrice Farnsworth*

By the turn of the twentieth century, the Russian revolutionary movement had evolved far beyond its early beginnings in the Chaikovskii Circle. Populism had gone through a "back to the people" movement as well as an assassination and terror phase and had developed into the underground party of the Social Revolutionaries. Socialism had been "Europeanized" by Plekhanov who founded the Russian Social Democratic party in exile. Despite appeals to unity, in 1903 it split over the form of organization into Bolshevik and Menshevik factions. Bolsheviks were a small, elitist group, totally dedicated to revolution and unwilling to tolerate any diversity within the party. In vain did Aleksandra Kollontai, the one who did most to bring feminism to Bolshevism, argue for a separate women's bureau and mobilization of a female constituency in the pre-1914 period. Yet it was the Bolsheviks who capitalized finally on existing social tensions and the collapse of the monarchy in March 1917, making the world's first successful socialist revolution in November of that year. Thus they stood in a unique position to fulfill a decades-old promise to feminists who had linked their cause to revolutionary socialism. In December, the Bolshevik party enacted into Soviet law a series of reforms that sought to remodel the position of Russian women and restructure the Russian family. But such change in personal relations proved too radical even for Old Bolsheviks with the exception, Farnsworth shows, of Kollontai. In what fundamental way was her perception of women different from that of other Bolshevik leaders? When did it become apparent to Kollontai that Russian socialists lacked a true commitment to the liberation of women? Why, when it was obvious that the Soviet regime had

**KOLLONTAI ADDRESSING SECOND INTERNATIONAL
CONFERENCE OF COMMUNIST WOMEN, JUNE 1921.** From A. M. Kollontai,
Iz Moei Zhizni Roboty (From *My Life and Work*), ed. I. M. Dazhina et al. (Moscow, 1974).

183

no intention of dealing with the woman question on a genu-
inely socialist base, did she choose to capitulate to Stalinism
and abandon overt opposition?

The utopian socialist, Charles Fourier, believed that the emancipation of women was the best general measure of the moral
level of a culture, that the degree of feminine emancipation was
a natural measure of general emancipation. Karl Marx liked to
quote Fourier. So did Old Bolsheviks.[1]

The Russian intelligentsia had long been absorbed with the
problems of two oppressed groups: women and peasants. And
as the relationship of the backward peasantry to the Bolshevik
revolution underwent tortuous analysis, finally to become by
the mid-twenties a source of bitter factionalism, the "woman
question" seemed one of the few issues on which party leaders,
Left and Right, agreed.

I would argue that it was an unfortunate consensus, deriving
in part from a superficial commitment, in part from a limited understanding of the problem, so that at a critical time when the
regime was taking form, the woman question moved not in the
direction of a socialist solution, but rather toward conversion to
revolutionary myth. Only one leading Bolshevik, Aleksandra
Kollontai, the central figure in the socialist woman's movement,
fought singlemindedly for the socialist course. But by the mid-
twenties, having established herself as an oppositionist, she was
isolated from decision making. This article will suggest that her
capitulation to Stalin in 1927 ended the most serious attempt of
bolshevism to treat the woman question on the basis of socialist
theory.

This article is based on a paper presented at the annual meeting of the American Historical Association, San Francisco, December 29, 1973. I wish to thank
the National Endowment for the Humanities, the American Philosophical Society, and Wells College for funds to facilitate research. I would also like to thank
Bertram D. Wolfe, Sheila Fitzpatrick, Robert Daniels, Stephen F. Cohen, and
Charles Duval for helpful criticism and suggestions and Phyllis Andrews for lo-
cating materials.

The article first appeared in *The American Historical Review*, Vol. 81, No. 2
(April 1976). Reprinted with permission.

Revolutions generate myths. One is the assumption that the Russian socialists were, from prerevolutionary days, actively committed to working for the liberation of women. In fact, insofar as we can speak of a single attitude for so factionalized a group as the Social Democrats, the opposite was true. The liberation of women, part of the ideological equipment that the Russians inherited from a more humanistic, Western European tradition, was a concept they resisted adopting as a goal.

The reluctance of Russian Marxists to pledge themselves to solving the woman question was far from evident to Kollontai; she came from the upper-class background common to Russian revolutionary women and joined the party in 1898 chiefly because she believed socialism the surest means to achieve women's liberation.[2] Only in the era of the Revolution of 1905 did Kollontai begin to sense that her original perceptions had been over optimistic. She reminded the Petersburg Committee of the Social Democratic party that they must give more attention in their program to the miserable lives of Russian working women. The party was losing women from the ranks of the students and the intelligentsia to the impressively organized bourgeois feminists, and it needed as a counterbalance a base among the proletariat. The socialists rejected both Kollontai's idea for a special bureau in the party that would devise ways to reach women and her suggestion that they include in their aims the liberation of women. Finding herself "completely isolated" in her idea and demands, Kollontai realized for the first time how little the Social Democratic party in Russia was concerned with the fate of the women of the working class, "how meagre was its interest in women's liberation."[3]

What lay behind this negativism? The Russian working woman, the *baba* so backward an element in society, seemed an unlikely recruit to a secret political party, an inappropriate comrade. But the Petersburg Committee objected to Kollontai's ideas chiefly because they saw in them the diversionary danger of feminism. Although an alliance between socialism and feminism is referred to as one of the most enduring of nineteenth-century intellectual bonds, it was true only insofar as feminism was defined loosely to mean the equality of women and their incorporation into the mainstream of public life.[4] With the development of Marxism as a political movement, later in the nineteenth century, the term *feminism* became suspect in European socialist parties. It implied not simply equality for women but a union of women as a separate group, linked by bonds that transcended those of class. This was, of course, deviant thinking, the mere suggestion of which made Marxists uneasy. Specific clauses concerning women and separate institutions, whether bureaus in the party or working women's clubs, held for them the threat of dividing the working class. Therefore the Social Democrats preferred that the liberation of women be treated not as a specific, revolutionary goal but rather as an eventual result of the class struggle.

Both wings of the Social Democratic party, Mensheviks as well as Bolsheviks, male and female, tended to share this view: thus when Vera Zasulich, the veteran revolutionary, returned to Russia after the upheaval of 1905, she rejected Kollontai's request for help in devising ways to reach women. To find the usually warm and expansive Zasulich their opponent, instead of their aid, distressed Kollontai and the small group she had recruited—among them the working woman, Klavdiia Nikolaeva, later a prominent Bolshevik. But they proceeded even without the older woman's support to establish on their own a legal women's club. Affiliated with neither socialist faction, it was deceptively named the Society for the Mutual Help of Working Women. Zasulich came to the club one evening not, as Kollontai hoped, to rejoice at its success but to condemn it as a "superfluous enterprise" that divided the strength of the socialist party.[5]

The woman question brought Kollontai to Marxism—others came to the richly diverse movement by equally idiosyncratic paths—but in no sense was she a political feminist. From 1906 to 1908, when she fled into exile to escape the Russian police who were pursuing her for revolutionary agitation, Kollontai was the scourge of the bourgeois feminists, whom she attacked in a torrent of polemical speeches, articles, and a belligerent four-hundred-page book, *The Social Bases of the Woman Question* (1909). With revolutionary righteousness, she denied the

186

feminist premise that women were a group apart bound by special ties; rather, they were divided into classes just as men were. Occasionally overstating her argument, Kollontai contended that the feminists' program of reform was pitifully irrelevant for proletarian women, that despite their claims to be "nonclass" the Russian "Equal Righters," as she called the Union for Women's Equality, remained bourgeois. Determined to establish a basic truth, Kollontai portrayed the woman question not as a matter of political liberation or social reform but symbolically as a "piece of bread," which meant that for women to be truly free they had to be economically independent.[6] The heart of the matter, which feminists in Russia ignored, was the domestic and marital situation. How could independence be possible for women of the working class unless the family ceased to be a closed, individual unit? Were the feminists so unrealistic as to believe that the contemporary class state, however democratically structured, would take on itself all the obligations relating to maternity and child care that were fulfilled by the individual family? Kollontai insisted that only socialists could create the conditions that in turn could free the "new woman."

What Kollontai did not reveal to the Equal Righters was her difficulty in convincing either Bolsheviks or Mensheviks, as she moved between these two factions, to include the woman question in its goals. The Social Democratic party continued to suspect Kollontai of feminism as they viewed with unease her penchant to concentrate on the problems of women, an emphasis that theoretically they need not have feared, if the situation of women, rather than being divisive, was to serve as a measure of the moral level of a newly structured society.[7]

Only in 1917 when Kollontai was at the peak of her popularity as a revolutionary, having officially joined the Bolsheviks in 1915 and been elected to their Central Committee at the Sixth Party Congress a few months before the Revolution, was she able to establish a women's bureau in the Bolshevik party. By then she had acquired powerful allies: Lenin and Iakov Sverdlov, who was later chairman of the Central Executive Committee of the Soviet. Most of the unhappy encounters between

Kollontai and the Russian socialists had taken place before the Revolution with Lenin far from the scene. Yet there are indications that at least initially she questioned Lenin's commitment to the woman question. In the spring of 1914, while preparing for a proposed meeting in August of the Socialist International in Vienna where she was scheduled to report to the Women's Congress, Kollontai learned in confidence that the mandates of Menshevik delegates to the Women's Congress would be contested by the Bolsheviks. To Menshevik leaders she expressed indignation at the maneuvering of the Bolsheviks who in her view had never before been interested in the women's movement—after all she had been participating in these international meetings for years—but who were now trying to dominate the group.[8] A revealing charge, for when one criticized the Bolsheviks in 1914, one meant Lenin, the undisputed leader of the faction.

Kollontai took a proprietary attitude toward the Russian women's movement, understandable in view of her earlier isolation, but somewhat unfair. Among the Bolsheviks in exile were Krupskaia, Lenin's wife, and her close party comrades, Ludmilla Staël, Zinaida Lilina, and Inessa Armand, women who shared Kollontai's commitment if not her single-minded intensity.[9] As for Lenin, his concern was not quite so sudden, or opportunistic, as Kollontai suspected. While Lenin possessed that feel for reality, that marvelous sensitivity to the demands of the time, which prompted him now and then to adopt new tactics, his interest in the woman question had its source in an intuitive knowledge that for the revolution to succeed women had to support it, that women, the most backward element of Russian society, could best be reached by specially designed measures. If for him women's problems were not primary, but subordinate to the larger goal of revolution, they were dear to the hearts of the women closest to him: his friend Armand, first director of the women's section of the party in 1919, and his wife, editor of its journal, *Kommunistka*. It was Armand who urged in 1914 that propaganda work be widely developed among the women workers and that a special women workers' magazine be published in Petersburg. Lenin wrote to his sister Anna with this idea, and *Rabotnitsa* resulted.[10]

After the revolution, Lenin sought in 1920 to explain why there were so few women in the party and pointed to the party's past policy of rejecting separate bodies for work among the masses of women. Adopting as his own the argument Kollontai had been advancing since 1906 and separating himself from the party's narrow view, Lenin insisted that there must be commissions, party bureaus, whose particular duty it was to arouse the masses of women workers, peasants and petty bourgeois, to bring them under party influence. What he was advocating, he explained, was not bourgeois feminism, it was instead revolutionary expediency.[11]

If Sverdlov seemed an unlikely ally as head of the party's Secretariat, staffed primarily by women, he understood women's subordinate status. Anatoly Lunacharsky, the animated and generous commissar of education, considered that Sverdlov was "like ice ... somehow faceless."[12] But this same man responded with warm compassion to Kollontai's plea that the Bolsheviks commit themselves to bringing women into the party. Sverdlov helped Kollontai win acceptance for a women's bureau, and he became so vital to her work among women that upon his death in 1919 Kollontai wrote an emotional piece telling the working women of Russia that with the death of Sverdlov they had lost a comrade who was among their few convinced defenders, a comrade who really understood the need for political work among women and whose death meant special grief for their movement.[13]

Had Sverdlov lived, had Lenin not become incapacitated, would the woman question have been resolved in a different way? Among the Bolsheviks there was only one other leader, Leon Trotsky, whom Kollontai praised equally with Lenin and Sverdlov for his work on behalf of women.[14] Their initial support was invaluable. A measure of it was the party's pledge in its new program at the Eighth Congress in 1919 to replace the individual household with communal facilities for eating, laundry, and maternal and child care. Kollontai believed she had scored another triumph for the movement when despite opposition, she was able to get a resolution passed at the Eighth Congress concerning the need for the party to work more specifically among women to draw them in as active members. But within two years she was harshly critical of the party's failure to implement its decision to include women in areas of communist leadership.[15] Zhenotdel, the women's section, which was established officially in 1919 as a part of the Central Committee, was never able to overcome the forces that regarded its work with indifference or hostility.[16] Sophia Smidovich, an Old Bolshevik who headed the Moscow Regional Women's Section until she replaced Kollontai as director of the central Zhenotdel in 1922, described the situation. The efforts of Zhenotdel to raise socialist consciousness among women were proving expedient, but the party was failing to help. The few qualified and trained workers assigned to it were regarded with contempt by party comrades. Smidovich put the question directly: if Zhenotdel was not regarded as necessary, the party must say so; if it was needed, then qualified workers had to be provided. It would be better to liquidate the department than to allow it to drag out its miserable existence. Her dismal appraisal was shared by another Old Bolshevik, Viktor Nogin, who in his report to the Eleventh Party Congress called attention to the condescension, the abnormal, unhealthy attitudes toward Zhenotdel that caused its members to feel unequal.[17] But V.M. Molotov, a member of the Central Committee and one of the three party secretaries, observed that Zhenotdel's difficulties were due to its lack of a real leader. This colorless but methodical functionary, who was to rise to the highest positions as Stalin's right-hand man, implied that the trouble lay not in party attitudes but in the poor organization established by its previous directors, either Armand, who died in 1920, or perhaps Kollontai, who was her successor.[18] Kollontai was an ideal scapegoat. Having fallen from favor, she was already under fire at the Eleventh Congress, which was trying unsuccessfully to expel her from the party for her role as a leader in yet another unhappy cause, the Workers' Opposition.[19]

We come to the mid-twenties, a turning point. The Bolshevik party, having committed itself in 1919 with some reluctance to solving the woman question, found that its New Economic Policy (NEP) adopted in 1921 was in conflict with its social obligations. Nikolai Bukharin, earlier a leader of the radical left wing of the party, but now an exponent of the more moderate pace of the regime, stated it bluntly in the Bolshevik newspaper, *Pravda*: the official party program of 1919 was outdated and irrelevant.[20] The end of labor conscription, the rise in unemployment resulting from the partial restoration of private enterprise under NEP, meant that the number of women unable to find work and dependent now on men had increased. Simultaneously the government reduced its investment in child care. A resolution offered at a conference concerning woman's work in 1922 spoke of NEP's "catastrophic effect" on the work being done among mothers. For example, the number of homes for mothers and children fell sharply after 1922. Articles in *Kommunistka* reflected the sense of alarm among workers in social institutions, like nurseries, who under NEP did not know how much longer they could function.[21]

For the hundreds of thousands of unemployed women, living in *de facto* marriages or neglecting to register post-1917 church marriages, the situation was potentially perilous. Should their husbands leave them, they would be without means of support. The party, faced with a critical family situation, had to deal with the fundamental question plaguing it in the twenties: would it present a forward-looking solution to demonstrate that Soviet Russia, despite the NEP, was moving toward socialism?

In October 1925 the party reacted instead by introducing to the nominal governing organ, the All Russian Central Executive Committee, a new family code, which increased not society's but the individual's economic obligations by making unregistered marriages legal. The purpose, the commissar of justice, Dmitri Kursky, explained, was to safeguard women by extending to *de facto* wives the existing right to receive alimony. To protect women further, the government added to the original family law, by which a destitute spouse unable to work had been entitled to a husband's support, the right to alimony "during unemployment."[22]

Attitudes, traditional and personal, surfaced in opposition to the new law: peasants feared that the expansion of alimony meant a threat to their property,[23] women and men looked suspiciously at each other, and even in the party, opponents battled the proposed changes. Aaron Sol'ts of the Central Control Commission, the body responsible for enforcing moral and doctrinal standards in the party, pleased many urban men when he argued that only registered marriages should carry material consequences; but Sol'ts, who feared that women might be wrongly encouraged by the new law to enter sexual relationships in order to get alimony, had in mind enforcing stricter morality, while the townsmen sought protection against law suits.[24] The most controversial feature of the law—recognition of *de facto* marriage—created a demand in the Central Executive Committee for a more precise definition of marriage, since no one intended that casual relationships should entitle women to alimony. The difficulty of defining marriage was suggested by the deputy commissar of justice, Nikolai Krylenko, in his pragmatic view after a year of discussion, that if confusion still remained as to what marriage was it might be best to discard the official definition—the fact of living together, a joint household, and the announcement of such to a third party—and let the courts decide.[25]

Bolsheviks from left to right argued over details, but the party's ultimate purpose, the decision to protect women as the weaker members of society by means of alimony, remained unquestioned. In the middle of the nineteenth century, J. S. Mill had analyzed women's subjection and pointed out that the question was not what marraige ought to be, but a far wider question, what women ought to be.[26] Settle that first, the other will settle itself. Yet in 1925, among prominent Bolsheviks, only Kollontai publicly declared that the government was not dealing in a meaningful way with the woman question.

The Central Committee had failed in its effort to expel Kollontai from the party in 1922 on grounds of factionalism, but she had been effectively isolated by being sent with other dissidents into diplomatic "exile." The party assigned her to a post in Norway, where she quickly wearied of diplomatic life. Disheartened additionally by the failure of her efforts in the Workers' Opposition movement to establish genuine proletarian control in the workers' state, or to restore to the party the right to

192

open protest, the idealistic Kollontai resigned her diplomatic position and in 1925 contemplated a break with bolshevism. While close friends in the embassy disagreed as to the seriousness of her intention to leave the party, with Marcel Body advancing the theory and another friend denying it, it seems a possible explanation for Kollontai's rash political action in the winter of 1925–26 when she returned briefly to Moscow.[27] If she failed, she would break with the regime.

Studies of the opposition movement by Western historians suggest that Kollontai had abandoned protest by 1925, but the facts are otherwise. Upholding the revolutionary-heroic outlook of 1917 as though she had been neither censured nor exiled, Kollontai plunged at the end of 1925 into what would be her last struggle on behalf of the now virtually defunct revolutionary domestic program of 1919. Her effort, overlooked by historians because of its singularly independent nature—and its distance from the issues of the male power struggle—centered on opposition to the government's projected new marriage code.

Kollontai's analysis ran counter to the gloomy fears of workers in the women's section that with the adoption of NEP the possibility of a socialist solution to the woman question had been irrevocably lost. Kollontai believed rather that continued expansion of the private sector of the economy under the NEP would mean an eventual increase in employment opportunities for women and that growing government resources would make possible further investment in public facilities that would replace the individual household. Before offering a counterproposal, it was necessary first to explain why the regime's new family law was unacceptable in a society purporting to be socialist. She argued that rather than being a step forward, the proposal revealed the party's failure, after eight years in power, to evolve a socialist family policy: the government would be creating categories of women—registered, unregistered, and casual—and since the first two were now made equal in their rights, the third was necessarily deprived. The women the new law refused to defend were but peasant girls going to the city for work and working girls living in factories and shops in conditions of frightful congestion. Registered and unregistered wives, on the other hand, were being encouraged to abase themselves in court, begging for their legal sop from an unwilling man, probably too poor to pay.[28] She scoffed at the pointlessness of socialists defining marriage or seeking to strengthen it by legislation, as if by such means abandoned, unemployed women could be aided. In an approach radically different from that of those who agreed that alimony had failed but argued helplessly that the courts must find ways to enforce payment, Kollontai insisted that women who served society by providing it with future workers deserved collective support. Prior to NEP, Kollontai had proposed government protection for mothers in the form of state subsidies.[29] Discarding the idea of direct state aid, Kollontai responded to the slower pace of NEP by proposing to abolish alimony and to create instead a General Insurance Fund to which the entire working adult population would contribute on a graduated scale, the lowest contribution being two rubles a year. With sixty million adult contributors one could count on an initial sum of one hundred and twenty million rubles, which would make it possible to provide for the cost of children's crèches and homes, homes for mothers in need, support to single mothers unable to work and for their children at least until they were a year old, later, according to the size of the fund, until they were three or four.[30] Soviet society was poor, but its economic growth in the mid-twenties was increasing at a rapid rate so that within two or three years the General Insurance Fund would no longer be a burden.

Kollontai's idiosyncratic proposal, springing from the romantic socialism of 1917 and the revolutionary era, was rejected by all but her own small group and youthful students; they invariably responded to Kollontai's optimistic theories, which kept alive hope that revolution still lived in Soviet Russia. "For us young communist women," a party worker recalled, "Kollontai was a lofty example of a revolutionary fighter, and we aspired to imitate her." Writing in *Komsomolskaia Pravda*, the newspaper for party youth, a student who claimed that most students supported Kollontai suggested, as a temporary means of strengthening the General Fund, a five-kopek tax on bottles of wine, theater tickets, and other amusements.[31]

Kollontai's right-wing critics implied that replacing alimony with an insurance fund was unfair to the peasant majority who, hostile to the towns, would never willingly pay an extra tax to benefit city women and children, while to compel payment would run counter to the new economic policy of lessening burdens on the peasantry. This argument was inconsistent since it was the peasants who opposed as immoral and a threat to their property the government's own proposal to recognize *de facto* marriages. In urging increased taxation, Kollontai seemed to the Right to be thinking along the lines of Trotsky and Evgeny Preobrazhensky, the economic spokesman of the Left, who argued for systematic pressure on the peasants. But the Left oppositionists sought economic support for more rapid industrialization, not social experiments, which Trotsky, speaking now as a reformist, regarded as premature. Trotsky referred later—presumably with Kollontai in mind—to experiments so radical that one would simply fall on one's face and be embarrassed before the peasantry.[32]

Kollontai's critics failed to understand that, while seeking ways to preserve revolutionary domestic goals, she was willing to modify her position to work within the reconciliatory context of Bukharinism, the party's official ideology in the mid-twenties. With the failure of revolution in the West, she had come to accept Bukharin's view of the need slowly to build socialism in one country.[33] She liked Bukharin, who at the age of thirty-eight was at the peak of his political influence and whose concept of a more humane socialism she shared. In the early prerevolutionary days they had frequently been allies, even as they had been opponents during the Workers' Opposition crisis in 1921. With Alexander Shliapnikov, the first commissar of labor and one of the few genuinely proletarian leaders of the party, Kollontai warned in 1921 about the dangers of "peasantization" of the government. But this did not mean that in 1926 she advocated the Left's position of accumulating capital for industrial expansion by extracting it forcibly from the peasant. The Right's contention that Kollontai's plan to tax the peasant at a rate of two rubles a year ran counter to government economic policy and resembled the pressures of the Left was an absurd exaggeration. Kollontai was simply in line with Bukharin in advocating some "pumping over" of economic resources from the peasant sector.[34]

For socialism to succeed—as Bukharin now contended—a long period of harmony between peasant and proletariat would have to be established. This "harmonizing" had consistently been Kollontai's purpose as well as the goal of the much-scorned women's section, which, since its inception, had worked to raise the socialist consciousness of peasant women. It is true that the women were only part of rural society, but as Lenin explained earlier, the Soviet Union could not exercise the dictatorship of the proletariat unless the women were won over.[35]

Another aspect of Kollontai's proposal, which she saw as a gesture of support for peasant women, was her plan for marriage contracts that were to safeguard the interests of house-wives, both peasant and proletarian. By these contracts, a couple entering into a marital union would, instead of registering, voluntarily conclude an agreement in which they would determine their economic responsibilities toward each other and their children. A somewhat weak idea, which at first glance seems, in its revolutionary romanticism, to deserve the criticism it received, it assumed a herculean effort on the part of workers from the women's section who were somehow to teach backward peasant women how to safeguard their economic interests.[36] Yet it is necessary to keep in mind that Kollontai was thinking in long-range, socialist terms, trying to maintain a sense of left-wing revolutionary purpose within a right-wing evolutionary structure.

The assumption on which Kollontai's proposals were based—collective responsibility for those in need—aimed specifically at an increased socialist awareness among both peasant and proletarian. Trotsky argued that the state could not build new social institutions without cooperation from the masses, that the people themselves had to grow.[37] This was a valid position, but how else could socialist awareness be created other than by the party's gradual but steady introduction of socialist measures? The need for such ideological persuasion was underscored by

196

the reaction to Kollontai's plan as seen in letters from working women. "Comrad Kollontai's tax is altogether unsatisfactory. ... How can anyone speak of a general taxation of all men? What is it to do with *all* men, when only *one* man is concerned in the begetting of a child? What affair is it of the community? The matter is far simpler; if you are the father, you must pay!"[38]

Even Trotsky, curiously insensitive to the Thermidorian aspects of the government's new marriage code, was indignant at its opponents: how could one think that in Soviet society anyone could be so thickheaded as to deny a mother the right to help from the father simply because the woman was not a registered wife; women needed all the protection they could get. Describing Soviet marriage legislation as socialist in spirit, Trotsky regretted that society lagged so dismally behind it.[39] Society did lag; so, too, did party leaders.

Trotsky shared a view of women that caused him to praise as socialist the legislation Kollontai condemned as petty bourgeois. Nor was his perception "un-Marxist." Once, in a light-hearted moment, Karl Marx filled out a so-called confession for his daughter Laura revealing his strongest preferences. He wrote that the virtue he admired most in men was "strength." The virtue he admired most in women? "Weakness."[40] Both Marx and Engels believed that the weak must be protected from the strong. Men must protect women. This theme ran through the debates over the new family code, jeopardizing the socialist assumption that the collective should provide social security for its members. The Bolsheviks believed in equality for women, of course, but few understood that phrase with Kollontai's sensitivity. While not politically a feminist, she did share their view that women were inherently strong and needed freedom from the debilitating protection of men. She singled out Trotsky—a risky thing to do in 1926 when he was under attack from the Stalinists—as being of great help to the women's section in its work.[41] Yet not even Trotsky—and if I seem to concentrate on him it is because of the degree of his concern and commitment—understood that her plan was an opportunity for the party to raise the consciousness of the masses further toward socialism.

197

On this issue the women's section proved no more monolithic than other Bolshevik institutions. Here, too, Kollontai found opponents. Smidovich, the section's former director, willingly spoke for the party. Chosen in 1925 as a member of the powerful Central Control Commission, living confortably enough in a traditional family, she was reasonably free of tensions concerning the woman question. While Kollontai viewed the revolution primarily from the perspective of women's liberation, Smidovich regarded that problem as one among many. The two Old Bolsheviks, each age fifty-four, saw themselves as representing different constituencies, a fact that in itself proved a cause for suspicion. Smidovich, gray haired and grandmotherly, spoke as a member of an older, more staid generation that wanted to protect women from the sexual irresponsibility of men, a problem to which Kollontai seemed indifferent. Kollontai gazed, strikingly attractive and still youthful, from the cover of the popular magazine, *Ekran,* in whose pages she argued on behalf of socialist women who were strong and wanted to be free.[42] In contrast to Kollontai's unquenchable idealism, Smidovich sounded practical as she affirmed the theoretical superiority of communal raising of children but defended the party's abandonment of efforts to replace the individaul household. Her hostility toward Kollontai unconcealed, Smidovich argued that Soviet Russia could not yet afford Kollontai's dreams.[43] The Smidoviches were conservative, and Petr Smidovich, a senior member of the Moscow Committee of the Bolshevik party, responded on the eve of 1917 to Lenin's radical course by insisting: "There do not exist the forces, the objective conditions for this."[44]

The leaders struggling for power in 1926 knew that the woman question was not politically decisive. Kollontai's plan to replace alimony by a general fund, based on a progressive tax, was simply further evidence of her Left deviation. Part of the tragedy of bolshevism in the formative mid-twenties was that immediate pressures could so easily erode original hopes. Staunch revolutionaries—not yet broken or become Stalinist servants— were too ready to abandon the ideal and grasp the expedient solution. More specific a cause was the ambivalence with which the party in 1919 had adopted the woman question as a programmatic goal. Too few people were committed to its success. And among them were those like Sophia Smidovich and Trotsky, who for all their socialism, were unaware that they continued to think of women as in need of male protection. Habits of thought, even among revolutionaries, change slowly.

Some historians, notably E. H. Carr, suggest that the government's abandonment in 1922 of its original plan to support needy mothers and children indicates that those early steps had never been more than emergency legislation evolving spontaneously only to be discarded by the party with other features of war communism. Such an interpretation, insofar as it suggests a lack of a theoretical base, is misleading. Kollontai, who was chosen by Lenin as commissar of public welfare in 1917, in which office she could do little more with her meager resources than express aspirations, had for years been advocating measures of state protection that were based on commonly assumed socialist theory.[45] Insofar as Carr implies an inadequate commitment on the part of Bolsheviks to orthodox socialist assumptions or a variety of Bolshevik interpretations of social theory, his position, of course, is valid. Reporting in 1922 to the Eleventh Party Congress, Lenin remarked suggestively that "the economic forces under the control of the proletarian state of Russia are quite sufficient to ensure the transition to communism. What then is lacking? What is lacking is culture in the stratum of Communists that is governing." Elsewhere Lenin observed that many comrades were still "Philistines" in their mentality regarding women.[46]

Carr contends further that by the mid-twenties, the party membership had rejected Kollontai's position on the family, that it was already diverging in "practice and opinion" from Engel's doctrine on which it was based: the liberation of women from domestic labor. Carr cites Trotsky's symposium for party workers in 1923 as a source to illustrate a desire for traditional life.[47] More accurately, the symposium revealed the conflict between the conventional family attitudes of men and the desire for greater freedom on the part of women.[48]

Was it not a case of failure of the leadership to respond to a

199

slowly awakening sense among women of the possibilities inherent in Engel's theories, as elaborated by Kollontai in 1920 in *The Family and the Communist State?* Trotsky regretted in 1923 and again in 1925 that the woman question was not being given greater attention in the press and elsewhere.[49] Many men no doubt preferred the traditional family, but many women eagerly awaited fulfillment of the promises of party workers from the women's section who, recognizing the growing response to their efforts, could do little about the lack of government support for social institutions but express distress and frustration in the pages of *Kommunistka.* Where "officially" but in the clubs, lamented a woman worker, could one even summon the collective spirit? The overcrowded factory barracks, the overflowing communal houses, and the inadequate public dining rooms were not likely to win people over to the collective way of life.[50]

Opposition to Kollontai suggests that in fact she had raised a specter: the "withering away of the family." If in the West this concept was seen as a Communist truism, for the Soviet leadership, concerned mainly with politics and economics not with social experiments, what was soon to be known as Kollontai's idea had become an irritant.[51] The party knew in 1926 that it needed the family, meaning the women, to do what they had always done—raise children, cook, and keep house. So when Kursky, citing Lenin, gave assurances that someday under communism the state would undertake the upbringing of all children, when Smidovich agreed but insisted that for now "destruction of the isolated, individual household," useful as a slogan to rally women in 1918, was not applicable, when Mikhail Kalinin, chairman of the Central Executive Committee, referred to the new marriage law as deeply affecting Soviet life, seeming to assume the permanence of the family it protected, one sensed that for the government the "withering away" concept had become a socialist myth.[52] In the women's section it remained a reality. But instead of the family, the women's section itself would disappear, abolished by Stalin in 1929 on the specious ground that its tasks had been completed. In less than ten years, the slogan "withering away of the family" was to move from myth to heresy with Kollontai's *The Family and the Communist State* cited as its "undoubtedly harmful" source.[53]

In the moral and personal disapproval directed against Kollontai one saw further mythmaking. Although she criticized debauchery in terms similar to those used earlier by Lenin (but at the same time, questioned the supposed dissoluteness of Komsomol youth),[54] slashing attacks in the press accused Kollontai of trying to revive her "discredited" advocacy of Ultra-Left, decadent, free love by means of the General Insurance Fund, which would further encourage youthful irresponsibility.[55] The Komsomol journal, *Molodaia Gvardiia*, which had carried Kollontai's essays in 1923, now reflected the party's puritanical line by printing articles harshly critical of her. In one instance the editors were perhaps uneasy over publishing an attack on a comrade who invariably defended Soviet youth. In a footnote that implied their apartness from the assault, they invited readers to express their own viewpoints based on available, factual materials.[56]

With the contention that alimony was one of the best means to regulate and to restrain sexual life, with the charge that in advocating its abolition Kollontai was seeking to remove personal responsibility from the sexual life of men, Kollontai's critics suggested the development of new attitudes toward privacy. In 1883 the German Socialist leader, August Bebel, wrote that satisfaction of the sexual instinct was a private concern to be interfered with by no one.[57] Presumably, assigning legal consequences to *de facto* marriage was in itself a violation of personal privacy, but even before 1926 doubts were expressed in the party as to the feasibility of Bebel's assumption. Bukharin's attempt in 1922 to use his personal popularity with the Komsomols to urge youth to a more controlled sex life is one example.[58] Polina Vinogradskaia, a young Trotskyist who worked with Kollontai on *Kommunistka*, moved in a similar way when she viciously condemned Kollontai in 1923 as a bourgeois feminist who wasted pages of Soviet journals with articles extolling sexuality. The editors of *Krasnaia Nov'* were unhappy enough to apologize in print for this cruel attack on a "fighting com-

201

rade." Vinogradskaia affirmed socialist privacy but at the same time insisted, in a novel tribute to Trotsky's theory of permanent revolution, that it was absolutely "inadmissable" for a Bolshevik to dwell on sex in view of the political setback of the Communist party in Germany.[59] Giving assurances that someday under communism there would be no need for moral laws, Emilian Iaroslavskii, a Stalinist and a leading figure in the party's Central Control Commission, warned that it was for bourgeois not proletarian youth to flit from flower to flower indulging in Kollontai's "love of the worker bees." In fact, Iaroslavskii recalled, for eight or nine years he sat in prison and sexual abstinence had done him no harm.[60]

What caused this violation of privacy by Bolsheviks who simultaneously asserted their belief in the socialist promise of complete freedom in personal life? Invariably we have the answer: this is the transitional era. The poverty of Soviet society, the homeless children, and the need for the responsible family during the twenties were serious factors; yet there seems another explanation for the avidity with which party members relegated privacy to mythology. The founder of the Marx-Lenin Institute, David Riazanov—a Bolshevik of integrity and something of an eccentric in his penchant for speaking the truth bluntly—declared during the debates of 1926 what other comrades had merely suggested: "We should teach our young Komsomols that marriage is not a personal act, but an act of deep social significance, demanding interference and regulation by society."[61] Riazanov implied that in fact the party aimed at a science of human behavior.

Again, why? What was there in Russian bolshevism that impelled it as a movement to turn away from less restrictive European socialism? In a suggestive analysis, the social scientist Nathan Leites provides a clue when he refers to Bolshevik fear of loss of control.[62] In the rhetoric of attack against Kollontai, from Smidovich, through Iaroslavskii, to Vinogradskaia, there occurred over and over words like "irresponsibility" and "debauchery," which implied lack of order. In privacy there lurked the possibility that youth, expending its energy in sexual excess, might cease to work purposefully for the party.

Ironically, but in reality, work as the ultimate liberating force for women forms a persistent theme in Kollontai's own writing. She applauded the labor conscription that characterized the civil war years. Her projected commune, alarming to the party because of its suggestion of freer, less conventional marriage patterns, appears really to be a somewhat rigid, work-oriented institution. Years before Freud theorized about conflicts between sexuality and work Kollontai had intuited the same dilemma for the socialist commune.[63] Unlike Fourier's phalanstery where individuals would fulfill themselves in passion, Kollontai's people, although sexually free, would relegate sex to a second place—while on the rock of collective work they would build the new society. While Kollontai's collective seemed alarmingly loose to most Bolsheviks, Herbert Marcuse used it as but another example of Soviet repression.[64]

Kollontai's singular position derived from her emphasis, unique to bolshevism, in fusing sex and work. Yet where in Kollontai's collective was privacy? The loving couple, absorbed primarily in each other, would not be welcome. In rejecting this individual preference, Kollontai suggests that within the libertarian there dwelled something of the authoritarian. The ambiguity remained but it was of no interest to a regime intent in 1926 on crushing Kollontai's left-wing, social deviance.

Perhaps the intense experience of renewed party criticism, reminding Kollontai of the depressing days that followed the failure of the Workers' Opposition, had the countereffect of keeping her within the party. Thoroughly socialized, she dreaded the contempt of her comrades. She thought of another woman who had left Russia, Angelica Balabanoff, the first secretary of the Communist International, who broke with bolshevism in 1921. Kollontai knew she could not bear the vilification that had been directed against Balabanoff.[65] Her sense of identity with Balabanoff suggests that Kollontai saw herself not so much as a Bolshevik leader but as a Bolshevik woman. One wonders if this perception was general, if antagonism toward an aggressive female played a part in negative attitudes toward Kollontai and her theories, if a woman became more vulnerable when she invaded the masculine provinces where Bolshevik policies were determined. Certain episodes are suggestive.In April 1917 only Kollontai supported Lenin's opposition to working with Russia's provisional government, and the fact was regarded as amusing enough to be the subject of a popular jingle.[66] In 1921 not even Lenin was above making a snide reference at the Tenth Party Congress to Kollontai's private life.[67] Intimations that Kollontai was overaggressive could always produce a laugh from assembled Communists: an Amazon, Trotsky called her, a Valkyrie, added Karl Radek, secretary of the Comintern. Stalin had no use for intellectual women in the party, calling them "herrings with ideas."[68]

By early summer of 1926, sensing that she had used the last of her emotional resources and deeply disheartened by divisions in the party, Kollontai abandoned not only the fantasy of an independent life but the very self who more than once had boldly opposed Lenin. As Stalin prepared to crush the opposition, Kollontai for the first time became cautious. Reflecting an awareness of the narrowing of party attitudes, she revised a brief autobiography so as not to seem an advocate of a radicalism that opposed the Stalinists.[69] Claiming privately that she wanted most to live freely as a writer, she clung instead to familiar authority.[70] She agreed with much of the criticism the Trotskyists were directing against repression in the party, but in the summer of 1926 when Trotsky's emissaries came seeking her support, they came in vain. Despite her friendship with oppositionists like Christian Rakovsky, a member of the Central Committee and the ambassador to France, who chided her for not joining them, her attitude toward Trotsky himself was ambivalent. For his concern with the woman question she was grateful; but how could she believe that Trotsky in power would alter the mood that Stalin was brutally imposing, be more tolerant of disagreement? An authoritarian Trotsky, together with Grigory Zinoviev, the chairman of the Communist International, had ensured defeat of her appeal to the Comintern four years earlier in behalf of intraparty dissent.[71] In the end, the leaders in both camps failed her, neither side able to understand her attempt to supply much-needed evidence to disillusioned Soviet youth that the regime, despite the NEP, still worked toward socialism.

Kollontai's refusal to join the Trotskyists did not improve her position in the party; for daring to question its socialist commitment, for calling its new family legislation bourgeois, Kollontai still had to be punished. In the autumn of 1926 she was sent into even more distant exile in Mexico City. Her decision in 1927 publicly to denounce opposition may have had its impetus in anxiety to get out of Mexico, but it was also the price for remaining in the party, her only home. As the Left oppositionists were expelled in 1927, Kollontai openly condemned them in the pages of *Pravda*. Resentment against Trotsky and Zinoviev made the task easier. Her words ring with helpless anger: the masses do not trust the opposition. Does the opposition think the memory of the masses so short that the masses cannot recall that the oppositionists themselves helped build the defects they now attack? She renounced not only opposition but spontaneity —declaring that in the masses a collective will had matured to triumph over the spontaneous individualism necessary during the civil war but no longer needed now in a time of collective construction.[72] In joining the leadership in mythmaking, she was also stifling the diversity that prevailed in the early revolutionary era when in the name of Marxism innumerable ideas and alternatives to Stalinism flourished. Her sexual and communal theories ceased to appear in Soviet journals.

Publicly accepting Stalinism, choosing to support its myths, meant becoming a person of secret pain, affirming among much that she knew to be untrue the boast that Soviet women, liberated from bourgeois roles, had achieved the socialist goal. Advancements in communal child-care facilities and aid to mothers were made under Stalin—most notably in 1944—but from motives other than those promulgated initially by the women's section when the "withering away of the family" was a premise. Women were needed in the work force after 1929 in connection with the five-year plans—hence the day-care centers. But they were also being encouraged to have large families, which meant a less public role and a continuation of men in positions of power.[73]

Abolition of the Zhenotdel in 1929 and the condemnation of

Kollontai's interpretation of the woman question coincided with the Stalin revolution. Using the party and the secret police, Stalin inaugurated a full totalitarian state system marked by an end to NEP, the onset of coercive industrialization and the terroristic collectivization of peasant farming. Should we conclude that Stalin, the dominant force in the party, led the opposition to Zhenotdel? Not necessarily. More likely he shared in prevailing attitudes among the leadership that ranged from insensitivity to antipathy. As a final humiliation, Kollontai wrote in 1946 that the Soviet state "had provided woman with access to all areas of creative activity and at the same time provided all the necessary conditions to enable her to fulfill her natural duty as mother, educating her own children, as mistress of her own home."[74]

By the irony of history, the very failure of the socialist promise of full equality, its conversion to myth, seems a factor saving Kollontai from the deadly fate of other Old Bolsheviks. The myth needed its symbols: Kollontai, deprived of any influence in the party, served in Sweden as the world's first woman ambassador. And Stalin, who had spoken contemptuously of Lenin during his last illness as being "surrounded by womenfolk,"[75] may have enjoyed keeping alive, and subjecting to terror, the abject Kollontai—an indication that he did not believe Bolshevik women were important enough to shoot.[76]

NOTES

1. Charles Fourier contended that "the development of a given historical epoch is best of all defined by the relation between the progress of women and freedom, since in the relations between woman and man, the weak and the strong, is most clearly expressed the victory of human nature over bestiality. The degree of feminine emancipation is a natural measure of the general emancipation." Fourier, cited by Marx, as quoted in David Riazanov, "Marks i Engels o brake i seme" [Marx and Engels on Marriage and the Family], *Letopisi Marksizma* [Chronicles of Marxism], 1927, no. 3, p. 21; Trotsky makes the same observation in *Pravda* [Truth], Dec. 17, 1925.

2. A. M. Itkina, *Revoliutsioner, Tribun, Diplomat: Stranitsy Zhizni Aleksandry Mikhailovny Kollontai* [Revolutionary, Tribune, Diplomat: Pages in the Life of Aleksandra Mikhailovna Kollontai] (Moscow, 1970), p. 44.

3. A. M. Kollontai, *The Autobiography of a Sexually Emancipated Communist Woman*, trans. Salvator Attanasio, ed. Iring Fetscher (New York, 1971), pp. 13–14.

4. See for example, Martin Malia, *Alexander Herzen and the Birth of Russian Socialism* (New York, 1965), p. 266, and Simone de Beauvoir, *The Second Sex* (New York, 1953), pp. 112, 126.

5. Kollontai, "Avtobiograficheskii Ocherk" [Autobiographical Sketch], *Proletarskaia Revoliutsiia* [Proletarian Revolution], 1921, no. 3, p. 275.

6. Kollontai, *Sotsial'nye Osnovy Zhenskogo Voprosa* [Social Bases of the Woman Question] (St. Petersburg, 1909), p. 34. The Union for Women's Equality was the most successful of the bourgeois feminist groups in terms of organization and broad appeal. For a discussion of Russian feminism prior to the revolution, see Richard Stites, "Women's Liberation Movements in Russia, 1900–1930," *Canadian-American Slavic Studies*, 7 (1973): 460–74.

7. Typical of Kollontai's prerevolutionary writing was her essay, "Novaia Zhenshchina" [New Woman], *Sovremennyi Mir* [Contemporary World], 1913, no. 9, pp. 151–85.

8. Letters from Kollontai to Semen Semkovskii, Boris Nikolaevsky Archive, Hoover Library, Stanford, California, as quoted in M. H. Pertsoff, " 'Lady in Red': A Study of the Early Career of A. M. Kollontai" (Ph.D. dissertation, University of Virginia, 1968), p. 42.

9. Zinaida Lilina was married to Grigory Zinoviev, Lenin's chief lieutenant in these years of exile. As for Inessa Armand, another Old Bolshevik, it has been suggested that Lenin was deeply in love with her. For contrasting interpretations of this alleged relationship, see Bertram Wolfe, "Lenin and Inessa Armand," *Slavic Review*, 22 (1963): 96–114, and Adam Ulam, *The Bolsheviks* (New York, 1968), pp. 284–85.

10. Clara Zetkin, *Reminiscences of Lenin* (New York, 1934), p. 53; N. K. Krupskaia, *Reminiscences of Lenin*, trans. Bernard Isaacs (New York, 1970), pp. 269–70.

11. Zetkin, *Reminiscences*, p. 53.

12. A. V. Lunacharsky, *Revolutionary Silhouettes*, trans. Michael Glenny (New York, 1967), p. 107.

13. Kollontai, "Kogo Poteriali Rabotnitsy?" [Whom Did the Working Women Lose?], in Kollontai, *Izbrannye Stat'i i Rechi* [Collected Articles and Speeches], ed. I. M. Dazhina *et al.* (Moscow, 1972), pp. 266–67.

14. Kollontai, *Autobiography*, p. 42.

15. Kollontai, "Avtobiograficheskii Ocherk," 301. For Kollontai's criticism of the party, see her "Profsoiuzy i Rabotnitsa" [Trade Unions and Working Women], *Pravda*, May 22, 1921, reprinted in Kollontai, *Izbrannye Stat'i i Rechi*, p. 319.

16. Zhenotdel developed through several stages, the first being the Women's Bureau established in 1917. From the outset the work of the bureau was directed by Kollontai, Armand, and Kollontai's protégé, Varvara Moirova, who joined the Bolsheviks in 1917. In 1918 Sverdlov helped in creating commissions for agitation and propaganda among working women for the purpose

of helping to attract nonparty working women. See E. Bochkarëva and Sera-
fima Liubimova, *Svetlyi Put* [The Bright Path] (Moscow, 1967), p. 81. In the
autumn of 1919 the party reorganized the commissions into a formal section
of the Central Committee known as the Zhenotdel. A network of women's
sections were attached to each of the local party committees, extending
from the center in Moscow into city and provincial districts. For a full discussion of the Zhenotdel, see Richard Stites, "Zhenotdel: 1917–1930,"
typescript. Also see Bette Stavrakis, "Women and the Communist Party in
the Soviet Union, 1918–1935" (Ph.D. dissertation, Western Reserve University, 1961), 79–168.

17. *Odinnadtsatyi S"ezd RKP (b): Mart*–Aprel' 1922 g [Eleventh Congress,
Bolshevik Party: March–April 1922] (Moscow, 1961), pp. 456–57, 67.

18. *Ibid.*, 58. For an idea of the organizational work of the women's section
under Kollontai, see her *Rabotnitsa i Krestianka v Sovetskoi Rossii* [The
Working Woman and the Peasant Woman in Soviet Russia] (Petrograd,
1921).

19. The Workers' Opposition was a group based on the idea of trade-union
leadership in industry. Organized in 1920, it tried to resist the centralizing
trend of Soviet politics. Its leaders were Alexander Shliapnikov, Sergei
Medvedev, and Kollontai. As an Ultra-Left idealist, Kollontai added to the
movement a protest against the stifling of criticism within the party and the
failure of the regime to improve the living conditions of the proletariat. This
movement was crushed by the party leadership in 1922.

20. *Pravda*, Jan. 25, 1923.

21. Sophia Smidovich, "O novom kodekse zakonov o brake i sem'e" [About the
New Code of Laws Concerning Marriage and the Family], *Kommunistka*
[The Communist Woman], 1926, no. 1, p. 47, and Smidovich, "Nashi zadachi
v oblasti pereustroistva byta" [Our Tasks in the Area of Reconstruction of
Daily Life], ibid., no. 12, pp. 18–20; see, for example, Moirova, "Obshchest-
vennoe pitanie i byt rabochei sem'i" [Public Feeding and the Way of Life
of the Working Family], ibid., no. 10–11, p. 45.

22. In the wording of the legislation the term *spouse* was used, but Kursky
stressed that the purpose of the law was to protect women. Children were
already safeguarded by the original code insofar as they had a right to parental support irrespective of whether the marriage was registered. Now
with the new legislation they had increased protection. Kursky as quoted in
"Discussion of the Draft of the Code," in Rudolf Schlesinger, ed., *The Family in the U.S.S.R.* (London, 1949), p. 85, a useful collection of primary
sources (now out of print) containing reprints of Soviet debates and press
articles. Although in the West it was said that the new code was intended
as a Bolshevik attack on legal marriage, Kursky's aide, Ia. Brandenburgskii,
indignantly replied that the law was promulgated out of concern for the potentially abandoned mother and child and therefore encouraged marital responsibility. *Izvestiya* [The News], Jan. 14, 1926. In 1944 the law was
changed, and only registered marriage was made legally binding.

23. Under NEP the private peasant farms were encouraged to exist and to contribute to economic revival. The peasant, unlike the proletarian worker,
lived in an extended household, the *dvor,* in which all members shared in
the family economy. If one member of the household, perhaps a young son,
fathered a child and then separated from the woman to whom he had been

married, the alimony exacted from him—it might be a cow to help feed the child—meant a loss to the entire household since they all lived together. For peasant protests along this line, see excerpts from the discussion of the marriage code in the Second Session of the Central Executive Committee of the RSFSR, October 1925, as reprinted in "Discussion of the Draft of the Code," pp. 107–108. For further discussion of the new marriage code, see *Brak i Sem'ia: Sbornik Statei i Materialov, Molodaia Gvardiia* [Marriage and the Family: Collected Articles and Materials, Young Guard] (Moscow, 1926), pp. 3–162.

24. For report of a debate between Aaron Sol'ts and Nikolai Krylenko, see *Izvestiya*, Nov. 17, 1925. Another reason cited by those favoring recognition only of registered marriage was that to do otherwise would encourage church marriage, unrecognized since 1918. In the countryside, where unregistered marriage was seen as debauchery, opinion was said to be against the new proposal. Kursky, however, in a speech carried in *Izvestiya*, Nov. 1926, reported that young people in the villages were favoring the recognition of *de facto* marriage. Reprinted in Schlesinger, *Family in the U.S.S.R.*, pp. 125–26. In a speech to the women's section of the party, Krylenko claimed that the regime had not anticipated the opposition the new law met. Jessica Smith, *Woman in Soviet Russia* (New York, 1928), p. 109.

25. Krylenko as quoted in "Discussion of the Draft of the Code," pp. 93, 112.

26. John Stuart Mill, "Early Essays on Marriage and Divorce," in Mill and Harriet Taylor Mill, *Essays on Sex Equality*, ed. Alice Rossi (Chicago, 1971), p. 73.

27. For Marcel Body's view, see his article, "Alexandra Kollontai," *Preuves*, 1952, supp. no. 14, pp. 17–19. Another close friend does not believe Body's contention that Kollontai wished to leave the party. Interview with a long-time friend of Kollontai's, Aug. 24, 1973, Moscow.

28. Kollontai, "Brak i byt" [Marriage and Daily Life], *Rabochii Sud* [Workers' Court], 1926, no. 5, p. 371.

29. Kollontai, *Sotsial'nye Osnovy Zhenskogo Voprosa*, p. 230.

30. Kollontai, "Obshchii kotel ili individual'nye alimenty?" [A Common Pot or Individual Alimony?], *Komsomolskaia Pravda* [Komsomol Truth], Feb. 2, 1926, p. 2.

31. Party worker quoted in Itkina, *Revoliutsioner*, 203; "Obshchii kotel ili individual'nye alimenty?" (Otkliki na stat'iu tov. Kollontai) [A Common Pot or Individual Alimony? Responses to Comrade Kollontai's Article], *Komsomolskaia Pravda*, Mar. 21, 1926, p. 4.

32. Leon Trotsky, "Okhrana materinstva i bor'ba za kul'turu" [Protection of Motherhood and the Struggle for Culture], in *Sochineniia* [Works] (Moscow, 1927), 21: 49. For Trotsky's view that the time was not yet ripe for thought-out schemes, initiated from above, see his *Voprosy Byta* [Problems of Everyday Life] (Moscow, 1923), p. 46.

33. Stephen F. Cohen, *Bukharin and the Bolshevik Revolution* (New York, 1973), p. 233; Moscow interview.

34. Cohen, *Bukharin and the Bolshevik Revolution*, p. 174.

35. See Kollontai, *Rabotnitsa i Krestianka*, 19; Zetkin, *Reminiscences*, pp. 53–57.

36. Kollontai, "Brak i byt," p. 373. Kollontai suggested that out of the approximately five million babies born in the Soviet Union each year, perhaps a

million would not be provided for by the marriage contracts and be in need of government support. Her marriage contract idea was called unrealistic by Smidovich, "Otmenit' li registratsiiu braka i sistemu alimentov" [Whether to Change Registration of Marriage and the System of Alimony], *Komsomolskaia Pravda*, Feb. 14, 1926, p. 2. For further criticism, see E. Lavrov, "Polovoi vopros i Molodezh'" [The Sexual Problem and Youth], *Molodaia Guardiia* [Young Guard], Mar. 1926, no. 3, p. 145.

37. Trotsky, "Protiv Prosveshchennogo Biurokratizma (A Takzhe i neprosveshchennogo)" [Against Bureaucracy, Progressive and Unprogressive], in *Sochineniia*, 21: 71–72.

38. Quoted in Fannina Halle, *Woman in Soviet Russia* (London, 1933), p. 123. Another letter from a group of working women asked, "Why should a deserted mother become a burden on society?" It urged a system of alimony: "For if once a man has succeeded in fooling a woman . . . then he should pay. . . . He will take care to avoid another time." One factory group wrote that if Comrade Kollontai's tax were introduced, then men would lose all shame and universal license would be the result. Ibid., 124, 122. For the Russian version of these letters, see *Brak i Sem'ia*, pp. 143–44.

39. Trotsky, "Okhrana materinstva i bor'ba za Kul'turu" and "Kul'tura i Sotsializm" [Culture and Socialism], in *Sochineniia, 21:* 50, 434. Emilian Iaroslavskii expressed identical views in his "Moral' i byt proletariata v perekhodnyi period" [Morality and Daily Life of the Proletariat in the Transitional Era], *Molodaia Guardiia*, May 1926, no. 3, pp. 15–151. Supporters of the marriage law liked to picture its opponents, in Krylenko's words, as philistines. Krylenko argued that Soviet policy was moving toward economic and political equality of the sexes despite opposition from philistines and peasants. Krylenko's arguments in favor of the new marriage law, "Obyvatel' nastupaet" [The Philistine Advances], *Pravda*, Jan. 15, 1926, are quoted in Trotsky, *Sochineniia*, 21: 514n.

40. From "Confession," a manuscript by Marx's daughter printed in Erich Fromm, *Marx's Concept of Man* (New York, 1962), p. 257.

41. Kollontai, *Autobiography*, p. 42.

42. *Ekran* [Screen], 1926, no. 5.

43. See Smidovich's conversation to Smith, in Smith, *Woman in Soviet Russia*, pp. 102–103; Smidovich, "O novom kodekse zakonov o brake i sem'e," pp. 45–46; and her "Nashi zadachi v oblasti pereustroistva byta," pp. 22–24. Smidovich argued that homes for mothers and children were too expensive for the state to carry, and she recommended local initiative on the part of working women to establish less expensive communal facilities such as day nurseries. She criticized the attitude of those who believed that the liberation of working women must come only from the strength and money of the state. It is difficult to determine the amount of real support for Kollontai in the women's section, since Smidovich may have exerted considerable influence because of her position on the Central Control Commission. But judging by the articles that did appear in *Kommunistka*, support was not widespread. Varvara Golubeva was one of the few voices in opposition to the new marriage law. "K diskussii po voprosam brachnogo i semeinogo prava" [Toward a Discussion of the Marriage and Family Law], *Kommunistka*, 1926, no. I, pp. 50–53.

44. As quoted in Cohen, *Bukharin*, p. 50.

45. E. H. Carr, *Socialism in One Country* (Baltimore, 1970), I: 39–40. The term "war communism" refers to the policies of the era of civil war, 1918–21. Many radical measures adopted during this period, such as labor conscription and forced requisitioning of grain from the peasants, were ended with the NEP; Carr himself cites Marx and Engels to the effect that women must be relieved of domestic care through the institution of communal dining halls and nurseries. Ibid., 38.

46. Lenin, *Sochineniia* (4th ed.; Moscow, 1951), 33: 258. For Lenin's observation concerning attitudes toward women, see Zetkin, *Reminiscences*, p. 56.

47. Carr, *Socialism in One Country*, I, 43.

48. Trotsky, *Voprosy Byta*, pp. 84–88.

49. Ibid., p. 81, and Trotsky, "Okhrana Materinstva i bor'ba za Kul'turu," p. 55.

50. Z. Rakitina, "Byt po zametkam rabotnits," [The Way of Life According to Notes of Working Women], *Kommunistka*, 1926, no. 12, pp. 32–36. Letters from working women to the journal, *Raboinitsa* [The Woman Worker], quoted in these pages in *Kommunistka* suggest their eagerness for social change. The enthusiasm of working women for child-care institutions and for the work of clubs trying to raise their political and social level is also documented.

51. The concept itself had been left vague by Marx and Engels, as Lenin explained when he chided Kollontai in 1919 for assuming prematurely to specify the future form of the socialist family. The Eighth Party Congress rejected incorporating in its new program Kollontai's proposals concerning the future disappearance of the individual, isolated family—proposals that she suggested despite Lenin's prior objection. Itkina, *Revoliutsioner*, p. 208. In her recollections, Kollontai refers to her proposals being rejected but also to her victory in getting passed a resolution concerning the need for the party to work more specifically among women. "Avtobiograficheskii Ocherk," p. 301.

52. For Kursky's remarks, see "Discussion of the Draft of the Code," p. 91; for Smidovich, "O Novom Kodekse zakonov o brake i sem'e," p. 46; for Kalinin, "Discussion of the Draft of the Code," p. 119. It is of interest that the 1918 legislation on the family had provisions for state care of dependents that were omitted from the 1926 legislation. For example, the section stating that parents were obliged to provide board and maintenance for their minor children, if they were in need and unable to work, was followed by a notation that the parental obligations here stated were to be suspended in the event of the children being maintained by public or governmental care. This notation was not included in the 1926 legislation. Similarly in 1918 it was stated that children were obliged to provide maintenance for needy parents unable to work unless the latter were to receive maintenance from the government in accord with the law of insurance against illness, old age, or social security. This proviso was omitted in 1926. See the text of the 1926 legislation in Schlesinger, *Family in the U.S.S.R.*, p. 163; compare with the 1918 family law, ibid., p. 40. Further indication that the state was moving away from assuming the burdens of the family was given in 1924 when Aleksei Rykov, chairman of the Council of Commissars, attacked the idea of children's homes as obviously inadequate and also unwise since they separated the child from productive labor. Carr, *Socialism in One Country*, I: 45.

53. See V. Svetlov, "Socialist Society and the Family," *Pod Znamenem Mark-sizma* [Under the Banner of Marxism], 1936, no. 6, translated and reprinted in Schlesinger, *Family in the U.S.S.R.*, p. 333. S. Volfson, renouncing as erroneous his thesis published in 1929 that socialism entailed the extinction of the family, now wrote that "assertions that socialism leads to the extinction of the family are profoundly mistaken and harmful." This renunciation is found in his "Socialism and the Family," in ibid., p. 315.

54. Kollontai, "Brak i byt," pp. 375–76.

55. For the most complete attack on Kollontai, see Lavrov, "Polovoi vopros i Molodezh'," p. 145. Calling Kollontai's statements an example of precisely the wrong kind of thinking, Lavrov accused her of trying in 1926, with her idea for abolishing alimony, to take revenge for the attacks on her sexual theories in 1923. The reference is to Kollontai's article, "Dorogu Krylatomu Erosu!" [To the Winged Eros!], *Molodaia Guardiia*, 1923, no. 3, pp. 111–24, and her novella, "Loves of Three Generations," which appeared in the collection, *Liubov pchel trydovykh* [Love of the Worker Bees], trans. Lilly Lore (Moscow, 1923), pp. 180–243. The notion that alimony acted as a restraint on the conduct of men was echoed in a letter to *Komsomolskaia Pravda*, Mar. 21, 1926, p. 4.

56. Lavrov, "Polovoi vopros i Molodezh'," p. 136.

57. August Bebel, *Die Frau in der Vergangenheit, Gegenwart und Zukunft* (Zurich, 1883), trans. by Daniel De Leon as *Woman under Socialism* (New York, 1971), p. 343.

58. *V Vserossiiskii S"ezk RKSM* (Moscow, 1927), pp. 114, 124–25.

59. Polina Vinogradskaia, "Voprosy morali, pola, byta, i tov. Kollontai" [Questions of Morality, Sex, Daily Life, and Comrade Kollontai], *Krasnaia Nov'* [Red Virgin Soil], 1923, no. 6, p. 190. For the apology to Kollontai, see ibid., no. 7, p. 306.

60. Iaroslavskii, "Moral' i byt proletariata v perekhodnyi period," p. 150. Without using Kollontai's name, Iaroslavskii referred to the collection of stories by Kollontai with that title. The distortions concerning her views were so widespread that her titles alone had come to signify debauchery.

61. As quoted by an observer at the meeting, in Smith, *Woman in Soviet Russia*, p. 117. Riazanov insists that even in the Communist future there would be registration of marriage, but it would then be regarded as an obligation as natural as the obligation to work. His views are explained in his "Marks i Engels o brake i sem'e," pp. 34–35. That same year, 1927, the views of party leaders concerning personal morality were published in Izrail Razin, ed., *Komsomolskii byt* [Everyday Life for Komsomols] (Moscow, 1927). Bukharin, Lunacharsky, and Iaroslavskii were among the many who advocated greater sexual restraint—the orthodox party view.

62. Nathan Leites, *A Study of Bolshevism* (Glencoe, Ill., 1953), p. 186.

63. Freud analyzed the problem in 1930 in his *Civilization and Its Discontents* (New York, 1930), pp. 56–57. For Kollontai's glorification of work conscription that existed during the war communism era and her view that it was the best hope for women's true liberation, see her *Polozhenie Zhenshchiny v Evoliutsii Khoziaistva* [The Position of Women in Connection with the Development of the Economy] (Moscow, 1923), pp. 152, 166. For suggestions as to the primary place work, rather than love, would have in the proposed commune, see "Brak i byt," p. 376. Elsewhere, however, Kollontai

suggests that love was for her a source of energy. *Autobiography*, p. 22.

64. For Herbert Marcuse's view, see his *Soviet Marxism* (New York, 1961), pp. 233–34.

65. Body, "Alexandra Kollontai," p. 17.

66. "Lenin Chto tam ni boltai. Soglasna s nim lish' Kollontai" [No matter what Lenin babbles, only Kollontai agrees with him]. Kollontai, "Avtobiograficheskii Ocherk," p. 296.

67. *X S"ezda Rossiiskoi Kommunisticheskoi Partii (8–16 Marta 1921 g) Stenograficheskii Otchet* (Petrograd, 1921), 48. Lenin implied that Kollontai had resumed her former liaison with the commissar of labor, Alexander Shliapnikov. This was particularly awkward because Kollontai was married to Pavel Dybenko, also in the Soviet government.

68. Trotsky and Karl Radek as quoted in *Tretii Vsemirnyi Kongress Kommunisticheskogo Internatsionala Stenograficheskii Otchet* (Petrograd, 1922), p. 372; Stalin as quoted in Svetlana Alliluyeva, *Only One Year* (New York, 1969), p. 381.

69. Kollontai wrote to Elga Kern, editor of the series, Leading Women of Europe, apologizing for the extensive revisions she had made in her manuscript. It could not be otherwise, she explained. The changes had to be made because she was an "official person." Since her revisions were so drastic, Kollontai offered to bear the cost of any additional expenses they might cause. This letter, dated July 19, 1926, appears as a center insert in Kollontai, *Autobiographie Einer Sexuell Emanzipierten Kommunistin* (Munich, 1970). It is omitted in the English edition, thus allowing for a somewhat disingenuous introduction speculating as to why the revisions were made.

70. Michael Futrell, *Northern Underground* (New York, 1963), pp. 113–14.

71. After her exile, in part to disassociate herself from the supporters of Trotsky, Kollontai sent to the party archives letters written by Lenin during the prerevolutionary period. Some passages, highly critical of Trotsky, were later used as part of the campaign to discredit him. But Lev Kamenev, who edited the first edition of these letters, omitted the most damaging words, "What a swine that Trotsky." See Lenin to Kollontai, Feb. 17, 1917, in *Leninskii Sbornik* [Lenin Miscellany] (Moscow, 1924), 2: 282. Compare this letter with the complete version that appears in Olga H. Gankin and H. H. Fisher, *The Bolsheviks and the World War: The Origin of the Third International* (Stanford, 1940), p. 576.

72. Kollontai, "Oppozitsiia i partiinaia massa" [The Opposition and the Party Rank and File], *Pravda* Oct. 30, 1927.

73. Alliluyeva, *Only One Year*, p. 381.

74. Kollontai, "Sovetskaia Zhenshchina—Polnopravnaia Grazhdanka Svoei Strany" [The Soviet Woman—A Citizen with Full Rights in Her Own Country], in her *Izbrannye Stat'i i Rechi*, p. 378.

75. Stalin quoted in Robert H. McNeal, *Bride of the Revolution: Krupskaya and Lenin* (Ann Arbor, 1972), p. 245.

76. Roy Medvedev writes of the humiliation and terror Old Bolsheviks like Kollontai were subjected to but kept alive in his *Let History Judge: The Origins and Consequences of Stalinism*, trans. Colleen Taylor, ed. David Joravsky and Georges Haupt (New York, 1971), p. 200. Like Krupskaia, Kollontai was a useful symbol. A Moscow friend recalled that when Kollontai

returned to Moscow during her last years in the late forties she was regarded as an "internal exile"; friends kept away, afraid to visit the old woman. This same man, who spoke of Kollontai's close friend, Elena Stasova, another Old Bolshevik, as also isolated from the party, attributes their survival in part to the fact that they were women. Moscow interview. Robert Daniels suggests that it was a streak of Georgian chivalry that kept Stalin from purging Old Bolshevik oppositionists Kollontai and Nikolaeva. *The Conscience of the Revolution* (Cambridge, Mass., 1960), p. 389. I think, rather, that it was Stalin's contempt for women more than his supposed chivalry that enabled these two former oppositionists to survive. Stalin, of course, did not hesitate to purge the wives of Bolsheviks. And there may be one notable exception to the survival of oppositionist women. Medvedev writes that Varvara Iakovleva, an oppositionist in 1918 who was forced to testify against Bukharin in 1939, was later shot. *Let History Judge*, p. 181. Robert Conquest reported that Iakovleva supposedly survived until 1944. *The Great Terror* (New York, 1968), p. 400.

8 • Five Socialist Women: Traditionalist Conflicts and Socialist Visions in Austria, 1893–1934

• Ingrun Lafleur

The Bolshevik Revolution split European socialism into two hostile groups—communists who sided with Lenin's slogan "from dictatorship to democracy" and his tactic of working-class seizure of power through soviets; and socialists, committed to the acquisition of power through democratic, parliamentary means. The Austrian Socialist party, however, proved an exception. Known in the prewar period as the second pillar of Social Democracy in the International, the party preserved unity by speaking a revolutionary language and performing a cautious and pragmatic act. This delicate balance, known as Austromarxism, reconciled moderates and radicals in the organization. After the war, which saw the transition of Austria from a multinational empire to a small, conservative, traditional society, the party engaged in radical social reform in the capital city, Vienna. Its socialist women, who had reneged on the issue of women's suffrage in 1907, came into their own. Unlike many continental socialist feminists who gave up their radicalism in the postwar decade, Austrians kept alive the association of radical feminism with socialism. Austrian socialist feminists were trying to bring working women into public life. Following the self-educated working woman Adelheid Popp, socialist feminists sought to teach them about self-worth, the necessity of work outside the home and about hygiene, child care, clothing, and religion. Did this signify a process of integrating working women into modern urban life or was it more— part of an integrated socialist vision in which the awakening of women was seen as necessary to the transformation of society? What different approaches characterized leading Austrian socialist feminists? Why did this party, with its revolutionary and pragmatic mix, adopt a program of radical feminist reform fifty years in advance of its time? What effect did socialist feminist deliberations have on the greater Austrian society?

━━━━━━━━━━━━

In clerical, conservative, traditionalist Austria, a socialist women's movement grew to become one of the largest, most active, and most innovative in Europe. By 1925 the Austrian proletarian women's movement counted 165,000 adherents. Women comprised 29.7 percent of the total membership of the Social Democratic party, a proportion exceeded only by Denmark among European socialist parties.[1] In the following year, at the Linz party congress of 1926, women contributed to a party program, which included a wide-ranging, integrated section on the position of women in society: in work, education, religion, and family law. For the first time for any political party, a section on population policy advocated the legalization and free availability of abortion, as well as the free distribution of birth control information and contraceptive devices.[2] The population policy was considered crucial for the emancipation of women, which, in turn, was recognized as essential to the transformation of society and culture.

This program was propounded in one of the most polarized countries of Europe. Liberal forces were overshadowed by a powerful socialist movement that confronted (and avoided) a politically influential Catholic Church, nascent fascist movements, and an apparently stolidly conservative peasantry. Women of all classes were thought to be under the sway of the clergy. The urban small bourgeoisie nourished a sentimental admiration for the old Habsburg monarchy and its cosmopolitan aristocracy.

The women's movement within Austrian Social Democracy in many ways expressed the characteristic virtues and dilemmas of that party as a whole. These virtues and dilemmas have been called, collectively, Austromarxism. A typical appraisal has

216

been that "the Social Democratic party of Austria attracted some of the keenest minds to espouse socialism anywhere."[3] The party was organized and unified by Viktor Adler and developed by such brilliant theorists as Otto Bauer, Karl Renner, and Max Adler. It was much admired in the prewar Second International and led efforts to revitalize and radicalize international socialism after World War I. Austromarxists viewed themselves as standing between the reformism of the German Majority Socialists (and other Western Social Democrats) and the bolshevism of the Russians. In principle, they refused to accept revisionism, Bernstein's theory of the gradual transformation of society through reform. Nor did they look upon the Bolshevik example as a viable alternative for a developed European country. Still, they considered themselves revolutionaries dedicated to class struggle and the socialization of the economic system.[4]

The party was a powerful network, systematically organized to penetrate every aspect of working-class life. The party coordinated a strong trade-union movement, educational and cultural associations, youth groups, choral societies, sports clubs, consumer cooperatives, and a system of cadres (*Vertrauensmaenner*) that held these various organizations together. In her discussion of socialism and feminism, Sheila Rowbotham observes that "socialism was not seen only as public ownership, or the control of the worker over the product of his or her labor, it was also the search for a new ethic, a new culture, a new life."[5] This was nowhere more true than in Austria. G.D.H. Cole concludes that "even more than in Germany, socialism became, above all in Vienna, a way of life and developed its own cultural institutions in both the intellectual and the artistic fields. It had its own music. . . . It had its own educational services, extending over a wide field." Indeed, "the Austrian, or at any rate the Viennese socialists became the most highly cultured and instructed body of proletarians in the entire world."[6] A recent work, *Dionysian Art and Populist Politics*, by William J. McGrath, explores the relationship between art and politics in Austria, documenting the particular commitment that Austrian socialists made to cultural change because of their assumption of the coherence of social and cultural developments. He

217

quotes an 1887 article by Viktor Adler, in which the party founder, who was also a medical doctor and psychiatrist, "saw two sides to the coming world revolution." "In a purely mechanical fashion the economic revolution goes its inexorable way . . . but a revolution in the consciousness of mankind goes forward at the same time. . . . The revolutionizing of the brain is the real assignment, the immediate goal, of the proletarian parties of Social Democracy."[7] Another commentator observed that "the social-democratic agitators became missionaries who first had to save humans and humanity. . . ." Viktor Adler was "an incomparable educator [who] constantly worked to elevate the working class morally and culturally. . . ."[8] When the socialist International resolved to adopt May Day as a tool for organization and propaganda, the Austrian socialists were among the most enthusiastic. They turned the observance into a mass drama, a spiritual celebration to electrify the working classes. A frightened church and state responded with more resplendent ceremonies: the sovereign was moved to march in holy day processions as an exercise in popular politics.

What the party prized above all was unity, and it took care not to split like the unfortunate German Social Democratic party. The emphasis on unity caused the party to behave, in actual practice, and under crisis conditions, with hesitation and ambivalence. Revolutionary rhetoric appealed to party radicals while frightening the middle classes with the bugbear of bolshevism. Pragmatic reform confirmed the loyalty of party moderates without dissipating the paranoia of the bourgeoisie, or lessening the dangers of civil war and fascism. It has been remarked that Austrian physicians valued diagnosis above cure, and a similar accusation may be leveled against Austromarxist theoreticians.[9] Socialist cultural organizations served to assimilate and integrate workers into modern life, but there remained a gap between the learned revolutionary "doctors" who ran the party and the workers who often looked in vain for the implementation and actualization of socialist measures.

The party's attitude toward its own women's movement, too, was marked by ambivalence and hesitancy. In theory women enjoyed all manner of equal rights, but in practice they were

218

hindered and inhibited. Working women were held to be apathetic and clerical; they were obstacles to the political activity of working men. The proletarian women's movement, by its own accounts, encountered limitations and suspicion from male socialists, yet it always remained within the discipline of the Social Democratic party. Class differences, after all, and not sexual oppression sped the motor of social change; women would be emancipated when the socialist revolution had eliminated capitalist exploitation. In most cases, therefore, socialist women subordinated their demands and their interests to party policy and party unity.

What were the alternatives? In Austria, the Christian Social party, the Pan German nationalists, and even the liberals generally opposed extending political rights to women. Only the Social Democratic party, in its programs and policy declarations, if not always in tactics and practice, supported civil and social rights for women. The middle-class women's movement, though it contained some internationally recognized figures, was apolitical, small, and limited in influence.[10] The best-known female public figure was Bertha von Suttner, the aristocratic pacifist, who believed women had a special role to play in supporting and promoting peace, but was not a feminist. Also prominent was the moderate Rosa Mayreder, author of *Zur Kritik der Weiblichkeit* (1905; *Toward a Critique of the Feminine*, translated in 1912 as *A Survey of the Woman Problem*). Mayreder founded the General Austrian Women's Association in 1893, supporting greater rights for women, but believing that women had a special civilizing mission. She disputed patriarchal psychoanalysis and advocated androgyny and harmony between the sexes. Her influence, however, tended to be limited to intellectuals.[11]

Basically, the Austrian bourgeois women's movement consisted of two strands. The more conservative wing, led by Marianne Hainisch, devoted efforts to gaining women admission to higher education and the professions. It was cautious, gradualist, and patriotic. For a long time Hainisch kept her distance from the women's suffrage movement, because she was reluctant to see women engage in "dirty political struggles."[12] Auguste Fickert represented the more liberal bourgeois movement

but never joined a political party.[13] Despite occasional cooperation between the liberal women and the socialists, differences
of policy and approach remained. There was particular suspicion of the more conservative bourgeois feminists who, socialists believed, "would never accept laboring women's views on
illegitimacy and prostitution" and who often did not support the
suffrage for women of all social classes, and expressed anti-Se-
mitic overtones.[14] The largest women's movement in Austria,
however, consisted of various Catholic organizations, led by the
devout Princess Pauline Metternich. While supporting protective legislation, the Catholics firmly upheld the sanctity of
woman's place in the home and family, deploring the necessity
of outside labor for some women.[15]

Socialist women leaders, then, maintained that it was left to
the proletarian women's movement to defend suffrage and
equality—as well as to fight for better working conditions for
women and to participate in the struggle for the social revolution that would remove all exploitation and make emancipation
possible. The origins of the Austrian proletarian women's
movement were modest: at the founding congress of the Austrian Social Democratic party at Hainfeld in 1888–89, the sole
woman delegate was turned away by the other members, who,
however, proceeded to place a demand for the political and social equality of women into their first party program.[16] In the
early 1890s only a handful of women met as a "Working
Women's Educational Society," while young female industrial
workers initiated several strikes.[17] At the 1907 meeting in Stuttgart of socialist women from many countries, the Austrian delegation was reprimanded by Clara Zetkin for having abandoned
the demand for women's suffrage during the 1906 compaign to
extend the suffrage to all adult males in Austria.[18] Soon thereafter, the Austrian socialist women energetically extended their
recruitment efforts and increased their political demands. During World War I, women swelled into the industrial labor
force in unprecedented numbers, and the socialist women's
movement expanded as well. Women received the franchise,
and socialist women leaders were elected to parliament and the
national leadership of the party.

220

ADELHEID POPP. Fotokopie aus dem Bestand des Dokumentationsarchiv des Österreichischen Widerstandes.

Just as the male Austromarxists were deemed the radical leaders of the international Social Democratic movement (the communist split having taken place), so Austrian socialist women took the leadership in the European socialist women's movement as well. The founder of the socialist women's movement in Austria, Adelheid Popp, revived the international socialist women's movement that encompassed more than 900,000 women in 1925. She succeeded its first leader, Zetkin, who had become a communist.[19] The German socialist movement had relegated the "woman question" to a low-priority position. Indeed, reaction had set in, both in theoretical discussions of women's issues, and in the continuing actual behavior of socialist leaders and workers. Popp observed that the postwar German Social Democratic party did not like to see women going in independent directions. She asserted that socialist women in all countries needed an organization to discuss and defend matters of special interest to women.[20]

For socialist women leaders, as for the Austromarxist men, socialism represented not simply a political and social movement, but a high ideal, a new culture. And, the transformation toward that culture did not await the revolution, but had to begin with and within the movement itself. In an essay (1911) entitled "Women are Awakening," Adelheid Popp wrote that it was the task of socialism to touch "the most oppressed, poorest and most deprived among humanity," and to "awaken them from their spiritual sleep." Popp thought that socialism would be important for women not primarily because of its theoretical explanations, but because it could "speak to their hearts, develop their consciousness, give them endurance, strength and self-respect."[21] To socialist organizers, culture did imply bringing some of the positive aspects of bourgeois culture to women; hence their sponsorship of working women's educational and literary societies. But culture, for them, also dealt with the daily lives of women: attitudes toward one's household, birth control, child rearing, attitudes toward one's work, working conditions, and fellow workers. While the socialist women's movement did not substantively explore ideas current in today's women's movement about sexuality, sex roles, and patriarchal culture, it did go beyond demands for economic and political change. It did express concern for daily relationships and attitudes.

The particular quality of the problems faced by Austrian socialist feminists and their approaches to these problems reflected both the traditionalism of Austrian society and the ambiguities of radical-moderate Austromarxism. The socialist women's movement shared some of the characteristics and conflicts of Austromarxism—ambivalence between radical theory and moderate practice, an emphasis on cultural education as well as on political organization. The conflicts faced by socialist women and the approaches they proposed, can best be understood by examining some of the leaders of the Austrian proletarian women's movement and some of the issues to which they devoted the most energy. The relationship between feminism and socialism was expressed in several conflicts in which different groups of women in the movement advocated varying approaches.

Five women very well represent the varieties of emphases, concerns, and activities of the Austrian socialist women's movement from 1893 to 1934, and helped shape that movement. Some worked untiringly to bring feminist concerns to the attention of the party; some organized the trade-union and cooperative movements; others sought to involve women in politics and policymaking at all levels. Adelheid Popp, Therese Schlesinger, Gabriele Proft, and Emmy Freundlich devoted half a century to the cause of working women; they were leaders of the movement from the beginning of the twentieth century to the end of their lives. Kaethe Leichter was relatively younger and met her death in a Nazi concentration camp. She provided a radical critique of the socialist movement and its tactics in the era of fascism.

Without question, women in the Austrian movement and those internationally, considered Adelheid Popp-Dworak (1869 –1939) their leader and "awakener." Popp first received international attention with her *Autobiography of a Working Woman* (1909), a strong, simply written account of her childhood among impoverished urban workers and of her involvement in the causes of women and socialism.[22] The book became a best-seller, going through six editions by 1930. Popp was known as an energetic organizer and bombastic speaker, and was often characterized as an enthusiastic, naive, and clever personality.

Popp came from a poor working-class Viennese background. She received a scant third-grade education and soon became a factory girl to help support her family. A frustrated student, she read widely in her spare time, moving from sentimental romances to newspapers and political tracts. Overcoming a basic shyness, she began to read aloud to her workmates and aroused the suspicion of her superiors. Popp was drawn to the socialist movement because it spoke to the concerns of female as well as male workers. When her brother took her to a socialist meeting she heard the speaker describe "the conditions of women's labor," and go on to show that "the holding back, the absence of wants, and the contentedness of women workers were crimes which drew all other evils in their train."[23] There were only a few women present and Popp "felt great shame at the indifference and backwardness" of her fellow women. She was impressed by the party's concern for the most exploited group, women, and was moved to make her first impromptu speech at this meeting. She encouraged other young women to engage in organizational work, strikes, and demonstrations, and was chosen editor of the *Arbeiterinnenzeitung* (Working Women's Newspaper) in 1892. In short, Popp became a socialist because of the movement's concern for women and the urban poor.[24]

Adelheid Dworak had married the party cashier, Julius Popp, who was twenty years her senior. They had two sons, and Adelheid was left widowed after seven years of marriage. After World War I, Popp became a member of parliament and devoted herself to social legislation, party organization, and the revival of the international women's movement. She became ill in the early 1930s, and resigned her major posts. At the time of the suppression of the Social Democratic party by Engelbert Dollfuss's clerical-authoritarian regime in 1934, she was in the hospital and escaped arrest, remaining sickly until her death in 1939.[25]

Though Popp differed with male party leaders on some issues

—she wished for a more vigorous opposition to World War I, and she wanted to participate in an international women's conference called by Clara Zetkin in 1915—she usually remained loyal to party discipline.[26] She occupied a position similar to that of Viktor Adler in the general party: she was the organizer, the uniter, the centrist, who smoothed out differences of opinion or pushed them under the rug in the interests of party unity. While she did not make any theoretical contributions to socialist feminism, she attempted to publicize the conditions of working women and to popularize socialist theory and feminist history. In her *Autobiography* she wrote that "socialism had given me so much, had lent my life so much peace, that I had strength to go through much without succumbing. To be inspired to serve a great cause gives so much joy, and lends so much high worth to life, that one can bear very much without losing courage."[27] The socialist party then, made it possible for women to engage in public life, and gave them structure and meaning for the exercise of courage. Despite Popp's preoccupation with organizational and parliamentary problems, she continued to grapple with women's issues. Her last writing, an unpublished manuscript called "Leni," dealt with the coming to feminist consciousness of a young girl who leaves her husband. Having overcome fear and hesitancy, she longs "to cry out for what she would like to achieve for her sex," resolving "to study in order to acquire the intellectual weapons" she would need in order to work for the "spiritual awakening of women."[28]

Therese Schlesinger (née Eckstein, 1863–1940), more than any other leader of Austrian Social Democracy, concerned herself with the relationship of feminist ideology to working-class women. The daughter of a wealthy, liberal Viennese industrialist, she became active in the middle-class women's movement. Her husband died early of tuberculosis; she herself was sickly and had difficulty walking most of her life. Together with her brother, Schlesinger wrote "The Woman in the Nineteenth Century." She had a humanitarian interest in working women and with Rosa Mayreder was elected by the Women's League to a commission studying the condition of female labor. Schlesinger met Popp and other socialist women at parliamentary hearings on this topic. When she proposed adding the problems of working women and issues such as prostitution to the public agenda of an international bourgeois women's gathering, she was rebuffed. Disappointed with the middle-class feminists' lack of understanding for the problems of working women, she concluded that the bourgeois women's movement would never achieve any influence if it remained aloof from political parties. Schlesinger joined the Social Democratic party, retaining a liaison role to the bourgeois feminist movement. In the theoretical journals *Sozialistische Monatshefte, Neue Zeit,* and *Der Kampf* she spoke out on feminist issues. She belonged to the party's left wing during World War I, and sympathized with Friedrich Adler's assassination of the Austrian prime minister in 1916 as a revolutionary act. After the war, she collaborated with Friedrich Adler in attempts to create an International (the 2½ International) that was more radical than the old Second International without being dominated, as was the Third, by Moscow and bolshevism. Schlesinger worked closely with Otto Bauer in the development of the radical 1926 party program, especially the section on women. Forced to emigrate during the fascist period, she died in exile in France shortly before the entry of German troops into Paris.[29]

Like Popp, Schlesinger emphasized that socialism was a "cultural movement intended to lead us out of misery and barbarism toward true humanity."[30] Schlesinger agreed that the pioneers of the bourgeois women's movement had pointed to the profound common problems which confronted women of all social classes and nations. In her view, however, bourgeois women did not consider how these problems (which are today described as sexism and ascribed to the structure of patriarchal society), affect women of different classes in different ways. She criticized the bourgeois movement for being too cautious and vacillating, for not probing deeply enough beyond such issues as political disfranchisement to more fundamental problems such as marriage and family rights, and the double standard of morality. It was bourgeois men, Schlesinger declared, who prevent women from having their own work, and keep them in a

226

state of social and economic dependency. The contemporary social order, she stated, rested to a large extent upon the serfdom of woman, buttressed by bourgeois moral prejudices.[31] While she criticized the bourgeois women's movement, Schlesinger believed that all women's movements inherently contained revolutionary potential. Even the attempts of women to gain access to higher education and the liberal professions, she noted, everywhere encountered obstinate opposition from men. This opposition originated not only from the fear of female competition, but also from the "habitual clinging to old concepts and dogmas" that restrict women to the narrowness of domestic life, such as the "ideal of true womanhood."[32] Schlesinger maintained that both male and female opponents of the women's movement do perceive, however dimly, that "to free woman from her bonds would mean to lay the axe to the roots of the existing order." Of all the Austrian socialist leaders, Schlesinger comes closest to radical feminism, for she declared that the ultimate emancipation of women, "the first slaves in history," would make impossible all other discrimination, subordination, and exploitation.[33] To her, therefore, the women's movement was not ancillary, but central, to the revolutionary and cultural mission of socialism.

Gabriele Proft (1879–1971) came from a poor Silesian shoemaker's family. Typically, she left school at the age of thirteen to become a domestic servant and was trained in needlework and dressmaking. Proft was impressed by massive May Day demonstrations in the 1890s. Anxious to extend her meager education, she joined groups of working women first in educational and then in trade union organizations. She met Adelheid Popp and discovered women of similar backgrounds and ideas with whom she could collaborate. She became Popp's assistant in forming the women's political organization within the Social Democratic party.[34] Proft was a stout internationalist during World War I and became vice president of the Karl Marx Society, the left wing of Austrian socialism led by Friedrich Adler. After Adler's *Attentat* and imprisonment, Proft became the spokeswoman of the party's left wing. In the first Austrian republic that followed the war she entered parliament, joining with Popp in proposing bills for the reform of the family laws that emphasized absolute patriarchal authority. Though Proft participated in the women's movement, her primary activities lay within general party politics. She did, however, defend the feminist policies laid out by Schlesinger in the 1926 program. Proft was arrested after 1934 and engaged in underground activities upon her release; her last arrest was in January 1945. After World War II, she played a leading part in reconstituting the Austrian Socialist party and devoted more time to women's issues, chairing the central committee of socialist women. In parliament in the 1950s, she found herself presenting some of the same bills on family law, abortion, and women's rights that she had sponsored with Adelheid Popp in the 1920s.[35] In the 1950s, however, relatively fewer of the younger women in Austria were willing to commit themselves to feminist demands.

Emmy Freundlich (1871–1948) grew up in a bourgeois family in Bohemia and early showed interest in politics. Of her youth, she wrote, "For many years I only had one wish: to be a boy, so that I could be the center of a circle of people interested in public affairs.... Instead, I was the daughter of the house, whose life goal was intended to be marriage."[36] She married a Jewish social democrat, from whom she was later divorced. Freundlich was particularly concerned with child welfare, acting as secretary of the Kinderfreunde (Friends of Children). She worked in the socialist consumer cooperative movement, and in the international consumer co-op movement as well. In 1929 she became the only woman in the Economic Council of the League of Nations. Freundlich was arrested in the 1930s, later freed, and emigrated to London after the *Anschluss*. She lived in New York in 1947, becoming an observer to the International Cooperative Guild.[37]

In 1912, Freundlich wrote a pamphlet, "The Woman Question," which was intended as a primer or guide to lectures and discussions for women party organizers. The pamphlet followed traditional socialist thinking, that is, Engels and Bebel, on the subject: "Just as social conditions have changed with every stage of human development, so also has the position of woman and her valuation by any given society." Freundlich discussed the earliest stages of history, the period of "mother right," when men and women had "equal rights and equal duties." But man the hunter needed a legitimate heir for his property, and thus woman gradually became the property, the slave of man.[38] Freundlich outlined the history of women in antiquity, in the Middle Ages, and went on to discuss the development of technology as well as women's work and motherhood in the industrial revolution.

Freundlich supported protective legislation for women workers and was a strong advocate of the rationalization of the household, of mechanization and of communal household facilities. As a member of parliament after World War I, she often presented socialist women's demands on a wide range of issues. For example, she protested that women were punished for prostitution while men went free, and demanded decriminalization and greater education about sexuality and sexual diseases in the public schools as better approaches to the problem. Women were entitled to sex education: "Woman, too, must learn to be true to herself; she must learn that she should not merely be the object of sexual life, but the leading, directing personality, who will educate society to purer morality and honor. Woman should no longer be a slave, but an equal human being, who can defend her honor and dignity."[39] This demand for greater freedom for women, it must be noted, was accompanied by the assumption that woman, being purer, would take the lead in moral regeneration. Though Freundlich personally led a very independent life, some of her views on women's roles and natures were rather traditional.

Kaethe Leichter (1895–1942) belonged to the younger generation of socialist women, the generation of postwar economic and political turmoil and disillusionment. She was the brilliant daughter of a cultivated, wealthy Jewish Viennese family. Leichter interested herself in the problems of the poor at an early age and became a socialist during her studies of political economy at the University of Vienna. Her views on the relationship between feminism and socialism were the traditional socialist ones: women could only achieve their emancipation in the struggle against the existing social order. Though angered

229

by the discrimination against women at the University, Leichter remained suspicious of and hostile to bourgeois feminists:

I have never had a comfortable relationship to the women's movement. I was much too normal for any kind of one-sided eccentricity. The struggle of the women's movement consisted of wearing new styles of clothing, of smiling condescendingly at the mention of the word *men*, of petitioning the parties in parliament, of organizing women's club evenings as the center of the lives, it seemed to me, of frustrated old-maidish types of creatures. Furthermore, these women always sought to give assurances that they were in no way provocative or radical, that they hoped to achieve their rights peacefully without touching the existing social order. They were overjoyed if, somewhere in the world, a woman became a professor or government minister or achieved some sort of leading role. These women did not realize that the issue was not opportunity for a few privileged women, but the raising of the miserable conditions of working women.[40]

No matter how appropriate some of Leichter's criticisms were, the condescending tone indicates a lack of sympathy and understanding for the dilemmas faced by middle-class women. Leichter certainly was no radical feminist. But she did belong to the radical left wing of the Social Democratic party in 1918 and 1919. She was sympathetic to the Austrian workers' council movement modeled on the Russian soviets, and worked on the Socialization Commission to reconstruct the economy. When the socialists left the coalition government in 1920, Kaethe Leichter went to work for the Chamber of Labor *(Arbeiterkammer)*, turning to the problems of working women. She published several theoretical works on socioeconomic problems as well as a collection on the conditions and attitudes of working women. She married Otto Leichter, the editor of the social newspaper, *Arbeiterzeitung*. They had two sons, one of whom is now active in New York politics. After 1934 Leichter went underground as a revolutionary socialist. Though her husband and two sons escaped the country, she was arrested by the Gestapo. She wrote a moving autobiographical memorandum in prison and perished in Ravensbrueck concentration camp in 1942.[41]

These five women were chosen for this study because they all participated prominently and over a long period of time in the socialist women's movement and enjoyed respected leadership positions in the party as a whole; they all gained international reputations and they all grappled with the effects of World War I and the postwar period on women. They all dealt, however, with the relationships between feminism and socialism in different ways and they held contradictory points of view. Popp and Freundlich were centrists in the party and devoted most of their time to women's issues and organizations. Schlesinger contributed equally to the general party and to the socialist women's movement, both in the development of theory and in practical organizational work. Proft, a left-wing socialist, put work among women second to general party activity, insisting that women must be integrated fully and equally into the party, not relegated to a special position. Leichter was a radical socialist. As with Zetkin, this did not imply a consistent radical position on feminist issues such as sex roles and the family. Class was overarching, not sex, and the point for Leichter was to bring women to working-class consciousness.

The ways in which these five women related socialism and feminism can be discerned by examining the kinds of issues which engaged them, and how their actions and ideas developed with changing political contexts. The suffrage, the role of women in politics, women's work, protective legislation, and the cultural changes required to fulfill a vision of the future socialist society involved Austrian socialist women in conflicts with tradition, with their male party comrades, and with the bourgeois women's movement.

Before World War I, the attention of the socialist women's movement focused upon the suffrage and working conditions of proletarian women. Its most significant prewar meeting (the Third Conference of 1908) was entitled "Women's Suffrage and Protective Legislation." [42] From the first, party programs had demanded the "abolition of all laws which discriminate against women." During the 1890s and early 1900s the socialist women's newspaper consistently carried articles to educate working women about the suffrage. Adelheid Popp told a parliamentary commission that sexual differences were given no consideration in the workplace and that therefore sex should not be taken into consideration in the distribution of rights. Woman was a coworker and participated in the productive life of society; she contributed taxes, and therefore she should have the same rights as the working man.[43] The suffrage question was also used to educate working women about feminist issues in general. In an 1899 article on women's suffrage, Popp discussed the historical reasons for the inferiority and oppression of women. When women were granted the franchise, she hoped, they would develop their intellectual abilities and self-consciousness, so that instead of presenting their children with "an image of humility and subordination, they would teach them to value the independent, spiritually developed personality."[44]

In trying to reach working women, socialist women could not count on the practical support of socialist men; indeed, they were often met with hostility and the suspicion that they were bourgeois "women's righters." Socialist women decried the indifference of "even radical and freethinking men who don't mind at all that their wives and daughters get their instructions in the confessional."[45] Even as women were acknowledged to have equal rights theoretically, women socialists complained that in practice "male comrades often were not mature enough to accept the demand for women's suffrage and the necessity that women participate equally with men in the struggle for socialism."[46]

That even sympathetic male colleagues considered women's suffrage a distant, somewhat impractical goal became evident in 1905–1906, when the Social Democratic party decided to push for the expansion of the franchise, but only for universal manhood suffrage. The outbreak of the Russian revolution in 1905 and the Habsburg emperor's continuing difficulties with the Hungarians made the moment propitious. The pragmatic Social Democratic leadership now asked socialist women to participate in the strikes, meetings, and demonstrations for universal manhood suffrage and to keep their demands for the female franchise in the background. There was little question of breaking party discipline for socialist feminists. Freundlich justified their subordination to party policy by pointing out that in engaging wholeheartedly in the male suffrage campaign, the socialist women's organizations did not act as isolated, separate, and ineffective auxiliaries, but rather were helping to organize men, and participating fully in enacting the policies of the party as a whole. Further, she maintained that under contemporary political pressures, the demand for women's suffrage, which had been too little analyzed and discussed in the general public, would only seem diversionary and confusing.[47] Popp explained that socialist women were not withdrawing the demand for women's suffrage, but were choosing temporarily not to emphasize it. Participation in the struggle for general suffrage would help to raise the political consciousness of women and make them better prepared to participate in public life.[48] Schlesinger was uncomfortably aware that the bourgeois parties, who had long opposed women's suffrage, now accused the socialists of hypocrisy and opportunism. In an era of mass politics, even Catholic conservatives were beginning to favor women's suffrage, both to confuse the campaign for universal manhood suffrage, and to be able to manipulate the votes of unenlightened women. Nonetheless, Schlesinger steadfastly supported the policy of the party—but she continued to hold women's suffrage meetings during the 1906 campaign.[49]

More telling criticism was leveled at Austrian socialist women at the first international conference of socialist women in 1907, in Stuttgart. There they were engaged in debate with the leader of the international movement, Clara Zetkin. It was mistaken, Zetkin insisted, to postpone the struggle for women's suffrage until male suffrage was achieved. The proletarian women's movement of all countries had an immediate task: to educate women to socialism and to the class struggle so that they could become fighters for their own liberation. It was the duty of proletarian women to struggle energetically and immediately for the greater democratization of society in general, and for the women's franchise in particular.[50]

In their defense, Schlesinger and Popp reiterated that their tactics had not harmed or hindered the fight for women's suffrage in Austria, that the special conditions of Austrian society had to be taken into account, and that the women had never surrendered the principle of women's suffrage. The victory of socialist men would also be a victory for women, for when socialist deputies were elected to parliament, they would work to fulfill the demand for women's rights.[51]

Reconciliation of the Zetkin and the Austrian positions took place at the Austrian socialist women's conference of 1908. A resolution was passed declaring political rights for women absolutely necessary. When a Social Democratic parliamentary deputy suggested that though the suffrage for women was important, socialists would have to consolidate their position in parliament before pressing for it, the women were not so easily appeased. Popp recalled that women had demonstrated their solidarity by working enthusiastically for manhood suffrage even though this meant holding back on their own rights. Perhaps, she added, women should not recriminate against their male comrades for procrastinating, but against themselves for their caution.[52] Schlesinger, too, took a more assertive stance, declaring that the time was past for declarations of principle— the time had come for action. She acknowledged that many men feared women's suffrage because women were thought to be too much under the influence of clericalism and would set back the cause of socialism. But women must take the weapon of the franchise in hand and learn to use it. Proletarian men were once passive and conservative: the suffrage was an educational tool for them. Proft added that if women were politically immature, it was precisely the struggle for the suffrage which would mature them.[53] From her vantage point in Germany, Zetkin now complimented the Austrian women on their energetic participation in the struggle for male suffrage and on their current resolutions. At this time, the Austrian Social Democratic party rewarded its women's efforts by expanding their organizations and establishing a system of female cadres, the famous *Vertrauenspersonen,* who were responsible for bringing women into the party. Their movement grew more rapidly thereafter, attaining a membership of 15,000 by 1910.[54]

Women's suffrage was achieved much earlier in Austria than

either female or male politicians had expected. It came, of course, as a result of World War I, which had stimulated a great influx of women into industry, and of the proclamation of the Austrian republic. Seven women, including Popp, Proft, Schlesinger, and Freundlich, entered the National Council, or parliament. Though these leaders knew that political equality did not automatically mean social or psychological emancipation, they set about drawing up proposals dealing with working hours, protection of domestic servants, social insurance, reform of marriage laws, and education, and the legalization of birth control and abortion. While an extensive system of social welfare and municipal public works was erected in socialist-controlled "Red Vienna," most of the national parliamentary proposals came to naught because of the bitter opposition of the Christian Socials and other conservative parties.

Indeed, women's suffrage did not benefit the Social Democratic party, just as had been feared. When the Social Democrats left the first republican coalition government, thus producing a purely Christian Social regime under Monsignor Ignaz Seipel, the socialist women's newspaper commented that "in 1920 it was the women who have decided for Mr. Seipel."[55] In 1927, 55 percent of male voters chose non-Marxist parties, whereas 60 percent of the female electors voted nonsocialist. In 1930, 57 percent of the men and 61 percent of the women voted against the socialists and communists.[56] This seemed to bear out the stereotype of the conservative nature of women and their tendency to vote for bourgeois rather than socialist parties even though the socialists had more success in politically organizing women than other parties. In an excellent study on women in the Weimar Republic, Renate Bridenthal and Claudia Koonz have provided a subtle explanation for the conservative female vote. Women were not rejecting emancipation and clinging mindlessly to tradition. Rather, they were responding to promises of progress and equality that sounded transparent and shallow within the context of patriarchal structures and attitudes. They were reacting to the immediate effects of industrialization that put women in positions of disadvantage and weakness both in the labor force and in the home. Traditionally, the home meant status and a recognized niche that now was exchanged for unskilled labor at very low pay and uncertain status. Simply put, women were affected by economic modernization and politicization in contradictory ways.[57] But the socialist women leaders in Austria could not understand this and felt puzzled and frustrated, for they had been working for goals intended to benefit women. Yet they realized that there existed a large mass of apathetic and unorganized women and that the Christian Socials could exert powerful influences over them. A more practical and energetic commitment to women's suffrage in earlier decades might have brought more women to their cause. Their sacrifices to benefit universal male suffrage seemed to have been made in vain.

Despite setbacks and frustrations, the Austrian Socialist women's movement became much more radical in its programs and educational efforts in the 1920s than it had been before World War I, and it became a much larger movement as well—this while other socialist and communist movements were becoming more conservative on women's issues.

At the outset of the Austrian republic, socialist women hoped that the suffrage would help bring about legal and social reforms relating to women. All five socialist women leaders were particularly concerned with women and work, both on the level of protective legislation, which preoccupied them in the prewar period, and long-range terms of the future socialist society, which came increasingly into consideration in the 1920s.

As women began to expand into the labor force from agricultural work and household duties into industry in the 1890s, they were met by great hostility from male workers, who considered women to be unfair competition and responsible for the lowering of wages. This hostility was more than matched by the exploitation of women workers by employers, an exploitation that included not only long hours at heavy labor in unhealthy surroundings, but disrespect and sexual advances by superiors.

Austrian socialist women's organizations very early began to demand protective legislation for women workers, and the women working in textile, chemical, and paper factories, and household servants as well, responded to these concerns. Adelheid Popp attended the 1893 International Socialist Congress in Zurich where protective legislation for women was demanded: the eight-hour day, prohibition of night work, female factory inspectors, and leaves of absence for pregnant and nursing women.[58]

Socialist women's organizations held positions that differed from both the Catholic trade unions and bourgeois feminists. Catholics demanded even greater protective legislation (or prohibitions on women's work) than did the socialists. To the Catholics, Freundlich explained that many tasks that once were the function of men and women in the household were now done commercially. Working-class women and men knew that women's work could not be forbidden because proletarian families could not survive on one income. Freundlich added that it was a myth that the woman who works at home has more time for her children than the factory wage workers: neither could care for children as well as a crèche or kindergarten.[59]

Bourgeois feminists, on the other hand, fought vigorously against any legal limitations upon women's work, including exclusion from those jobs "especially deleterious to the female constitution." These limitations were considered attacks upon the freedom and equality of women, putting them in a less competitive position in qualifying for all sorts of jobs. Indeed, some socialist feminists, particularly those from Belgium and the Scandinavian countries continued into the 1920s to oppose protective legislation for women.[60]

Austrian women socialists like Popp and Freundlich insisted that their support for protective legislation was based on "no separate protection for women as such, but protection for woman as mother.... This lies not only in the interests of women, but [is] significant for the whole proletariat."[61] Their ultimate concern was the protection of children. Leichter observed that even more than men, women were subject in actual factory conditions to a rapid use of their labor power as the work process was intensified, because women were placed in the "most soulless, tiring, monotonous, nerve-wracking jobs which they must perform at a higher and higher tempo."[62] Socialist women, concluding that female employment must not be used to lower wages for men, called on women to join men in trade-union organizations.

Popp and Proft also devoted attention to domestic workers, domestic servants, and housewives. They lamented the fate of the housewife who worked without pay, vacations, or limitations on working hours. The housewife, wrote Popp, received no recognition, and her only wages were derision and disrespect. "Women have not only the right, but the duty, to rise up against the Cinderella-like fate assigned to them."[63] Women, in this view, would find relief only when they did not have to be housewives and wage workers at the same time, and when household work would be looked upon as valuable and necessary for the culture of the family and of society. Particular sympathy went out to female domestic servants, who had perhaps the least protection of all, working irregular hours for abysmal wages. They were subject to feudal restrictions from their employers, who could limit their individual freedom, impose corporal punishment, and deprive them of human dignity. Socialists demanded regulation of the hours, wages, and working conditions of domestic servants.

The demands that socialist women made with regard to women and work were in some respects contradictory. They asked that household work be given social value, but were unclear whether housewives or professional people were to be paid for this labor. Women were not to be burdened with housework and industrial work; yet free Saturday afternoons were demanded precisely because Sundays were not days of rest for proletarian women, but filled with domestic chores. They demanded equal pay for equal work, yet protective legislation might make women less competitive in the job market.

Socialist women also discussed long-range goals of the transformation of society, which required changes in the relationship of women and work. Such long-term goals were developed implicitly in the 1926 program of the Social Democratic party. The women's section of it was outlined by Therese Schlesinger, working with Otto Bauer. The section on women opened with the statement that "Social Democracy . . . demands for women full opportunity for the development of their personality."[64]

238

The assumption was that working women needed relief from the triple burden of employment, household work and child raising in order to have the time and independence for personal development. Schlesinger insisted that a capitalist society could not solve the problems of women and work, or specifically wage work and motherhood.

What was the socialist solution? While some bourgeois women demanded that housework within the family be paid, this was not Schlesinger's emphasis. The 1926 program did demand "a greater respect for the social function of woman as mother and housewife and protection against the double burden of work in employment and household." [65] But it went further, insisting not only on the right of women to work, but on the necessity. Certainly, proletarian women had to work in order that their families could survive. But the family, as Freundlich had emphasized earlier, was no longer the unit of production it had been before the industrial revolution—it was now limited to consumption. Since it had lost many of its old functions, the traditional family could be modified radically.[66]

Work outside the home was necessary for other reasons as well. Popp had deplored women "who are accustomed to see in their husbands the 'provider' who is their only support in life, and who do not yet understand that women must get used to seeking their support somewhere else, no longer in the form of the husband, but in society as a whole. . . ."[67] Schlesinger opposed returning women to the "narrowness of the household," where woman is "locked within four walls, in profound dependence, not only dependent upon the man, not only dependent upon the children she must care for, but in spiritual bondage as well." The proper approach was first of all to demand equal pay for equal work, and equal access for women to all jobs "except those which are particularly harmful to the female organism."[68] Thus far not much was new.

But Schlesinger continued that equal pay would make possible a greater income for the family; it would increase wealth, which would then be available to provide for an increased rationalization of the household. By a rationalized household, socialist women meant not only the introduction of labor-saving technology into the home, or the application of scientific principles of home economics. They also advocated the avoidance of wasteful duplication through the construction of architecturally planned housing, the centralization of facilities such as cooking and laundries, and the engagement of professional cleaning and child-care services. Social welfare support, such as health insurance, work leaves for pregnant women and nursing mothers, and child care were obvious concomitants to this approach, which was explored as well in Leichter's collection on women's work.[69]

Socialist women did recognize that the conversion of the housewife into a professional worker and the transformation of the household into an industrial operation would take place slowly and not occur everywhere in the same way. "The education of women is today so backward, that women themselves often do not desire to try new methods of household management. To win women for public action, however, means to free them from the toil of daily housekeeping."[70] The socialists seemed to stress the mechanical organizational approach that came out of nineteenth-century notions of material progress shared by Marxists. Recognizing that progress has come about through division of labor, however, they held that the time had come to take advantage of division of labor among women as well—indeed, the time had come to investigate the sexual division of labor in the household. Timidly, Austrian women socialists began to devote attention to what we now call sex roles.

Schlesinger noted that there were still men and women who believed that housework was the lot assigned by nature to women and had an indissoluble connection with motherhood. In Leichter's 1930 collection, Schlesinger observed that all the jobs that had been regarded as the natural tasks of woman could easily become male tasks if they were to be paid for in money: there were male cooks, bootblacks, window washers, barbers, janitors. "It never enters the head of a male worker to clean his own apartment, to wax the floor, to wash the windows, to cook his own meals, to darn his clothes. . . ." Men, even those who work in factories alongside of women, are still used to seeing in women household servants. And women thoughtlessly never question this: if household work were to be shared by men and women, men would soon come up with the idea of rationalization of household chores through more centralized organization and labor-saving devices.[71]

But if patterns of work and if the household were to be reorganized, if women were not to be confined to the domestic sphere so that they could participate more fully in society, changes would be required in child rearing, population patterns, family law, education, and culture. In Juliet Mitchell's terms, changes would be required not only in production, but in reproduction and socialization and sexuality as well.[72]

The Linz Conference, at least, addressed itself to reproduction and socialization. One of the gravest problems of proletarian women, in the opinion both of Otto Bauer and Therese Schlesinger, was their overburdening with too many children and an even larger number of childbirths. This was continuing at a time when the middle classes were limiting their families.[73] The 1926 program demanded the distribution, free of charge, of birth control devices and information; it asked for the legalization of abortions, free of charge, in public hospitals upon the demand of the pregnant woman with the approval of a commission of physicians. Many socialists had been wary of, or vehemently opposed to birth control and abortion. Zetkin, for example, "refused to consider birth control and abortion as legitimate solutions to women's oppression and, in fact, criticized both harshly on moral and political grounds."[74]

In Austria, however, some socialist women wanted to go further than Schlesinger and to permit legal abortions without restricting them to public hospitals and requiring consultation with medical commissions. Here, both Popp and Proft were more conservative. Popp did not agree with those radicals who insisted that every woman had the right to decide for herself what to do with her own body. Proft cautioned that the state of medical science was still uncertain and divided in the field of abortion and that women socialists must not venture too far beyond the values and opinions of their working-class constituents. Freundlich took the most traditionalist and bourgeois approach. Men should have something to say in the decision of

241

whether or not to have children, she maintained. Although she claimed that she was opposed to women having more than three children, Freundlich also did not approve of women who refused to have any. "For I am convinced that a woman who really wishes to develop herself in every direction, who wishes to unfold her full personality, must have children. And I pity the woman who has no children, for she lacks a true content of life, and a true woman will not feel herself happy in absolute childlessness."[75]

Thus, as in Germany prior to World War I, on such fundamental feminist issues as birth control and abortion, there were deep disagreements among Austrian socialist women. In the end, going beyond their German sisters, they all supported Schlesinger's compromise in the 1926 program of the legalization of abortion in public hospitals. Furthermore, in addition to production and reproduction, the program considered socialization, containing sections on marriage, family law, religion, and education, for all these issues were related to the emancipation of women and the transformation of society that would change women's consciousness.

After all, Popp had written that Social Democracy was the party of the oppressed, whose purpose it was "also to free the female sex from a position of humility and subordination."[76] This freeing involved all aspects of life. In 1929, for example, *Die Frau* contained an article entitled "The Liberation of Women Through Sport." The article explained that a healthy body, encouraged by sport, would be a sign of spiritual emancipation, something Rosa Mayreder had maintained as well in lauding the bicycle as an instrument of women's liberation.[77] But this kind of cultivation of the body had nothing to do with the kind of bourgeois ill-breeding that looks upon lipstick and powder as the ultimate in feminine pulchritude. Rather, engaging in sport and exercise would improve health and provide women with the psychological benefits of greater self-consciousness and self-confidence.

The themes of self-worth and self-confidence had been touched upon by Austrian women socialist leaders for forty years. A brief article in *Die Frau* in 1930 summarized some of the views socialist women held on the future. It was entitled "A Glimpse into Yesterday, Today and Tomorrow," and examined the position of women in 1830, 1930, and 2030. The sketch of 1830 described working women in English textile mills and bourgeois ladies riding in stagecoaches to exchange coffee visits. The year 1930 was characterized by technological improvements: the railroad, bus, running water, gas, and electricity; much former household production was now done in the factory, as both father and mother were lured out of the household into the struggles of the world—and this had made their expectations rise, but increased their dissatisfaction as well. Despite this, the structure of the household, the state and the capitalist economy had not really changed. In 2030 the article depicted the era of a more organized, fulfilled individual and social life— the machine had been placed in the service of socialized man. The provision of food was a function of society as was the cleaning of apartments and laundry. Women had become independent and educated. Motherhood was regarded as a social contribution. The economy was not run for profit; working hours and the birth rate were low. Finally, it concluded, "the formerly reactionary element of society, woman, has become integrated into the mainstream of development and has now become an active transformer of society."[78]

In the 1920s the Austrian women socialists were the most advanced on social issues of any socialist party in Europe, with the exception of the temporary experiments in family and social legislation occurring in Soviet Russia. How could the Austrian women's movement, which in 1907 had defended its sacrifice of women's suffrage, have become the propounder of radical proposals? The Austrian Socialist party confronted a traditional society and a Catholic political movement. Its identity was forged in this conflict. Women socialists, whether their origins were middle class or working class, frequently pointed out their conflict with the Church and its values when they recounted the process of their politicization. Trade-union leaders and political organizers like Popp, Proft, and Schlesinger testified that the issue of clericalism always evoked a strong response from their audiences on agitational tours. Recruitment of new women members often took the form of mutual recounting of past injuries and abuses in the home and the work place and of the drastic break with tradition necessary to become a socialist. It may be, therefore, that in the confrontation with clerical attitudes, the emphasis on the personal and the cultural stimulated the development of radical positions on social issues. The stress which the Social Democratic party in general placed upon cultural life was a response to the massive influence of the Church and to intellectual currents at the time, including the psychoanalytic movement. Public life in the 1920s became polarized between a politically canny but socially conservative clerical party and the socialists who retained the loyalty of urban workers through a network of cultural organizations while retaining a revolutionary perspective within the International. As part of this network, Austrian socialist feminists shared the emphasis on cultural transformation rather than restricting their focus to economic change.

It was not until 1975 that even the minimal demands of the socialist feminists' program of the 1920s were enacted in Austria—that abortion became legal, that husband and wife were given legal equality in marriage, and that divorce was reformed. These partial measures continued to be vigorously opposed by the Catholic People's party (the *Volkspartei,* successor to the Christian Socials) and did not contain the far-reaching integrated outlook of the Austrian women socialists of the pre-fascist era.

When the Austrian Social Democratic movement was destroyed in 1934, the socialist women's organization disappeared as well. Though individual women socialists were important leaders in the party, the women's movement had been an adjunct, exercising minimal influence over the party as a whole. The socialist women's movement should have penetrated more deeply into the lives of working women and gained greater political influence within the party. The times, however, made this almost impossible.

After World War I, suffrage was to have been only the beginning. Socialist women hoped that their patience and discipline would be rewarded. Instead, they were increasingly forced to defend even the most minimal and basic rights of women as human beings. The postwar economy was especially hard on women. The new ideologies of clerical conservatism, fascism, and Nazism were specifically antifeminist. More and more in the late 1920s and 1930s, women socialists were preoccupied with economic crises, with unemployment and the exclusion of women, as well as the rise of fascism, which gained support from many females. International Women's Day in 1933 was framed by three slogans: "Against Fascism; For Freedom and Bread; Against Section 144" (the criminal abortion statute).[79] Public discussion about women, however, was put more and more in terms of the sacred natural duty of women to devote themselves to the home as wives and mothers. A report to the 1931 international socialist women's conference noted that "great unemployment on the one hand and fascist tendencies on the other have nearly everywhere led to attacks or attempted attacks upon the rights of women."[80] In the 1920s the bourgeois feminists continued to refrain from partisan politics and instead concentrated upon propaganda for international peace and disarmament. Popp, speaking for her colleagues, commented angrily that pacifism and international disarmament would only be possible after the defeat of fascism and after the disarmament of that enemy.[81] Political trends overwhelmed the women's movement and destroyed individual leaders who had devoted their lives to the ideals of socialism and the expansion of the experiences of working-class women.

NOTES

1. *Frauenarbeit und Bevoelkerungspolitik.* Verhandlungen der sozialdemokratischen Frauenreichskonferenz, 29. und 30. Oktober, 1926 in Linz. (Vienna, 1926), pp. 49, 56. Hereafter abbr. *FB.*
2. Ibid., pp. 14–16ff.
3. William M. Johnston, *The Austrian Mind: An Intellectual and Social History, 1848–1938,* (Berkeley, Los Angeles, London, 1972), p. 99.
4. See Norbert Leser, *Zwischen Reformismus und Bolschewismus: Der Austromarxismus als Theorie und Praxis* (Vienna, 1968); *Austromarxismus: Texte zu "Ideologie und Klassenkampf"* (Vienna, 1970); and Ludwig Brue-

gel, *Geschichte des oesterreichischen Sozialismus*, 5 vols. (Vienna, 1925).

5. Sheila Rowbotham, *Hidden From History* (New York, 1974), p. 91.

6. Quoted in William J. McGrath, *Dionysian Art and Populist Politics in Austria* (New Haven and London, 1974), p. 218.

7. Ibid., p. 214.

8. Ibid., p. 215.

9. Johnston, *The Austrian Mind*, discusses the "therapeutic nihilism" of the medical faculty of Vienna, an attitude that radiated out into other areas of intellectual life at the turn of the century.

10. See Anne Marie Strasser, "Publizistik und Agitation der oesterreichischen Frauenbewegung" (Ph.D. dissertation, University of Vienna, 1971).

11. Johnston, *The Austrian Mind*, pp. 156–58.

12. Hildegard Laessig, "Marianne Hainisch und die oesterreichische Frauenbewegung" (Ph.D. dissertation, University of Vienna, pp. 87–88.

13. Ibid.

14. *Gleiches Recht fuer die Frauen.* Eine Werbeschrift von E. Freundlich, S. Nestriepke, A. Popp (Nuernberg, 1914), pp. 5–6.

15. Johnston, *The Austrian Mind*, pp. 100, 130.

16. Adelheid Popp, *Der Weg zur Hoehe: Die sozialdemokratische Frauenbewegung Oesterreichs: Ihr Aufbau, Ihre Entwicklung, und ihr Aufstieg*, 2d ed. (Vienna, 1930), p. 51.

17. Ibid.; also see Thomas Lewis Hamer, "Beyond Feminism: The Women's Movement in Austrian Social Democracy, 1890–1920" (Ph.D. dissertation, The Ohio State Universtiy, 1973), pp. 65–67.

18. *Internationaler Sozialisten-Kongress zu Stuttgart, 18–24 August 1907: Anhang: Erste Internationale Konferenz Sozialistischer Frauen* (Berlin, 1907), pp. 40–47, 122–47.

19. *FB*, pp. 56–57.

20. *Die Forderungen der Frauen an Parlament und Verwaltung: Verhandlungen der dritten deutschoesterreichischen Frauenkonferenz Wien 13. und 14. November 1923* (Vienna, 1923). Popp's opening speech, p. 3.

21. Adelheid Popp, "Die Frauen Erwachen" (typescript prepared for International Women's Day, March 19, 1911, in Verein fuer die Geschichte der Arbeiterbewegung, Vienna, Lade 22, Mappe 69: Adelheid und Julius Popp).

22. Adelheid Popp, *The Autobiography of a Working Woman*, trans. by F.C. Harvey (London, 1912).

23. Popp, *Autobiography*, p. 106.

24. Adelheid Popp, *Freie Liebe und buergerliche Ehe:* Schwurgerichtshandlung gegen die *Arbeiterinnen-Zeitung* (Vienna, 1895).

25. See Popp, *Autobiography*, as well as: Adelheid Popp, *Erinnerungen: Aus meinen Kindheits-und Maedchenjahren: Aus der Agitation und Anderes* Berlin, 1923); Edith Kurz, "Die Sozialistin Adelheid Popp-Dworak," in *Frauenbilder Aus Oesterreich: Eine Sammlung von Zwoelf Essays* (Vienna, 1953), pp. 177–201; and Gabriele Proft, "Adelheid Popp," in *Werk und Widerhall*, ed. Norbert Leser (Vienna, 1964), pp. 297–307.

26. Proft, "Adelheid Popp," p. 302.

27. Popp, *Autobiography*, p. 133.

28. Adelheid Popp, "Leni" (manuscript in Adler Archiv, Verein fuer die Geschichte der Arbeiterbewegung, Vienna, Mappe no. 146), pp. 35–36.

29. Yvon Bourdet, Felix Kreissler, Georges Haupt and Herbert Steiner, *L'Autriche*, vol. I of Jean Maitron and Georges Haupt, *Dictionnaire biographique du mouvement ouvrier international* (Paris, 1971), pp. 275–76. Hereafter cited as *Dictionnaire*. Also see, Therese Schlesinger-Eckstein, *Die Frau im 19. Jahrhundert* (Berlin, 1902); Therese Schlesinger, *Die Geistige Arbeiterin und der Sozialismus* (Vienna, 1919); Therese Schlesinger, "Mein Weg zur Sozial-demokratie" in *Gedenkbuch, Zwanzig Jahre oesterreichische Arbeiterinnenbewegung*, ed. Adelheid Popp (Vienna, 1912), pp. 125–31; and Stella Klein-Loew, "Therese Schlesinger," in Leser, *Werk und Widerhall*, pp. 353–61.
30. Schlesinger, *Die geistige Arbeiterin*, p. 40.
31. Therese Schlesinger, "Buergerliche und proletarische Frauenbewegung," *Sozialistische Monatshefte* II (1898): 465.
32. Ibid.
33. Schlesinger-Eckstein, *Die Frau im 19. Jahrhundert*, p. 31.
34. *Dictionnaire*, pp. 241–42; Popp, *Der Weg zur Hoehe*, pp. 86–87.
35. "Gabriele Proft"—papers and documents in Verein fuer Geschichte der Arbeiterbewegung, Vienna, Lade 22, Mappe 73; also, Gabriele Proft, *Der Weg zu Uns: Die Frauenfrage im Neuen Oesterreich* (Vienna, 1945); and *Die Frau* (Vienna, no. 9, Sept. 1, 1925), "Antrag Proft und Popp."
36. Anette Richter, "Emmy Freundlich," in Leser, *Werk und Widerhall*, p. 160.
37. *Dictionnaire*, pp. 102–103.
38. Emmy Freundlich, *Die Frauenfrage* (Vienna, 1912), pp. 12–14.
39. *Die Forderungen der Frauen*, p. 10.
40. Herbert Steiner, ed., *Kaethe Leichter: Leben und Werk* (Vienna, 1973), p. 376.
41. Ibid., pp. 251–340; also see Otto Leichter, "Kaethe Leichter," in Leser, *Werk und Widerhall*, pp. 234–45.
42. *Frauenwahlrecht und Arbeiterinnenschutz*. Verhandlungen der dritten sozialdemokratischen Frauenkonferenz in Oesterreich (Vienna, 1908).
43. "Das Maedchen aus der Fabrik," *Wiener Tagblatt* (Vienna), Aug. 6, 1893, vol. 43, no. 215.
44. Adelheid Popp, "Das Wahlrecht der Frauen," (1899 printed article, source unknown, Library of Austrian Socialist Party, Vienna).
45. Popp, *Weg zur Hoehe*, pp. 38–39, 126–30.
46. *Arbeiterinnenzeitung* (Vienna), vol. II, no. 15, Aug. 4, 1893.
47. *Arbeiterzeitung* (Vienna), vol. XI, no. 236, Aug. 29, 1907.
48. Adelheid Popp, "Die oesterreichische Wahlreform und das Frauenwahlrecht," *Sozialistische Monatshefte* (Vol. I, Heft 4, April, 1906), pp. 301–305.
49. *Arbeiterinnenzeitung*, vol. XIV, no. 24, Nov. 28, 1905, p. 2.
50. *Internationaler Sozialisten-Kongress Stuttgart*, pp. 40–47, 122–142.
51. Ibid.
52. *Frauenwahlrecht und Arbeiterinnenschutz*, pp. 9–10, 15–19, 26, 32.
53. Ibid., pp. 27–32.
54. Hamer, *Beyond Feminism*, pp. 94–95; Popp, *Weg zur Hoehe*, p. 51.
55. *Arbeiterinnenzeitung*, vol. 32, no. 8, Aug. 7, 1923.
56. Hedwig Hoenigschmied, "Der Einfluss des Frauenwahlrechtes auf das politische Geschehen Oesterreichs unter besonderer Beruecksichtigung der Gesetzgebung" (Ph.D. dissertation, University of Graz, 1952), p. 53.

57. Renate Bridenthal and Claudia Koonz, "Beyond Kinder, Kueche, Kirche: Weimar Women in Politics and Work" in *Liberating Women's History*, ed. Berenice Carroll (Urbana, Chicago, London, 1976), pp. 301–329.
58. *Arbeiterinnenzeitung*, vol. II, no. 17, Sept. 1, 1893.
59. Emmy Freundlich, *Arbeiterinnenschutz* (Vienna, 1913).
60. Fourth Congress of the Labour and Socialist International, *Reports and Proceedings*. Fourth International Women's Conference of the Labour and Socialist International, Vienna, July 23 to 25, 1931 (Zurich, 1931), pp. 43–61.
61. *Frauenwahlrecht und Arbeiterinnenschutz*, p. 40.
62. Kaethe Leichter, ed., *Handbuch der Frauenarbeit* (Vienna, 1930), pp. 38–39.
63. Adelheid Popp, *Frauenarbeit in der kapitalistischen Gesellschaft* (Vienna, 1922), p. 20.
64. *FB*.
65. *FB*.
66. Freundlich, *Arbeiterinnenschutz*, pp. 9–10.
67. Adelheid Popp, "Die Familie und der sozialistische Staat," *Arbeiterinnenzeitung*, Vol. 29, no. 16, Aug. 17, 1920.
68. *FB*, p. 9.
69. *FB*, p. 10; also, Therese Schlesinger, *Die Frau im sozial-demokratischen Parteiprogramm* (Vienna, 1928), p. 13.
70. *Forderungen der Frauen*, p. 14.
71. Therese Schlesinger, "Die Forderungen der Frauen an Gesetzgebung und Verwaltung," in Leichter, *Handbuch;* also see Schlesinger, *Die Frauen im sozialdemokratischen Parteiprogramm*, p. 7; and *FB*, p. 10.
72. Juliet Mitchell, *Woman's Estate* (New York, 1973), pp. 100–122.
73. *FB*, pp. 59–60.
74. Karen Honeycutt, "Clara Zetkin: A Socialist Attempt at Analyzing Women's Oppression and Raising Feminist Consciousness Among Proletarian Women," paper presented to Second Berkshire Conference of Women Historians, Radcliffe College, Oct. 24, 1974, pp. 10–11.
75. *FB*, pp. 17–44.
76. Adelheid Popp, *Frau, Arbeiterin, Sozialdemokratie* (Vienna, 1916), p. 6.
77. Marie Deutsch-Kramer, "Die Befreiung der Frau durch den Sport," *Die Frau*, Vol. 38, no. 6, June 1, 1929. Rosa Mayreder, too, emphasized sports, regarding the invention of the bicycle a giant step toward the emancipation of women.
78. *Die Frau*, Vol. 39, no. 3, March, 1930, pp. 6–8.
79. *Frauentag 1933* (Vienna, 1933), commemorative pamphlet.
80. Fourth Congress of the Labour and Socialist International, pp. 65–83.
81. *Die Unzufriedene* (Vienna), Vol. 10, no. 4, Jan. 30, 1932.

The Contributors

BOXER, MARILYN J. Received a Ph. D. in European History from the University of California, Riverside, in 1975. She is currently chairperson of the Women's Studies Department at San Diego State University where she also teaches courses on women's history. She has contributed articles on women's history to the *Proceedings of the Second Annual Meeting of the Western Society for French History* (College Station, Texas, 1975) and a forthcoming special issue of *Third Republic, Troisième République*. With Jean H. Quataert she is beginning a comparative study of the artificial flowermakers of Paris and Berlin.

ENGEL, BARBARA. Obtained a Ph.D. in Russian History from Columbia University in 1974. She taught European women's history at Sarah Lawrence College for several years and is currently an Assistant Professor of Russian History at the University of Colorado. She is co-editor of *Five Sisters: Women Against the Tsar* (New York: Knopf, 1975), has an article entitled "Women as Revolutionaries," in *Becoming Visible: Women in European History*, eds. Bridenthal and Koonz (Boston: Houghton-Mifflin, 1977), and is preparing a book on Russian women of the intelligentsia.

FARNSWORTH, BEATRICE. Obtained a Ph.D. in history from Yale University in 1959. Her specialty is the early soviet period. She has taught history at Hobart and William Smith Colleges and Wells College, where she is now an Associate Professor teaching women's and Russian history. The author of *William C. Bullitt and the Soviet Union* (Bloomington, Indiana University Press, 1967), her current interest is in social history of the early soviet period. She is writing a political biography of Aleksandra Kollontai and the Bolshevik Revolution.

LAFLEUR, INGRUN. Received a Ph.D. from Columbia University in 1972 where she worked in East Central European history. She teaches at William James College in Michigan and coordinates the Women's Studies Program. She was executive producer of a local PBS–TV program on women called "A Nature to Nurture," and has published an article on "Adelheid Popp and Austrian Socialist Feminism" in *Frontiers: A Journal of Women's Studies*, Fall 1975.

LaVigna, Claire. Received a Ph.D. in history from the University of Rochester in 1971. She is an Associate Professor at Erindale College, University of Toronto where she teaches courses in modern Europe and modern Italian history. She has published an article on Anna Kuliscioff in Italy in the Summer-Fall 1976 issue of the *Italian Quarterly* and is currently revising for publication a full-length biography of Kulisioff.

Moon, S. Joan. Received a Ph.D. from Wayne State University in history in 1968. She has been a Lecturer at the University of California, Los Angeles; Assistant Professor at California State University, Long Beach; Visiting Faculty at the University of Wisconsin at Eau Clair; and is currently Associate Professor of History at California State University, Sacramento. She teaches the history of women in Western civilization and graduate seminars in historiography. She has an article, "Saint-Simoniennes and the Moral Revolution," to appear in the *Proceedings of the Sixth Annual Meeting of the Consortium on Revolutionary Europe 1976.*

Quataert, Jean H. Obtained a Ph.D. in German history from the University of California, Los Angeles, in 1974. She is currently Assistant Professor of Humanities at the University of Houston at Clear Lake City and teaches courses in the Women's Studies concentration. Previous to this appointment she taught European history at Loyola Marymount University, Los Angeles. She has completed a book manuscript, "Reluctant Feminists: Socialist Women in Imperial Germany 1885–1917," and has published an article "Feminist Tactics in German Social Democracy 1890–1914: A Dilemma," in *Internationale wissenschaftliche Korrespondenz zur Geschichte der deutschen Arbeiterbewegung,* March 1977. With Marilyn J. Boxer she is beginning a comparative study of the artificial flowermakers in Berlin and Paris.

Index

Abortion: and Austria, 235, 241–42, 244; and Madeleine Pelletier, 104; Social Democrats on, 216

Adler, Friedrich, 226, 227

Adler, Max, 217

Adler, Viktor, 217, 218, 225

Alarchin courses for women: 65; limitations, 54–55; opening, 53–54

Aleksandrov, Vasilii: on labor issue, 67, and Marx, study of, 62; press of, 70; proposal to Kornilova, 64–65

Alessandria, Anna Maria Mozzoni in, 173

Alexander II, Tsar, 55

Alimony, and Bolsheviks, 191–92

All Russian Central Executive Committee, 191

American Historical Association, 184*n*.

American Philosophical Society, 184*n*.

Anarchists: Bakunists, 150; and Madeleine Pelletier, 103–104; in P.O.F., 78

Andrews, Phyllis, 184*n*.

Angelucci, Armando, on free love, 173

Anna, Hauptmann character, 132

Anna, sister of Lenin, 188

Anschluss, 228

Aptekman, Osip, 57

Arbeiterinnenzeitung, 224

Arbeiterkammer, 230

Arbeiterzeitung, 230

Armand, Inessa: exiled, 188; and Zhenotdel, 190

Atelier: described, 35–36; on suffrage, 39; universality, 40; warning to typographers, 43

Attentat (Adler), 227

Augsburg, Lily Braun at, 121

Austria: birth control in, 17; Social Democrats in, 216ff., 234, 235, 238, 244; and women, 15–16, 215ff., 228

Austrian Social Democracy. *See* Social Democratic women's movement

Austromarxism, 216–17, 222, 223

Autobiographies, male attitudes in, 138–39

Autobiography of a Working Woman (Popp), 223–24

Avanti!, 160

Baader, Ottilie: memoirs of, 118, 119–20, 211

Bachofen, J.J., 10, 11

Balabanoff, Angelica, 203

Bauer, Otto: 217; on birth control, 241; and Therese Schlesinger, 226, 238

Bäumer, Gertrud, 138–39

Bebel, August: 116, 228; impact, 120; and Italian socialists, 148; marriage, 138; on sexuality, 202; on socialism and feminism, 10, 11–12, 161–62

Bebel, Julie, eulogy on, 138

Belgium: feminists, 237; suffrage in, 15–16, 94

Berlin, Clara Zetkin in, 127

Bernsteinian revisionism, 123, 163, 160–70

251

253

French League for the Rights of
Women, 76
French Revolution of 1789, 2
French Section of the Workers'
International (S.F.I.O.), 78, 79, 98,
100, 103
French Workers' party (P.O.F.): 79;
funding congress, 77–78; on illegal
candidates, 86; Valette in, 87, 90, 91;
women in, 75, 78–79
Freud, on sexuality and work, 203
Freudian perspective, on Flora
Tristan, 30
Freundlich, Emmy: 223; on abortion,
245–46; background of, 228; and
Catholics, 237; as centrist, 231; on
family, function of, 239; in
parliament, 229, 235; on party
loyalty, 233; on protective
legislation, 241; on women in
society, 228–29
Friends of Children, 228
Fronde, La, 90

Garin, Eugenio, on women's
liberation, 164
Gazette des femmes, on suffrage, 39
Gebärstreik, 126
Gebärzwang, 126
General Austrian Women's
Association, founded, 220
General Insurance Fund, 194, 201
Genio e Lavoro, 157
Genoa, Italian Socialist party at, 154–55
German Ethical Culture Society, 123
German Majority Socialists, 217
German Social Democracy, 2, 8, 15,
94, 112, 115, 218, 222
Gestapo, 234
G.F.S. *See* Feminist Socialist Group
Gilman, Charlotte Perkins, 90
Gioberti, Vincenzo, on women, 164
Gioia, Melchiorre, on women, 164
Giolittian period, Italy, 159
Gleichheit, 130
Glickman, Rose, xi
"Glimpse into Yesterday, Today and
Tomorrow, A," 243
Gosset, union plans, 36
Goudeman, Alphonsine Caroline
Eulalie. *See* Valette, Aline
Griboedova, Vera (Vera Kornilova), 69
Group of Milanese Socialist Women,
165–66

Group of Women Socialists, 97
Groupe féministe socialiste (G.F.S.),
92, 97
Grünberg, Helene: on female labor
force, 122, 124, 125; feminism, 118
*Gruppo delle donne socialiste
milanese*, 165–66
Guerre sociale, La, 103
Guesde, Jules: 88, 101, 102, 105; and
Aline Valette, 87, 90, 91; faction of,
103; on feminist principles, 80;
political strategy, 85; on Rouzade,
78–79
Guesdist faction, of socialists, 103
Guindorf, Marie-Reine, 27
Guizot Law of 1833, 34

Habsburg monarchy: admiration for,
216; and Hungarians, 232
Hainfeld, Social Democratic congress
in, 220
Hainisch, Marianne, and bourgeois
women's movement, 219
Hanna, Gertrud, 118
Harmonie sociale, L', 87
Hauptmann, Gerhart, 132
Havre, Le, 82
Hervé: faction of, 103; and Madeleine
Pelletier, 103
"History of Women in Society, The"
(Mink), 83
Homosexuality, latent, and Flora
Tristan, 30
Housewife, rights of, 238
Humanité, L', 102
Humanity, as Marxian term, 8–9
Hungarians, and Habsburg emperor,
232

Iaroslavskii, Emilian: on Aleksandra
Kollontai, 202; on sexuality, 202
Ibsen, criticized, 132
Ihrer, Emma: 133; on bourgeois
feminism, 118; on Edmund Fischer,
134; on female disadvantages, 125;
on male egoism, 138; obituary on,
124
Illegitimate children, legal issues,
97–98
Imperial Germany: feminists in, 15;
Socialist women in, 6
Infant schools, French, 34
International Congress on Injuries on
the Job, 158

International Congress on the Condition and Rights of Women, 95, 96
International Cooperative Guild, 228
Internationalism, and Flora Tristan, 40
International Review of Socialism, 151
International Socialist Congress, 237
International Women's Day, 2, 245
International Workingmen's Association, 9
Italian Socialist Party (PSI): 6, 15, 150, 154, 156, 159, 160, 163; founding of, 151; unity, appeals for, 157; and women, 146ff.
Italy, feminist theory and practice in, 14, 15

Jaurès, Jean, 13, 102, 103
Jesus, indignation, 24
Juchacz, Marie, 118–19, 139
July Monarchy, of France, 19, 35, 42, 44, 45, 106

Kalinin, Mikhail, on Soviet marriage, 200
Kapital, Das (Marx), 62
Karl Marx Society, 227
Kauffmann, Caroline, 101–102
Kautsky, Karl, 130, 138
Kautskyism, 5
Key, Ellen, 90
Kharkov: 63; women workers of, 56, 61, 62, 63
Kiev, Sofia Perovskaia in, 64
Kinderfreunde, 231
Knizhnoe delo, 69
Kollontai, Aleksandra: autobiography of, 205; and Bolsheviks, 187ff.; and bourgeois feminists, 186–87; on class and sex, 13; commune of, 203; in diplomatic exile, 192–93; and family life, 16, 17, 199ff.; feminism of, 182; and Lenin, 204; in opposition movement, 193ff.; on sexuality, 198, 201; and Social Democrats, 184–85; and Stalinism, 205–206; on work, and sex, 203; and Zhenotdel, 190
Kommunistka, 188, 191, 200, 201
Komosomol youth, 201
Komsomolskaia Pravda, 194
Koonz, Claudia, on conservative female vote, 235

Kornilov, Aleksander, nililism of, 56
Kornilov, Ivan, 56, 63
Kornilova, Vera, 56, 63
Kornilova, Aleksandra: 53, 55; in Chaikovskii circle, 68–69, 71; described, 59–60; education of, 62–64; family life, 56; goals of, 58; on knowledge, value of, 59; on men, studying with, 66; proposed to, 65; and Sofia Perovskaia, loyalty, 64; teaching workers, 70
Kornilova, Liubov, 53, 56, 68–69
Kornilova, Nadezhda, 56
Koval'skaia, Ekaterina, 55
Koval'skaia, Elizaveta: 53, 62–63, 65, 69; Alarchin course attendance, 56–57; education of, 63; family life, 57; at Kornilova meeting, 59–60; memoirs, 58–59; on men, studying with, 66; as teacher, 62
Koval'skaia, Sol'ntsev, 57
Krasnaia Nov', 201
Kropotkin: on Chaikovskii circle, 71; on role of women, 100
Krupskaia, wife of Lenin, exiled, 188
Krylenko, Nikolai, on marriage, 192
Kuliscioff, Anna: activism, 156ff., 161; career significance, 7, 146, 148; committment, 168; on family, 170–72; on feminism, break from, 148–49; Italian support, 15; labor bill, 168–69; on law, 158–59; on marriage, 155–56; as Marxist, 163–66, 167, 169–70, 172–74; and Marxist-feminist clash, 151–53; personal life, 149–50; and Pope, 169; and PSI, 151; public life, 150ff.; at Second International, 155; on women's suffrage, 159–60
Kursky, Dimitri: on family life, 200; on women's rights, 192
Kuvshinskaia, Anna, 53, 61, 68, 69, 70, 71–72

Lafargue, Paul, 91, 101, 105
Lafleur, Ingrun: 153; on Austrian women socialists, 17, 215ff.
Lagano, Anna Kuliscioff in, 149
Lainé, Thérèse. *See* Tristan, Thérèse
Latin Quarter: socialist group formation, 94; socialist meeting place, 93
Lausanne congress, First International, 82

243; on abortion, 241–42; background of, 225–26; on birth control, 241–42; on capitalist limitations, 243; contribution of, 231; feminist views, 226–27; in parliament, 235; on rationalized household, 239–41; on sex roles, 240–41; on socialist hypocrisy, 233–34

Scientific socialism, 8

"Seamstresses on Corso Magnenta," appeal to, 156–57

2½ International, proposed, 226

Second International, 2, 14, 102, 112, 155, 217, 226

Seipel, Ignaz, 239

Sexual love, Russian feminists on, 58–59

"Sexualism," theory of, 87–89

Sexualisme (Bonnier), 88

S.F.I.O. *See* French Section of the Workers' International

Shishko, Leonid, teaching workers, 70

Shliapnikov, Alexander, 195

Simbirsk, Obodovskai, 65

Sinegub, Sergei, marriage of, 67–68

Skvortsova, Nadezhda, 68–69

Smidovich, Petr, on Lenin, 198

Smidovich, Sophia: on Aleksandra Kollontai, 202; on sexuality, 198; writings, 199, 200; on Zhenotdel, 190

Social Bases of the Woman Question, The (Kollontai), 186–87

Social Critic, 151, 155–56, 159, 173

Social Democratic women's movement: 114–15; Austria, 70, 216ff., 220ff., 226ff., 238, 239, 242, 248; concerns, 139–41; Germany, 122–23; impact, 130; Russia, 185–87; SPD, 115, 117, 127

"Social Movements in the Nineteenth Century" (Mink), 83

Social Warfare (Hervé), 103

"Socialism and Revolution' (Mink), 83

Socialist Feminist Group, of Paris, 75

Socialist International, Vienna, 188

Socialist Woman, 94

Society of the Mutual Help of Working Women, 186

Solidarity of Women, 85–86, 101–102

Sol'ntseva, Elizaveta, *See* Koval'skaia, Elizaveta

Sol'ts, Aaron, 192

Soviet Russia, family experiments, 243

Sozialistische Monatshefte, 130, 133, 226

Spalletti, Countess, 167

SPD: 138; Congress, 139; on familial equality, 137

Spencerian hypothesis, 88

Staël, Ludmilla, exiled, 188

Stalinists: 184, 200, 202; and V.M. Molotov, 190; revolution of, 205, 206; and Trotsky, 197

Stuttgart: Second International, 102; socialist women at, 220, 237

Subjection of Women, The (Mill), 163–64

Suffrage, female: 159; Austria, 220, 235ff.; France, 102; Germany, 125–26; Italy, 165–66

Suffragiste, La, 100

Sullerot, Evelyne, survey of, 171–72

Survey of the Woman Problem, A 219

Suttner, Bertha von, 219

Sverdlov, Iakov, 187, 189

Sweden, Aleksandra Kollontai, 206

Switzerland, Paule Mink in, 82

"Talent and Work" (Kuliscioff speech), 157

Tavrich, vice governor of, 55

Technological Institute, St. Petersburg, 63

Tenth Party Congress, Bolshevik, 204

Tertullian, on women, 12

Theses on Feuerbach (Marx), 166

Third Conference of 1908, 231

Third International, 226

Third Reich, German, 139

Third Republic, France: formation, 75, 76; and Left, 106; survival of, 85

Thought and Action, 167

Toward a Critique of the Feminine (Mayreder), 219

Trade unions: Austria, 243; Catholic, 237; and feminism, 118, 122; Italy, 156

Tristan, Aline, 31

Tristan, Flora: 2, 9; childhood of, 21–22; on children, 33, 34; female rights, 13–14; feminist-socialist synthesis, 40–42; illegitimacy, 22; literary qualities of, 24–25; as messiah, 31; personal experiences, 22–23; and Russians, 53; sexless love of, 31; sublimation of, 30; Union of, 38–40, 42; and utopians, 19ff., 28ff.; and workingmen, 38, 41–42, 77; on workingwoman, 32–34, 37